From the
DESERT
to the
DERBY

From the
DESERT
to the
DERBY

The Ruling Family of
Dubai's Billion-Dollar
Quest to Win America's
Greatest Horse Race

Jason Levin

DRF PRESS

Published by
Daily Racing Form Press
100 Broadway, 7th Floor
New York, NY 10005

ISBN: 0-9700147-2-4
Library of Congress Control Number: 2001099913

Cover design by Chris Donofry
Text design by Pauline Neuwirth, Neuwirth & Associates, Inc.

Printed in the United States of America

Contents

Acknowledgements

Many people view writing as a lonely task, when it is actually a total team effort. First and foremost, I want to thank the love of my life, Sandy Kobrin, for her consistent support in the face of the obstacles the project presented. You believed in me and helped from proposal to finished product and I could not have done it without you. To my father, Michael, a racing fan as well as a man of letters, sincere thanks for your thoughts, opinions, and being the best sounding board a son could ask for. Finally, to my mother, Loretta, thanks for your support and instilling in me a love and respect for language, books, and libraries. Grandpa Vahe, this one's for you.

Thanks to the professionalism and support of *Daily Racing Form*'s Charlie Hayward and Bonnie Britt of the National Writers Union, this project quickly went from a verbal agreement to a contractual reality.

Once things got going, the Hollywood Park PR crew, led by Mike Mooney, helped ease me into the project, as did the intelligent, opinionated trio of Donny Abrams, Mike Willman, and Kurt Hoover.

At Del Mar, Dan Smith, crack PR man, jazz fan, and boxing aficionado, was gracious to a fault, as was his entire crew, especially Mac McBride. Ditto for the folks in the press box and near the paddock, never shy with an opinion, such as Steve Andersen, Jay Privman, Brad Free, Bob Ike, Bruno de Julio, Toby Turrell, and Larry Weinbaum. A special thank-you goes to the eminent author and racing fan William Murray, for his encouragement and friendship. Also, special thanks to radio king Felix Taverna, who took me in and showed me around the town he knows so well. To fellow Gaucho Dan Sbicca, thanks for gastronomical assistance at key times. To Jeff Sotman and Tom Quigley, the men behind *HorsePlayer* magazine, many thanks for your help and support, as well as the occasional winner. To the hard-working librarians of Del Mar and Solana Beach, many thanks.

At Keeneland, everything starts with the hospitality and generous spirit of Ken Kirchner, his wife, Kelly, and their boys, Derek and Justin. Thanks for making me feel at home during the stressful days following September 11. Jim Williams and Nick Nicholson, the men behind Keeneland Association, thanks for your candor and help in leading me down the right path. The same goes for DRF writer Glenye Cain, who introduced me to some of the key players in the breeding game and helped me navigate unfamiliar surroundings.

In Europe, I could not have survived and prospered without the hospitality and good humor of the one and only "Uncle D.," David Bennett, of my Internet friend, the well-informed Jeremy Edge, and his racing cronies, Bob, Mike, and Nigel, who proved invaluable. The same goes for Shauna Campbell, who volunteered to be my first Newmarket tour guide. The Ascot PR crew, headed by the redoubtable Nick Smith, and his assistant, Jayne McWilliam, went above and beyond the call of duty in making this Yank feel welcome. Bookmaker Simon Clare was always a pleasure to talk to, as was writer Jamie Reid. The good people at the International Racing Bureau were most helpful, and while those at Longchamp were not, it sure made things lively in France.

In New York, my path was cleared by the NTRA's Jamie Haydn and Eric Wing, McKay Smith of Breeders' Cup Ltd., and many others who exemplified the term grace under pressure. New York is also home to Bert Sugar, whom I thank for his wit, wisdom, experience, and ability to judge and nurture young talent.

There are many *Daily Racing Form* people to thank, from writers like Lauren Stich, Alan Shuback, and David Grening to my New York office contact and right hand, Dean Keppler. I thank Mandy Minger and Tim O'Leary for their enthusiasm for the project.

Back in Los Angeles, I got help getting out of the gate and coming down the stretch from Wayne Wilson, Michael Salmon, Shirley Ito, and everyone at the Ziffren Sports Library; also Dick Russell, Dave Davis, Bruce Bebb, Raphael Greene, Steve Siu, Mike Lazarus, Benjamin Berman, Jason Roach, Bill Wallace, John Hough, Rob DeLorenzo, the good people at the Brentwood Library, and my cat, Fast Eddie.

Thanks also to Martin Sexton, Red Garland, Hank Mobley, Jonny Lang, Sublime, Bob Marley, Bob Dylan, and Little Feat for musical inspiration while driving up and down the 405 and flying around the world.

Sincere thanks as well to the owners, breeders, trainers, jockeys, jockey agents, grooms, and horseplayers who took time out of their busy schedules to answer my questions and were open and gracious with their thoughts.

Finally, thanks to Steven Crist for giving me this opportunity. In addition, thank you for allowing me to find my own way, and providing solid editorial assistance from beginning to end. Lastly, thanks to Robin Foster for your diligence and love of the sport. You were a pleasure to work with and the book is far better for your having copyedited the manuscript.

Introduction

In the summer of 2000, I was working as the horse-racing and boxing writer for FOXSports.com when I noticed that Godolphin Racing, the operation run by Dubai's Sheikh Mohammed bin Rashid al-Maktoum, had sent a huge number of 2-year-olds to America. The group was being trained by Eoin Harty, formerly the top assistant to Bob Baffert, the hottest Thoroughbred trainer of the late 1990's and a man I had frequently written about. I knew Harty and Baffert had been good friends and wondered how their relationship had been affected by Harty's leaving to work for the sheikh. I followed the Godolphin juveniles closely for about a month, then suggested to my superiors, Rick Jaffe and Mike James, that I go down to Del Mar and dig a little deeper.

Once they gave me the go-ahead, I began looking into exactly what Godolphin Racing was all about. The closer I got, the more intriguing it became. The ensuing time spent with Harty and Baffert at their stables on the Del Mar backside only served to whet my appetite for the story further, as did the presence of the $25 million of gorgeous Godolphin juveniles. The portrait that emerged of Sheikh Mohammed, the crown prince of the tiny Persian Gulf emirate, was of an intensely competitive man driven by the desire to prove to American horsemen that he could not only win the biggest race in America, the Kentucky Derby, but also do it his way. The story about Harty, Baffert, and the sheikh ran for a few days, then disappeared into the dot-com void.

A few months later, most of the FOXSports.com staff, me included, was laid off. I also work for *HorsePlayer* magazine, and did an interview in the spring of 2001 with Steven Crist, chairman and publisher of *Daily Racing Form*. In the course of our discussion, he made it clear that he wanted to do more with DRF Press, to put out more books, not all of which would be handicapping oriented. With nothing but time on my hands and a nudge from my girlfriend, I wrote a book proposal that focused on Sheikh Mohammed's ego-driven, money-is-no-object quest to win the Derby. Crist and I met in New York in June, I pitched him the idea, and, ever the gambler, he called my bluff. Three weeks later the deal was signed and the work began. I presented the idea to Sheikh Mohammed, hoping that he would arrange special access to Eoin Harty and other key members of his operation. He declined, but I got what I needed by traveling to Del Mar, Kentucky, New York, and overseas.

The key to becoming a good teacher is the ability to listen, and I believe the same to be true of writing. The more you listen, the more you learn. Here is what I found.

1

9-11

September 11, 2001, was a day many people in the Thoroughbred-racing business had circled on their calendars for a year. It was the second and final day of the "select" portion of the fall yearling sales at historic Keeneland racetrack, in the heart of the Bluegrass country in Lexington, Kentucky. For a good number of breeders, September 11 was payday.

Until the early 1940's, anyone looking to sell a well-bred racehorse under the age of 2 at auction in

America did so in the summer at Saratoga Springs in upstate New York. In 1943, that all changed. The country was at war and Saratoga's race meeting was canceled, forcing the Kentucky breeders to seek another venue. That August, under a tent on the racetrack grounds, the first Keeneland sale was held. They've been doing it every year since, and Keeneland is now known around the world as the place to find the best young Thoroughbreds money can buy.

The annual September sale is a two-week affair, but the yearlings with the best pedigrees are grouped together in the "select" segment, which takes place the first two days. Getting your yearling into the select sale is the equine version of having your high school senior accepted to the right college, with bloodlines and conformation, or physical appearance, taking the place of grade-point averages and SAT scores. It's a highly subjective process, and the decisions, which are made behind closed doors, have serious implications: During the intense 48-hour period, more money flows through the Keeneland sales ring than the Gross National Product of some small nations. In 2000, 443 yearlings were sold for an all-time September select-sale record of $162,142,000.

In 2001, the big-money train was rolling even faster. The average price of the 156 yearlings sold on September 10 was a hefty $386,737 and it was widely acknowledged that the horses scheduled for sale on Day Two were superior to the first group, so hopes were sky-high.

The ultimate goal of most yearling buyers is to get a colt or filly who will win the Kentucky Derby two years later. That is exactly what happened to Fred W. Hooper, who spent $10,200 at Keeneland's inaugural 1943 sale on a son of imported European sire Sir Gallahad III, named him Hoop, Jr., and a year and a half later watched the colt win the Derby. Long recognized as one of the true gentlemen of American racing, Hooper spent the next 50 years, and millions of dollars, buying more horses and breeding his own in an attempt to duplicate the feat, to no avail. Through 2001, 15 Derby winners had been purchased at Keeneland sales, ranging from bargain-basement buys like 1971 winner Canonero II ($1,200) and 1998 winner Real Quiet ($17,000) to the 2000 winner, Fusaichi Pegasus, who cost an even $4,000,000. Ironically, Fusaichi Pegasus is the only one of well over 100 million-dollar-plus yearling purchases to have won America's most famous race.

The sales start promptly at 10 A.M., but the Thoroughbred business rises well before the rooster. Grooms arrive at Keeneland's weather-beaten green-and-white wooden barns around 5 A.M. to prepare the horses for their coming-out party. They bathe, brush, and walk the skittish youngsters, all under the watchful eyes of the sales agents. Known as consignors, they arrive with the grooms or soon after. It is their job to promote and show the horses to potential buyers, so they closely monitor the morning activities, knowing they have only a few hours before the day begins in earnest.

Just after 7 A.M., the prospective buyers begin making their morning rounds. The agents enthusiastically tout their horses, pumping up their pedigrees and praising their conformation. The buyers, catalogs in hand, stand silently, gesturing or grunting to have the horses turned this way or that, trying to find a flaw. Occasionally, a question or two is asked, then another horse is brought out of its stall for inspection.

Horse racing has become a truly international sport in the past 20 years, and on September 11 there were representatives of Japan, Canada, Mexico, France, Italy, Ireland, England, Germany, Argentina, Brazil, India, and Saudi Arabia looking at horses at Keeneland. There was, however, one billionaire buyer every sales agent hoped to see in person that morning: Sheikh Mohammed bin Rashid al-Maktoum, the crown prince of the tiny Persian Gulf emirate of Dubai.

On September 9, he had stopped by the Eaton Sales barn and looked at three or four horses, but only actually touched one, a calm chestnut son of the top stallion Storm Cat.

"When Sheikh Mo touched the Storm Cat, I felt like we were in good shape," recalled Tom VanMeter, the agent in charge of the Eaton barn that day and a master of understatement. The next day, September 10, the Storm Cat colt, his chestnut coat gleaming, was led into the sales pavilion.

Most of the yearlings are visibly nervous and scared when led into the small roped-off area that serves as the sales ring. They whinny loudly, fight against the groom trying to keep them calm, and often release a sizable bowel movement. Standing in the middle of a brightly lit amphitheater filled with 1,000 people while an auctioneer seated a few yards above and behind them rattles off numbers into a microphone is an experience that makes most young horses decidedly uncomfortable. The Storm Cat colt let the groom slowly walk him into the ring and stood stock still, looking at the assembled crowd as a king would survey his subjects. When the groom gently tugged at him, he moved accordingly, then resumed his lordly stance. Five minutes later, the calm, athletic colt became the ninth-most-expensive yearling ever sold at auction, bought by Sheikh Mohammed for $5.5 million.

ELEVEN HIGHEST-PRICED YEARLINGS IN SALES HISTORY
(ALL SOLD AT KEENELAND)

PRICE	BUYER	YEAR	SIRE
$13,100,000	COOLMORE	1985	NIJINSKY II
$10,200,000	MAKTOUM	1983	NORTHERN DANCER
$8,250,000	COOLMORE	1984	NORTHERN DANCER
$7,100,000	MAKTOUM	1984	NORTHERN DANCER
$7,000,000	MAKTOUM	1985	NIJINSKY II
$6,800,000	COOLMORE	2000	STORM CAT
$6,500,000	MAKTOUM	1984	SEATTLE SLEW
$6,400,000	COOLMORE	2001	STORM CAT
$5,500,000	MAKTOUM	2001	STORM CAT
$5,400,000	COOLMORE	1984	NORTHERN DANCER
$5,300,000	MAKTOUM	2000	KINGMAMBO

The 53-year-old Sheikh Mohammed is the third oldest of the four Maktoum brothers who rule Dubai, a tiny country of just 1,500 square miles located on the southern shore of the Persian Gulf and one of the seven sheikhdoms that make up the United Arab Emirates. His official title is minister of defense for the UAE. His oldest brother, 61-year-old Sheikh Maktoum al-Maktoum, is Dubai's ruler and vice president of the UAE. The second-oldest, 58-year-old Hamdan, is the UAE's finance minister and its representative to the Organization of Petroleum Exporting Countries. The youngest of the four, Ahmed, runs the national airline, Emirates Air, and is the least involved in horse racing.

The UAE was formed in 1971 when Britain formally withdrew its presence from the oil-saturated region, but the Maktoum family has ruled Dubai since the early 1800's, when they led about 800 members of the Al Bu Falasah group of the nomadic Bani Yas tribe into the area.

At that time, England was the military power in that part of the world, having taken control from the Portuguese some 50 years earlier. In 1820, the Bani Yas signed a general treaty of peace with England, which had been having trouble with local attacks on its trade ships in the area, a region the English referred to as the Pirate Coast. Dubai, which is bisected by a creek, is the only natural deepwater port on the 400 miles of Persian Gulf coastline. That agreement, followed by another treaty in 1852, made it a key link on the active England-India trade route.

The Maktoums have been known as master traders since their arrival in Dubai, and upon establishing formal relations with England, they made it plain that they were open for any sort of business. As a result of its geography and the open-door, anything-goes policy of its rulers, Dubai quickly became the commercial hub of the area as well as a haven for smugglers. Under the Maktoum family, the policy was that all trade was good trade, as long as they got their cut, and the British agents in the area had no problem with the laissez-faire attitude.

In 1892, the Trucial States, as the group of sheikhdoms was then known, signed yet another agreement stating that England would be its only diplomatic and foreign contact. The agreement stipulated that while England would assume responsibility for defense and foreign affairs, the local rulers would maintain control over domestic affairs. It was a deal that solidified the power of paternalistic and authoritarian tribal rulers such as the Maktoums. The 1892 treaty was the formal beginning of a long-standing and mutually beneficial relationship between the Maktoum family and England, one that would prove pivotal in the development of Sheikh Mohammed's intense interest in horses.

Around 1900, there were only a few thousand people in all of Dubai, more than half of whom were involved in the pearl trade. There were thousands of pearl-bearing oyster beds off the Dubai coast, and they contributed heavily to Dubai's status as a trade center. Other than pearls, everything else that went in and out of Dubai was "re-exported," or smuggled, mainly to Iran, Pakistan, and India. In the 1930's, Japanese cultured pearls hit the world market, a major blow to Dubai, but one it weathered under the free-trading leadership of Sheikh Saeed, grandfather of the four brothers and leader of Dubai from 1912-58.

In 1932, oil was found in nearby Bahrain, and six years later the world's largest oil field was discovered in Kuwait. In 1939, two other branches of the Bani Yas tribe attempted to overthrow Sheikh Saeed at the wedding of his son, Rashid, but the coup was unsuccessful and served only to strengthen the power of the Maktoum family. Though exploration was slowed soon after by World War II, it wasn't long before oil made its presence felt all over the Persian Gulf region. Sheikh Rashid became the ruler of Dubai upon his father's death in 1958, a time when the majority of the inhabitants of what was little more than a busy fishing village were either Iranian, Pakistani, or Indian. The same is true today.

When oil was discovered some 60 miles off Dubai's coast in 1966, it was Sheikh Rashid who had positioned Dubai to take immediate advantage of this stroke of luck. A businessman by nature, he was aware of Dubai's unique role as the commercial and trade center of the region and was busy planning what he would do if and when the oil money began flowing his way. It didn't take long.

By 1969, Dubai began exporting crude oil all over the world. It was during this period that England formally withdrew from the region, leading to the formation of the UAE in January 1971. Since Dubai's neighbor, Abu Dhabi, is by far the largest of the seven emirates, as well as the richest, its leader, Sheikh Zayed, was named president of the UAE. Sheikh Rashid was made vice president and immediately went about reinvesting the billions of dollars that flew into his coffers into his country's infrastructure. He built a major airport, a 15-berth deep-water port, the largest dry-docking facilities in the Persian Gulf, and set up a free-trade zone to attract foreign companies, continuing the family tradition of encouraging wheeling and dealing.

The UAE joined OPEC in 1971, and after the Arab-Israeli war of 1973, Sheikh Rashid was a pivotal player in the ensuing oil embargo against all countries that were sympathetic to Israel. The embargo caused the price of oil to increase dramatically, and as a result, the Maktoums became instant billionaires. Whereas in 1965, the Maktoum family had zero income from oil, by 1975 they were banking over a billion dollars a year from the black gold that just happened to be located in their waters. In 2000, *Forbes* magazine ranked Sheikh Maktoum as the 27th-richest man in the world, with a worth of just over $12 billion.

Dubai has grown so rapidly it defies all logic. Forty years ago only the Maktoum family and a select few of the 150,000 people in Dubai had electricity. In 2001, they opened "Internet City," which they have positioned as a rival to Northern California's Silicon Valley as a hotbed of Internet development. Dubai now boasts a population of more than 900,000, some 85 percent of which are foreigners, and it has more five-star hotels per square foot than anywhere in the world. Sheikh Rashid became ill in 1980, and by the time he died in 1990, Sheikh Maktoum had been effectively running the tiny emirate for a decade. For the purpose of comparison, Dubai, much of which is uninhabitable desert, is the same size as Lexington, Kentucky.

Without question, Mohammed is the one brother truly obsessed with dominating the Thoroughbred horse-racing business. He bought his first horse, a filly named Hatta, in 1977 and hasn't stopped buying since. Until recently, the Maktoum brothers had concentrated on English racing, and as a result of their monumental spending, had been phenomenally successful. Sheikh Mohammed was the leading owner in England, based on purse money won, every year but two between 1985 and 1999. The leader the other two years was his brother Hamdan. Since their first buying spree of Kentucky yearlings in 1980, the Maktoum brothers have spent well over a billion dollars of their new money on the Sport of Kings.

Maktoum and Hamdan are physically soft men of medium height, unlike their father, who was over six feet tall and a robust individual. Both shake hands gently, carry more than a few extra pounds around the waist, and act as if physical exertion is a distant and not particularly fond memory. That is not the case with Sheikh Mohammed. Whereas Maktoum and Hamdan will look at someone who is speaking to them, Mohammed is more likely to look right through him. He too is of medium height, but in better physical shape than his older brothers and fiercely competitive at everything he does. A horseman from a very young age, he prides himself on leading the Dubai team, which includes his two teenage sons, to victory in endurance-riding (50 miles or more) competitions around the world.

As a result of his lifelong business relationship with England, Sheikh Rashid became quite an Anglophile, and he sent his sons to be educated at Cambridge in England. The role of defense minister is a vital one in an area of the world where war is never far away, and after Mohammed finished at Cambridge, Rashid sent him to Mons, the British officer-training school, grooming him for the position.

It was while in school in England that Mohammed first attended the horse races. Newmarket racecourse is located just minutes from Cambridge, and there he was captivated, as many were at that time, by the brilliance of the colt Nijinsky II. A son of 1964 Kentucky Derby winner Northern Dancer, Nijinsky II swept the 1970 English Triple Crown, consisting of the one-mile 2000 Guineas, the mile-and-a-half Epsom Derby, and the mile-and-three-quarter St. Leger. No horse has duplicated the feat since.

An intense man with dark hair, a closely shaven beard, and piercing dark eyes, Sheikh Mohammed was the biggest buyer on Day One of the 2001 Keeneland September select sale, spending just over $10 million for seven horses. Sheikh Hamdan was second on the list, spending $5,575,000 for six horses. Between the two, the Maktoum brothers accounted for more than 25 percent of the total amount of money spent on September 10.

By 8:30 A.M. on September 11, the Keeneland grounds were buzzing with activity. The staff was in the process of rounding up the first batch of yearlings to be brought to the large walking ring just outside the sales pavilion. Buyers and sellers were all over the grounds, making their final preparations for the day, which was clear and comfortable, with the temperature on its way into the low 70's.

One of the quirks of the Keeneland sale is the preponderance of television sets on the grounds. The idea is for people to be able to follow the sale no matter where they are, and it works. There are televisions installed in every barn, in the track kitchen, the library, and in every nook and cranny of the sales pavilion and walking ring. Since the sale was still more than an hour away, the televisions were on a variety of different channels that morning.

At 8:45 A.M., American Airlines Flight 11 was flown into the north tower of the World Trade Center in New York City. Within minutes, every single television at Keeneland was switched to CNN, Fox News, or MSNBC, but nobody was quite sure what was happening. When the second plane hit the south tower 18 minutes later, all activity in the barn area stopped.

Keeneland President Nick Nicholson, in only his second year on the job, was the man on the spot. He immediately went into his office in the sales pavilion, turned on the television, and conferred with other Keeneland officers as the tragedy unfolded. He knew he had to talk with one nonofficial as well.

"I talked with people whose opinions I respect, including Sheikh Mohammed, and ultimately decided the only thing to do was to postpone Tuesday's sale," said the 53-year-old Kentucky native. Nicholson is a tall, sturdy man with a soft voice and pleasant manner, and the weight of the decision made his shoulders slump inside his suit.

Had the Maktoum brothers chosen to leave the sale at that moment, the impact would have been devastating. Longtime breeder Bob Courtney put it bluntly when asked how the Maktoums' departure would have affected the Kentucky economy. "Tobacco's dead. The government killed it. Coal's dead too, so in Kentucky right now, the horse bidness is it. If he and his brothers left, it would have been one helluva hit."

As the tragic events of September 11 unfolded, Nicholson wasn't the only one in an awkward position. As the defense minister of the UAE, Sheikh Mohammed is the person responsible for making the military decisions for the area and a powerful voice in the Arab world. He is also on a mission to win the Kentucky Derby, and had flown to Lexington personally in the hope of spotting, and buying, the 2003 Derby winner.

By virtue of the titanic amount of money he spends, Sheikh Mohammed could be considered the most powerful man in Thoroughbred horse racing. Despite having occupied that role for two full decades, however, he has no close personal relationships with anyone in the sport. He spends only a few days a year in America and does not socialize when he does come. He is all business, all the time. As more than a few longtime Kentucky breeders made clear, it's a good thing he's a man who does his business professionally, because there's nothing they could do about it if he didn't.

Keeneland is located directly across the street from Bluegrass Field,

Lexington's small airport. Both Mohammed and Hamdan had their private 747's parked in plain sight, ready to fly at a moment's notice. Shortly before 10 A.M., however, the FAA halted all takeoffs nationwide, a decision that was without precedent in American history, and nobody knew how long that ban would last. The Maktoum brothers were grounded.

Nicholson had conferred with Sheikh Mohammed a few more times on September 11. With over 1,000 horses on the grounds and over 1,000 more on the way, the Keeneland president was facing a total meltdown if he attempted to postpone the sale to a later date. He also didn't know how long it would be before air travel resumed, or how long Sheikh Mohammed was going to be in town. After much hand-wringing, he decided to reopen the sale on Wednesday.

"I have tremendous respect for Sheikh Mohammed, because unlike a lot of folks, he has a way of saying very little but communicating exactly what he means," Nicholson recalled, adding, "He came up to me Wednesday morning just before the sale and told me I'd made the right decision to postpone, and the right one to reopen, then he walked away. When he left, I felt a whole lot better about how the day was going to go."

Before the sale of the first horse at 10 A.M. on September 12, everyone in attendance observed a moment of silence. Immediately afterward Nicholson read a prepared statement explaining what went into his decision and announcing the formation of a relief fund.

Many of the decisions Sheikh Mohammed makes in regard to horse racing are motivated by the desire to promote and publicize Dubai. That motivation stems from his knowledge that its oil supply, which only provides about 15 percent of the emirate's yearly income, could run out within the next 20 or 30 years. Consequently, the Maktoums have done everything within their considerable power to put Dubai on the world map and position it as a prime wintertime vacation spot for Europeans. Toward that end, they have continued unabated the building boom their father began 30 years ago. Dubai now has an airport that prominent American horse owner Mike Pegram called "the most unbelievable thing I've ever seen," three top-class golf courses, every kind of water sport imaginable, new roads, and brand-new, sparkling shopping malls in which everything is duty free.

As part of that overall plan, Sheikh Mohammed created Godolphin Racing in 1994. The idea was to form a stable that would select some of the best horses from each brother's string and send them out to compete in the world's most important races. The Kentucky Derby is the most famous race there is, and, not coincidentally, the one race Sheikh Mohammed wants to win most of all.

A key to the plan was the building of first-class training and racing facilities in Dubai. They already had the Zabeel training center, but it wasn't big enough to house what Sheikh Mohammed knew would be a massive operation. In America, a project of such magnitude would require years of environmental studies, committee meetings, and funding issues. In Dubai, the work started as soon as Sheikh Mohammed declared it was time.

By 1994 the Al Quoz stables had been built, as had the Dubai Equine Hospital, and the Nad Al Sheba racetrack updated. Interestingly, Nad Al Sheba was modeled after famed Churchill Downs in Louisville, Kentucky, home of the Kentucky Derby, a place Sheikh Mohammed had only visited once or twice. The track, originally built in 1983, was upgraded significantly in 1993, as was the grandstand. A sophisticated drainage system was put in place to ensure that the sand-based track would stay in top condition despite the severe weather conditions of the area, which feature high temperatures around 120 degrees from May through August. Luxury suites were installed in the new grandstand and a nine-hole golf course built in the infield area.

The Al Quoz stables are state of the art, featuring a 250-meter, one-lane equine swimming pool, a training track, screened and air-conditioned barns, shaded walkways, and spotless facilities for routine veterinary work to be done. Hall of Fame trainer Richard Mandella called the Al Quoz setup "a first-class country club for horses that puts anything else I've ever seen to shame." Likewise, the equine hospital features every possible instrument and machine necessary to assist veterinarians in their efforts to treat sick or injured horses.

Sheikh Mohammed is used to being in total control, and he wanted to be able to supervise the training of his horses, which until that time had taken place some 3,000 miles away in England. Since its inception, Godolphin has dominated top-class racing in Europe, winning 66

Group 1 races in seven years (1994-2000), more than double the victories of any other stable during that period.

In 1995, Sheikh Mohammed made another bold move designed to raise Dubai's profile around the world. He proposed an international sporting event. Dictators Mobutu Sese Seko and Ferdinand Marcos had done the same thing in the 1970's, featuring Muhammad Ali fighting for the heavyweight title as their hook. They got plenty of attention for their countries—Zaire and the Philippines, respectively—but the move backfired on Mobutu and Marcos when the world suddenly saw firsthand the havoc the dictators had wreaked on their own people. They paid big money, took a big one-time risk, and lost.

Sheikh Mohammed announced that in March 1996, he would put up a then-record $4 million as the purse for a mile-and-a-quarter race to be run at Nad Al Sheba. He called it the Dubai World Cup and happily paid the expenses of every owner, trainer, jockey, and journalist who made the lengthy trek to the desert. When the best horse in the world at the time, Cigar, flew from America to Dubai and won the inaugural running, it brought attention from the worldwide media and gave the Dubai World Cup immediate and total credibility, exactly what Sheikh Mohammed had hoped for. Like Mobutu and Marcos, he had paid big money, but unlike the two dictators, he was in for the long haul and shone the spotlight on a country that was crime free and prospering. The gamble paid off immediately and the event has grown every succeeding year, with the purse in 2002 reaching a record $6 million, and the total purse money for the seven races that day totaling a staggering $15 million.

With those building blocks in place, in 1998 Sheikh Mohammed turned his attention to horse racing's Holy Grail, the Kentucky Derby. He had been part-owner of the 1992 Derby favorite, Arazi, but had not been back to Louisville since watching the supposed wonder horse struggle home in eighth place. A student of the sport, he realized that, horse-racing fan or not, everyone has heard of the Kentucky Derby. To achieve that goal, Sheikh Mohammed knew his best chance would come from the best American yearlings.

While European racing takes place almost exclusively on grass courses, the Derby is run on dirt. Nobody in the world produces more talented young dirt horses than America, with the best of the best coming from Kentucky. Since making up his mind to focus on the Derby in 1998, Sheikh Mohammed has spent well over $100 million on unproven, unraced yearlings, and millions more buying proven 2-year-olds from American owners. The plan was to do more of the same in 2001, and as Sheikh Mohammed prowled the walking ring behind the Keeneland sales pavilion, he was accompanied by his hand-picked crew of experts.

Attached to his side was his bloodstock advisor, John Ferguson. An affable, if a bit harried, Englishman, the 41-year-old Ferguson is the person responsible for helping Sheikh Mohammed select yearlings. Before attending a given sale, the Godolphin bloodstock-research team has run the pedigrees of all the likely candidates through their computer, compiling a list of horses bred for success on American dirt. When Ferguson arrives in town, he heads out to inspect them firsthand. He checks their conformation, looks for horses that are well-balanced and athletic, makes notes in his catalog, and passes the information on to Sheikh Mohammed. His is the advice Sheikh Mohammed values above all when buying yearlings.

"As a bloodstock agent, working for Sheikh Mohammed is very exciting," said the self-effacing Ferguson a few weeks after the sale, adding quickly, "but I mustn't get carried away with being the biggest buyer at the sale. The pat on the back comes when the horses past the winning post, not when you sign the sales ticket."

Also in attendance, ear glued to his cell phone, was stable manager Simon Crisford. A handsome Brit with a quote ready for any question, Crisford began his career in racing as an assistant trainer, then became a racing writer. Three years later, in 1994, he went to work for Sheikh Mohammed, assisting Anthony Stroud, who had been Sheikh Mohammed's stable manager for a number of years. In 1995, Sheikh Mohammed decided it was time for a changing of the guard, and he put Crisford in charge of the day-to-day operations of his stable. When speaking about Sheikh Mohammed, Crisford refers to him, as many do to New York Yankees owner George Steinbrenner, as "the Boss."

Godolphin trainers Saeed bin Suroor and Eoin (pronounced "Owen") Harty were also part of the large Godolphin entourage at Keeneland. A soft-spoken Dubai native, the unassuming Suroor was plucked from obscurity by Sheikh Mohammed in 1995 and has been listed as the head trainer for Godolphin ever since. There has been much speculation about just how much input Suroor really has, but he's on his fifth full year at the helm and the results of the Godolphin horses in Europe have been excellent. The results of the Godolphin horses in the Kentucky Derby, however, have not. Suroor spends his winters in Dubai and the rest of the time shuttling between their stable in England and the various racetracks all over the globe.

Harty is the latest addition to the Godolphin team, hired in November 1999. Unlike Suroor, he had a track record with top-class horses, although not as the man in charge. From 1992 to 1999 he was the head assistant to top American trainer Bob Baffert, a time in which Baffert-trained horses won two Kentucky Derbies (Silver Charm in 1997 and Real Quiet in 1998) and a Dubai World Cup (Silver Charm in 1998). Sheikh Mohammed had observed Harty in action and obviously liked what he saw from the 38-year-old Irishman, a fifth-generation trainer. According to Crisford, "One of the things we were looking for was someone who was an excellent horseman familiar with classy horses but one not already set in his ways who would be willing to listen and follow our program. Eoin fit that profile beautifully." During the sales, Suroor did very little, while Harty was a powerful presence, conversing often with Ferguson.

There is one only one group that has no fear of getting into a bidding war with Sheikh Mohammed at the yearling sales. Known as the Coolmore group, Irishmen John Magnier and Demi O'Byrne, in tandem with Englishman Michael Tabor, are the other gigantic players in the high-stakes game of buying young horses. Magnier is a stud manager and deal maker with a nose for bloodstock who has been at the top of the game since the mid-1970's. A handsome, secretive 53-year-old who wears his thinning silver hair long underneath a variety of stylish hats, he was paying top dollar for American yearlings before Sheikh Mohammed bought his first horse. Over the past 25 years, he has built Coolmore into a worldwide power, both on the racetrack and in the breeding shed, and is the ultimate decision maker for the group. O'Byrne is a wily veterinarian whose ability to spot quality yearlings and to help correct whatever physical flaws they may have is legendary. For the past few years he has been the one responsible for doing the big-money bidding. Tabor is the moneyman, having sold his English book-making business five years ago for more than $50 million, and he already has what Sheikh Mohammed wants, having won the Kentucky Derby with Thunder Gulch in 1995.

"That was a classic old bidding war between Sheikh Mo and Coolmore on the Storm Cat," laughed VanMeter, whose company reaped a percentage of the rewards of that pitched September 10 battle of ego and money. Before the bidding, VanMeter had positioned himself some 20 feet away from Sheikh Mohammed. "Sheikh Mo and Ferguson didn't even bid until about two and a half million. Until then it was Coolmore and the Thoroughbred Corp. When they did jump in, Ferguson did the bidding until the low threes, then Sheikh Mo took over himself. The Thoroughbred Corp. was done about then and it seemed like it took forever from there. Sheikh Mo was very slow and deliberate but I'll tell ya, it took my breath away when Coolmore finally backed out and they dropped the hammer at five and a half."

The Thoroughbred Corp. is a stable owned by the Saudi Arabian prince Ahmed Salman, who owns the Saudi Research and Marketing Group, the largest publishing entity in his home country. A large man with a smile as big as his ego, Salman is as outgoing as Sheikh Mohammed is private. In the past few years, as Salman's horses have had more and more success in America, the two men have developed a real rivalry. The 44-year-old Salman is best known for his ownership of the top 3-year-old in America in 2001, Point Given. Fifth as the heavy favorite in the Kentucky Derby, the Bob Baffert-trained colt went on to win the Preakness and the Belmont Stakes, the next two of the three races that make up America's Triple Crown. After Point Given won the Preakness, Salman was quoted as saying he was proud to have become the first Arab to own the winner of an American classic race, a not-so-subtle dig at Sheikh Mohammed.

On September 12, all the major players were in place when the bidding began just after 10 A.M. The television sets in and around the Keeneland sales pavilion never showed one minute of news coverage that day. It was back to business as usual. Just before noon, things began to get interesting.

Coolmore got the action going, paying $1.3 million for a Storm Cat colt out of a mare that had already produced a champion American dirt horse named Lemon Drop Kid. Sheikh Hamdan was next, chipping in $325,000 for a Kingmambo colt, and Sheikh Mohammed then paid $440,000 for a son of Bertrando. One $55,000 colt later, the bidding battle was joined yet again. A striking bay filly entered the ring and the bidding jumped to a million dollars in a blink. It was Sheikh Mohammed, trying hard to look bored, standing in his usual spot just in the back of the pavilion and out of sight. His carefully placed informers in the pavilion got word to him that he was indeed bidding against the Irish. Finally, Coolmore quit and Sheikh Mohammed bought the filly for $2.3 million.

Next up was a Storm Cat colt many had predicted would be the sales topper of the day. This time the bidding began at a million and jumped straight to $2.5. After a protracted battle, Ferguson and Sheikh Mohammed conferred briefly, then turned away from the bid spotter, indicating that they would go no higher. The hammer dropped at $3.3 million and the Storm Cat colt was on his way to Ireland.

After a son of the quality sire Saint Ballado went for $1.55 million to Indian entrepreneur Satish Sanan, another strong chestnut son of Storm Cat entered the sales ring. He tossed his head as if to announce his presence, planted his feet much as the $5.5 million colt had done two days earlier, and Sheikh Mohammed and John Ferguson exchanged knowing looks. Two minutes later the colt was theirs, for $900,000.

In a half-hour period sandwiched by handsome sons of the highest-priced stallion in the world, Storm Cat, more than $10 million had been spent. Sheikh Mohammed smiled at his entourage, put on his sunglasses, and, hitching up his faded jeans and tucking in his white Godolphin T-shirt, walked briskly back out into the fresh air.

Sheikh Mohammed bought four more seven-digit yearlings before the sun went down on September 12, including a $3.8 million colt from the last crop of the late sire Mr. Prospector. The purchases ran his September 12 spending spree to just over $15 million. Coolmore was second on the list with $11.5 million spent, including the most expensive purchase of the two days, $6.4 million for yet another son of Storm Cat. Although the Day Two average of $385,721 was down from the all-time September record of $420,400 set in 2000, everyone in the industry breathed a massive sigh of relief at the end of the session. Despite the terrible events of the previous day and the uncertainty of what was to come, the major players had come to buy on the 12th. At least for one extremely important day, all was well in Kentucky. In the two days of the select sale, the Maktoum family had spent $36,042,000 on 47 horses, accounting for a bit more than 30 percent of the money spent on the 353 horses sold.

As soon as he was allowed to fly on Thursday, Sheikh Mohammed was on his private plane, headed back to Dubai. He would have much to do in the coming weeks, knowing that the UAE was one of only three entities to have officially recognized the Taliban regime in Afghanistan. One thing he did was have his people contact Keeneland finance man Buddy Bishop. Using Ferguson as his intermediary, Sheikh Mohammed pledged $5 million, less than he had paid for the one Storm Cat colt but more than any other individual contributor, to the relief fund Nicholson had set up the day after the attacks. The money was received just a few days after the two-week sale ended.

With their work done and the boss gone, Ferguson and Harty joined a large crowd celebrating the end of the emotional day at a bar inside the pavilion. It was a temporary bar, set up just for the two weeks, but nobody cared that the chairs were plastic because the beer was cold. The two settled in at one corner, their mission accomplished. Harty was thinking about the exciting prospect of training the large group of regally bred horses the next year. He was also awaiting word about whether or not his top 2-year-olds would be flown to New York that weekend to run the most important races of their young lives. The answer was no, but ultimately, it made no difference, as it was announced that all racing was canceled that weekend in New York.

Ferguson, having finished one of the most important, intense periods of his year, was worn out. Dressed casually in chinos and a rugby shirt, he looked like just another person celebrating the end of a long day, not the man who had signed the sales slips for millions of dollars of horses. As he recalled, "It was a tough day, but once we got going, we got focused on the task at hand and that was nice. We bought some beautiful horses that day, which was the idea and hopefully one of them will get Sheikh Mohammed the Derby."

Just outside the bar, Nick Nicholson stood in the quiet, empty hallway, staring into the pavilion. He was clearly still shaken by what had transpired in the past 48 hours. "I think what happened here today speaks well for not only our industry but also says something about the inner strength of a whole lot of people," he said quietly, adding with a shrug, "I guess I did the right thing. I sure hope so."

Whether or not one of the many young colts Ferguson helped Sheikh Mohammed buy the days before and after the terrorist attacks would make it to the 2003 Derby was anybody's guess. The far more pressing issue was the performance and potential of the group he bought the year before. Trained by Harty, they were racing in America as 2-year-olds, and the pressure already was squarely on their beautifully bred, well-muscled shoulders.

Before the 1999 Kentucky Derby, Sheikh Mohammed had held a wide-ranging press conference in front of the Godolphin barn at Churchill Downs. Only one quote, however, made it into nearly every paper in America. It was a bold prediction from a man familiar with making them and used to doing whatever it took to make them come true.

"We will win the Derby within four years," predicted Sheikh Mohammed.

Year Four would be 2002.

2

An American Tradition

The Kentucky Derby is a unique American sporting institution. First run in 1875, the Derby is the longest continually held sporting event in the country and rightfully known as the most famous two minutes in sports. When the gates open and the race begins, a roar emanates from the massive crowd that is both deafening and exhilarating, a sound born of months of anticipation mixed with hundreds of millions of dollars riding on the outcome. The final key to the power of the Derby is the immediacy of the event. Win or lose, it is over in two minutes.

No big events match the Derby in focused intensity. Heavyweight title fights can be as hotly anticipated, but the attendance is limited to about 20,000 people now that they are all held indoors. The same is true of the NBA Finals. The Super Bowl takes three hours, as does the Indianapolis 500, and the World Series lasts more than a week.

The Kentucky Derby was the brainchild of Meriweather Lewis Clark, grandson of explorer William Clark, of Lewis and Clark fame. An avid sportsman, Clark saw how quickly the popularity of racing was growing after the Civil War, and while on a business trip to Europe in 1872, had studied how the English Jockey Club conducted its racing. He also witnessed the running of the three new English classics. They were the 1¾-mile St. Leger for 3-year-olds, the 1½-mile Oaks for 3-year-old fillies, and the 1½-mile Derby for 3-year-olds. In contrast to the four-mile marathons that dominated American racing at the time, they emphasized speed over endurance. The focus on 3-year-olds was also different, placing a premium on precocity. Finally, the shorter races were far more exciting, which was not lost on Clark.

CLASSIC RACES FOR 3 YEAR-OLD COLTS IN THE U.S. AND ENGLAND

AMERICA	DISTANCE	TRACK	FIRST YEAR RUN
KENTUCKY DERBY	1¼m	CHURCHILL DOWNS	1875
PREAKNESS	1³⁄₁₆m	PIMLICO	1873
BELMONT STAKES	1½m	BELMONT	1867
ENGLAND			
2000 GUINEAS	1 m	NEWMARKET	1809
EPSOM DERBY	1½m	EPSOM	1780
ST. LEGER	1¹³⁄₁₆m	DONCASTER	1776

Upon his return to Kentucky, Clark formed the Louisville Jockey Club, leased land from his relatives, John and Henry Churchill, built his racetrack, and made its most important race a spring Derby, for 3-year-olds run at the English Derby distance of a mile and a half.

The first Kentucky Derby was run on May 17, 1875, before a crowd of around 10,000, larger than even Clark had hoped for. The race favorite was Chesapeake, who ran in the green-and-gold colors of Irishman H. Price McGrath. McGrath, who had been involved with the building of Saratoga Race Course in upstate New York 11 years earlier, was a big bettor and had entered a second horse, Aristides, to ensure a fast pace that would set up Chesapeake's furious closing kick.

There were 15 starters in all, and as per McGrath's orders, jockey Oliver Lewis sent Aristides immediately to the lead. Lewis was black, as were 13 of the 15 jockeys in the race, not an uncommon percentage in racing of that era in the South. Chesapeake was struggling in midpack, and Aristides, running free on the lead, took the field all the way to the wire. The startling result made it plain that in horse racing, especially those events featuring young, relatively inexperienced horses, it paid to expect the unexpected.

The Kentucky Derby gained slightly in popularity every year until 1886, when an incident occurred that threatened to relegate the race to a permanent position as just a local affair.

James Ben Ali Haggin owned the race favorite, a horse he had named, with little subtlety, Ben Ali. Haggin, a native Kentuckian who lived in New York at the time, was a betting man, and planned on laying down sizable wagers on his talented colt. He had also brought with him a number of wealthy friends looking to get in on the action.

Unbeknownst to Haggin, the Churchill Downs bookmakers were engaged in a licensing dispute with track management. After failing to resolve the dispute, the bookies were barred from the racetrack on Derby Day, leaving Haggin and his cronies unable to place the substantial bets they had planned on making.

Furious, the multimillionaire threatened the Churchill brass. He said that if the matter was not rectified, he would pull his entire stable, one of the largest on the grounds, out of their track. The threat was ignored. Ben Ali won the race, as Haggin, without the action he so craved, watched and fumed. The next morning, the man whose colt had just won the Kentucky Derby was gone, and so was his entire stable. It would be more than 15 years before another Eastern stable sent a horse to the Kentucky Derby, an unofficial boycott that was the main reason the race stayed little more than a blip on the national sporting scene until early in the 20th century.

Through the turn of the century, black jockeys dominated the Kentucky Derby, winning 15 of the first 28 runnings. The greatest of the lot was Hall of Famer Isaac "Ike" Murphy, who won the race three times (1884, 1890, and 1891). Two other notable black jockeys were Willie Simms, who won the only two Derbies he ever rode in (1896 and 1898) and Jimmy Winkfield. Simms was also credited with changing the style of riding in England, where he had gone at the turn of the 20th century in search of greater opportunity. Before his arrival, English jockeys rode high in the saddle, but Simms wore much shorter stirrups and hunched down closer to the horse, a style that is still preferred today. Winkfield was the last black jockey to win a Kentucky Derby, and actually won two in a row (1901 and 1902). After finishing second in the 1903 Derby, Winkfield, too, went overseas, riding first for Czar Nicholas in Russia before settling in France.

By 1910, black jockeys had been driven out of the sport. The rise to prominence of black heavyweight champion Jack Johnson had brought about a rise in overt racism, especially in the South. White riders became increasingly aggressive toward their black rivals on and off the track, often ganging up on the horse ridden by the black jock and making it impossible for him to win the race. In addition, the migration of blacks out of the South meant there were far fewer potential jockeys coming into the sport. A few, like Simms and Winkfield, found some success in Europe, but after they left, the era of the black jockey was over.

By 1903, the Eastern boycott of the Derby (which had been shortened to a mile and a quarter in 1896), combined with financial mismanagement, had gotten Churchill Downs in deep trouble. Even though a new group of investors had tried to improve the track in 1894, building a new grandstand topped by the now-famous twin spires, Churchill was still floundering. Its owners decided to cut their losses and went looking for a buyer. If they did not find one quickly, they planned on shutting down the track.

One of the men they approached was Matt Winn, a tailor by trade and a horseplayer by nature, and he seized the opportunity. He put together a group of prominent Louisville businessmen, including the mayor,

Charles Grainger, and ponied up $40,000 to buy Churchill Downs. They then sold 200 "Jockey Club" memberships at $100 apiece, and promptly built a new clubhouse with the $20,000. Grainger was installed as the track president, and Winn as general manager.

Having seen every Kentucky Derby ever run, starting with Aristides' upset win in 1875, Winn was determined to restore to prominence the Kentucky tradition he held so dear.

The energetic promoter quickly turned the track around, showing a profit after only one year. Emboldened by his success, the father of eight sold his custom-clothing business and began focusing all his boundless energy on his racetrack. Less than five years later, that gamble looked like a losing proposition.

Grainger was ousted as mayor in 1908, and the newly elected group of Louisville city officials wrote laws banning bookmaking. Winn knew that if the bookies were not allowed on the grounds, the fans would stay home and the track would go under.

After much research, Winn and his people found a loophole in Louisville law that permitted what is known as parimutuel wagering, a system that had been developed by the French. Instead of relying on individual bookies to set their own odds for each horse, parimutuel wagering used machines to take bets, and all the money bet on a particular race went into one pool. Odds were calculated by the percentage of money bet on each horse in relation to the entire pool.

A few parimutuel machines had been used briefly at Churchill in the late 1880's, but nobody knew what had become of them. An exhaustive search of the track uncovered two, rusted and broken, but repairable. Another was found in a pawn shop, and a fourth came from a local who had one in his garage. Winn called New York, tracked down a few more, and had them shipped to Louisville. A local handyman was then hired to get the metal bet-takers, 11 in all, in working order. Meanwhile, the court battle against City Hall to allow the use of the machines raged on. Finally, a few days before the Derby, Winn obtained an injunction from a Circuit Court judge, and the doors opened as scheduled.

The publicity generated by the controversy sent a huge crowd through the gates, and they bet a record total of $67,570 that day. Almost half of it was wagered on the Derby, won by a 23-1 longshot named Stone Street. Bets were taken in $5 increments, which remained the fixed unit until 1911, when Winn decided to lower the minimum wager to $2, still the standard for a win bet to this day.

Having survived that scare, the savvy Winn knew he needed the participation of the Eastern stables if he was to put the Derby at the forefront of the national racing scene. He began courting owners, using all his powers of persuasion to get them to break the unofficial boycott set in motion by the Haggin affair.

Winn's victory in court in 1908 and the implementation of the parimutuel betting machines had enabled Churchill to survive the antigambling movement that was sweeping the country. New York was not so fortunate. Governor Charles Hughes signed a bill prohibiting betting on the outcome of a horse race, and there was no racing in New York from August 1910 through 1912, during which time Churchill Downs thrived. Once the Hughes bill was pushed aside and the big Eastern stables got back in action, Winn made his move.

The Derby got a boost in 1913 when Donerail, sent off at 92-1, won and paid $184.90 for the newly created $2 win ticket, bringing tremendous publicity to the race, and Winn made the most of it. The following year, the heavy favorite was Old Rosebud, who had been a star as a 2-year-old. Winn tirelessly played up the colt's reputation, and Old Rosebud did not disappoint, winning by eight lengths and shattering the track record in the process.

Winn was on a promotional roll in 1914, and his successful courtship of a truly special filly that fall would propel the Derby to the forefront of the Sport of Kings. The filly's name was Regret, and the striking chestnut with a white blaze on her face was owned by New York millionaire Harry Payne Whitney. One of the wealthiest men in the world at the time, Whitney was a sportsman who loved horse racing. Winn had gotten to know him over the years, and despite their radically different backgrounds, the two men respected each other.

Regret had made her debut at Saratoga in the summer of 1914 in a stakes race against colts, and won without taking a deep breath. She then toted the heavy weight assignment of 127 pounds to victory in another stakes, and in her third and last start at 2, she slogged through the mud to beat the top colts in the East once again, despite spotting some rivals up to 20 pounds. She had accomplished all of that in just 14 days. Given the rest of the year off, Regret was named champion 2-year-old filly by the adoring Eastern press, who speculated all winter about what she would do as a 3-year-old.

Winn pushed and pushed until Whitney gave in. When Whitney announced that Regret would make her much-anticipated 3-year-old debut in the Derby, the focus of the racing world, and the influential Eastern writers, shifted to Kentucky and Churchill Downs.

Regret arrived at the Downs in the spring of 1915 a fresh horse, but with a truckload of unanswered questions. She had never raced around two turns, had never run more than seven furlongs, and had not competed in six months. Furthermore, she would be facing 15 quality colts at the testing distance of a mile and a quarter, and none of the previous 14 fillies who had run in the Derby had ever beaten the boys. Regret caused quite a commotion at Churchill Downs in the weeks leading up to the race, just as Winn had hoped. He knew that if she beat the odds and won, he and the Derby would be on their way.

Winn's promotional skills and Regret's talent brought a huge crowd through the gates at Churchill Downs, including more women than ever before. The Derby had been the social event of the spring in Kentucky since the first year it was run, but with the presence of the phenomenal filly, it reached new heights.

The bettors, many of whom were women placing sentimental wagers on Regret, made her the 2-1 favorite. Regret was known for her early speed, and she shot straight to the lead, bringing a roar from the crowd. She was never headed and won with her jockey easing her up at the finish. It would be 65 years before another filly, Genuine Risk, beat the colts in the Derby. Years later, Winn recalled, "The race needed only a victory by Regret to create some more coast-to-coast publicity to really put it over. She did not fail us. Regret made the Kentucky Derby an American institution."

By the 1920's, the Derby was flourishing, aided in large part by attention from big-name Eastern journalists such as Grantland Rice and Damon Runyon, whom Winn had courted for years. Winn treated them like kings when they came to Kentucky, supplying them with the best accommodations, bourbon, and everything else he had to offer, and he was repaid by their uniformly positive coverage of his event. In 1925, an inspired Runyon penned a famous poem about jockey Earl Sande, titled "A Handy Guy Was Sande." The jock lived up to the plaudits bestowed on him by the man who later wrote "Guys and Dolls" when he came out of retirement in 1930 to ride Gallant Fox to victory in the Derby, Preakness, and Belmont.

At the time, however, the races were not truly linked, as they would come to be just five years later. In 1935, Gallant Fox's son Omaha won all three, and after following the horse around for five weeks, sportswriter Charlie Hatton, who is credited with coining the term "Triple Crown" in reference to Gallant Fox's feat, described the whole experience as "a traveling road show."

The Derby was first broadcast over the radio in 1925 on WHAS in Louisville, but the live broadcast was soon picked up by CBS radio and made its way to a huge national audience. Before television, radio was it, and because of the immediacy of the action, no sport was better suited to the format. The Derby quickly became the one horse race everybody was familiar with and looked forward to every spring, adding tremendously to its cachet.

The Derbies of the 1920's and 30's, an era of tremendous popularity for racing in general, were dominated by Colonel E. R. Bradley, a Kentucky gambler who bred and owned four winners in a 13-year span (1921-33). While Matt Winn and others credited the 1915 triumph of Regret for making the Derby America's premier race, Bradley, ever the gambler, cited something closer to his heart. In 1917, bookmakers began taking future-book bets on the Derby, offering fixed odds on horses in the winter after they had finished their 2-year-old seasons. Bradley loved betting on his own horses, a record 28 of whom ran in the Derby, and by 1921, bookies in New York, St. Louis, Chicago, and Louisville were offering him, and other gamblers, the chance to lock in some large prices. Bradley believed that the fixed-odds betting, a staple of English racing since the early 1800's, went a long way toward creating interest in the preparation of the 3-year-olds in the spring and the race itself.

The 1933 Derby received enormous publicity, though not the kind Winn was looking for. The stretch drive featured a two-horse battle to the wire between Broker's Tip, ridden by Don Meade, and Head Play, ridden by Herb Fisher. Rough riding had been the norm since American racing began, but Fisher and Meade took it to another level, and were caught in the act by the camera of a photographer sitting underneath the rail at the finish. Fisher had grabbed Meade's saddlecloth nearing the wire, trying to slow his horse down. Meade had slashed at Fisher with his whip to knock his arm away as the two hit the finish just noses apart. Broker's Tip was determined to be the winner, and when Meade returned to the jockeys' room after the ceremony, Fisher jumped him and the two traded blows until they were pulled apart. If there was anyone in America who was not aware of the Derby by 1933, the dramatic picture and lively story that accompanied the Broker's Tip-Head Play battle took care of that.

Before 1940, trainers generally took it easy on their 3-year-olds in preparations for the Derby, racing them two or three times at most, usually over their home tracks in March and April. "Plain Ben" Jones used a decidedly different approach once he started training the Calumet Farm horses of Warren Wright, pioneering the practice of taking his top Derby prospects to Florida in the winter to take advantage of the warm weather. It was the same tactical advantage employed by Sheikh Mohammed over other European stables when he founded Godolphin and began training his horses in Dubai.

Jones had trained Lawrin to victory in the 1938 Derby, beating a Calumet horse in the process and prompting Warren Wright to make Jones an offer to become Calumet's trainer. He accepted, and in 1941, Whirlaway swept to victory and went on to win the Triple Crown.

While Sheikh Mohammed may have followed Ben Jones's lead in terms of taking horses to warm climates in the winter, his views on how to prepare a horse for the Kentucky Derby differ wildly. Jones believed in running his horses early in their 3-year-old seasons, and often. Sheikh Mohammed does not. Jones had started Whirlaway, known as "Mr. Longtail" because his flowing tail reached almost to the ground, 16 times as a 2-year-old, and his 3-year-old campaign was just as strenuous. He had run five times by April 11, then ran in the Blue Grass Stakes just nine days before the Derby, and again five days later in the one-mile Derby Trial at Churchill Downs. Despite losing both of his final Derby preps, he was the race favorite and blew away the field. He won by eight lengths and broke the track record, making headlines around the country.

Jones's son, Jimmy, his top assistant for most of his career and a two-time Derby-winning trainer in his own right, pointed to the preparation of 1952 Derby winner Hill Gail, who also ran in the Derby Trial, as an example of how his father went about his Derby business.

"My father knew that Hill Gail was as rugged as an oak and needed to be physically sharpened with a hard race a few days before the big one. Just as important, Hill Gail needed the mental sharpness that could only come from competition. It would bring him up to the Derby in the right frame of mind."

Under Jones's guidance, the "devil's red, blue collar, blue hoops on sleeves" colors of Calumet became racing's equivalent of the New York Yankees' pinstripes. They simply dominated the sport, and if you were going to win the Derby in the 1940's or 50's, you usually had to beat a Calumet horse to do it. In all, Ben and Jimmy Jones trained eight Derby winners between them, the last seven for Calumet. Even more impressive was the fact that they did so from only 15 starters. Ben Jones was often quoted as saying the Derby was the toughest race to win and one that could ruin a horse who wasn't prepared for the monumental challenge of going 10 furlongs in early May. He also said he never ran a horse he didn't think could win. His record proves that in addition to being the greatest Derby trainer of all time, he was a man of his word.

CBS put the Kentucky Derby on television in 1952, and the race exploded in popularity. The next year television found its first equine hero in the legendary Native Dancer, who was a gray, and therefore easy to spot on TV. Known as "the Dancer" or "the Gray Ghost," the big colt captured the fancy of fans across the country as he won every race he ran—except one. After a troubled trip in the early stages of the 1953 Derby, Native Dancer closed with a rush but fell a head short of 25-1 shot Dark Star at the finish. Native Dancer never lost again, retiring with 21 wins from 22 starts, but it was his only loss that many fans remember most.

Two years later, in 1955, a bicoastal battle shot the Derby even higher on the national radar. Nashua was clearly the best 3-year-old in the East, but Swaps was equally dominant in the West. No West Coast-based horse had won the Derby since Morvich in 1922, but owner Mesh Tenney and trainer Rex Ellsworth headed for Kentucky to try their luck. Swaps went straight to the lead under jockey Bill Shoemaker and stayed in front all the way to the wire, holding off Nashua by just a length and a half. Again, fate had conspired to give the television folks a perfect story line, and the race attracted more viewers than ever before.

While the Derby was growing in popularity, thanks in part to television exposure, the patrician powers of East Coast racing made a terrible mistake. They pulled away from the new medium, afraid showing their sport for free would detract from the ontrack attendance and wagering. The decision denied an entire generation of sports fans an opportunity to witness racing regularly, leaving them with the impression that the Derby was the only race that mattered.

They had made a similar tactical mistake regarding promotion of their big events. Unlike Matt Winn, who was always seeking new ways to publicize the Derby and was willing to spend money to do so, the rest of the racing world did next to nothing to promote their product in the booming postwar era. Their inability to see what the sport needed to compete with professional baseball, football, and later basketball, was the result of arrogance and they paid dearly when television made those sports their darlings. Winn, on the other hand, stepped into the breach and the Derby became more and more important with every move he made.

Another reason the Derby grew in popularity while other races stagnated was that it was open to all 3-year-olds. Every horse carried the same amount of weight, 126 pounds (with the exception of fillies, who received a five-pound concession), and any owner could put up the few hundred dollars necessary to enter. It appealed to the underdog mentality, the dreamers who believed they, too, could strike it rich, like Fred W. Hooper. The Derby was the race for the common man.

In 1971, an underdog horse the likes of which the Derby had never seen showed up and turned Louisville on its ear. Canonero II was a Kentucky-bred colt who had been prepped in the high altitude of Venezuela before coming to the Derby. Trained and ridden by Venezuelans (Juan Arias and Gustavo Avila) the colt was so lightly regarded that the Churchill officials made him part of the mutuel field, meaning that he was lumped together in the betting with the other horses that seemed least likely to win. (This was done out of necessity, since the track's wagering system could not accommodate each of the 20 horses entered as a separate betting interest.) They were right about the other field horses, who occupied the five final spots across the wire, but dead wrong about Canonero II. Eighteenth of 20 horses after a half-mile, he looped the field on the turn and drew off to win easily in front of 123,284, the largest Derby crowd ever at the time. Canonero II won the Preakness as well, but was worn out from the Triple Crown grind and finished fourth in the Belmont.

The Triple Crown winners Secretariat (1973), Seattle Slew (1977), and Affirmed (1978) took the baton from Canonero II and ran with it. The talented trio was just what racing needed, having faded from the public eye due to the increased competition from other sports and its lack of TV exposure.

In order to win the Triple Crown, a horse must first win the Derby, and 19 million CBS viewers saw Secretariat do just that. Just before the Belmont, the equine superstar was on the cover of *Sports Illustrated, Time,* and *Newsweek* magazines in the same week.

AMERICAN TRIPLE CROWN WINNERS

1919	SIR BARTON
1930	GALLANT FOX
1935	OMAHA
1937	WAR ADMIRAL
1941	WHIRLAWAY
1943	COUNT FLEET
1946	ASSAULT
1948	CITATION
1973	SECRETARIAT
1977	SEATTLE SLEW
1978	AFFIRMED

ABC took over coverage of the Derby in 1976, and its timing could not have been better as Seattle Slew and Affirmed followed Secretariat down the Triple Crown trail.

As racing entered the 1980's and 90's, it was spurred by the advent of simulcasting, which allowed bettors to watch and wager on races from all over the country. Ontrack attendance dropped off, but the overall handle grew, leading to larger purses. In addition, the creation of the Breeders' Cup in 1984, a day of championship-quality racing that showcased the best horses in each division, gave racing four hours of television coverage to reintroduce itself to the American sports fan.

Simulcasting helped the Derby because it allowed fans to watch the 3-year-olds as they raced down the road to Churchill Downs, a luxury they had been previously denied. What was already a closely monitored buildup was placed under an even greater spotlight. The Breeders' Cup helped the Derby as well, because in previous years, the best colts from around the country tended to avoid one another until a Derby showdown, but the fat $1 million purse and immediate prestige of the Breeders' Cup Juvenile made it nearly impossible for a top colt to pass the race.

The Breeders' Cup also gave Derby winners a chance to face off against their elders in a defining championship race, the Breeders' Cup Classic. Before the Breeders' Cup, the traditional fall handicap events in New York had served that purpose, but not in such an obvious, easily marketable package. An epic battle in the 1987 Classic between 1986 Derby winner Ferdinand and '87 winner Alysheba showed a national audience how exciting that could be, with the 4-year-old Ferdinand getting to the wire just a few inches in front.

Both the Triple Crown and the Breeders' Cup were dominated by one person in the 1980's and 90's, and his name was D. Wayne Lukas. His first experience with the Derby came while growing up in his native Wisconsin.

"I remember seeing the Calumet horses winning the Derby on the newsreels they played before the Saturday-night movies at our local theater," recalled the 66-year-old trainer. Lukas began his career with Quarter Horses, and he trained numerous champions before making the leap to the more lucrative, high-profile Thoroughbred world in the late 1970's. His first Derby starter, Partez, finished third, but that was as good as it got for the trainer through 1987, a span in which he ran 12 horses.

"I had some grandiose ideas in those days about sweeping the Triple Crown, and I was actually doing better in the Preakness," he recalled with a chuckle. Lukas won that race with Codex in 1980 and Tank's Prospect in 1985. "You learn more from losing than you do from winning," he continued, "and finally I realized my schedule was two weeks too late. I sure wasn't doing it on purpose, but I had been using the Derby as a prep."

Lukas broke through in 1988 with a filly, Winning Colors. Just as Regret had done in 1915, Winning Colors went right to the front and ran the Derby field into the ground, making number 13 a lucky one for Lukas. He won a record six straight Triple Crown races at one point, starting with the 1994 Preakness, and three more Derbies (1995, 1996, and 1999). His numbers in the Breeders' Cup are even more overwhelming, with 16 winners from 132 starters through 2000, more than double those of any trainer in either category.

When Sheikh Mohammed decided he wanted to win the Derby, he could have bought some top yearlings and sent them to Lukas, figuring he would be able to get the job done for him. According to Lukas, that will never happen.

"He's a genuine horseman, unlike a lot of dignitaries or owners, and my sense is that when he wins the Derby, and I think he will, eventually, he wants to stand on the viewing stand and be able to say he did it his way."

Drawing a Line in the Sand

3

The first move Sheikh Mohammed made once he decided to go after the Kentucky Derby in 1998 was one he had used often in Europe, with varying degrees of success. He bought someone else's horse. He had never made that power play in America, but when Sheikh Mohammed decides he wants something, he wastes little time, and money is never an object. In the fall and winter of 1998, he opened his wallet and spent more than $10 million for a small group of proven American 2-year-olds. The purchase that created the biggest buzz was that of Worldly Manner, a colt who had established himself as the top 2-year-old on the West Coast before the 1998 Breeders' Cup.

At a reported cost of $5 million, Worldly Manner was the most expensive colt Sheikh Mohammed bought, and it was no coincidence that the one that brought the highest price was trained by Bob Baffert. The 44-year-old trainer with the snow-white hair was in a groove in the fall of 1998, having come a long way in a short time.

KENTUCKY DERBY STARTERS
OWNED BY THE MAKTOUM FAMILY

1992	THYER	SHEIKH MAKTOUM	13TH
1992	ARAZI	SHEIKH MOHAMMED (Co-owned with A. Paulson)	8TH
1999	WORLDLY MANNER	GODOLPHIN	7TH
2000	CHINA VISIT	GODOLPHIN	6TH
2000	CURULE	GODOLPHIN	7TH
2001	EXPRESS TOUR	GODOLPHIN	8TH

MAKTOUM KENTUCKY DERBY ENTRANTS
INJURED WITHIN A WEEK OF THE RACE

1999	ALJABR	GODOLPHIN
2001	STREET CRY	GODOLPHIN

An Arizona native who grew up on a cattle ranch, Baffert had not even trained a Thoroughbred until 1988. Previously he had made his living, as Wayne Lukas had before him, training Quarter Horses. Quarter Horses are sprinters, bred for speed, never asked to run more than 870 yards, and they are not allowed to compete in Thoroughbred races. Baffert quickly proved to be one of the best in that competitive business, winning every big race in California and training two champions. In 1988, prompted by his growing friendship and working relationship with the McDonald's-owning, Coors Light-drinking Mike Pegram, he decided to try his hand in the potentially far more lucrative world of the Thoroughbred.

It didn't take him long to make an impact. He won the 1992 Breeders' Cup Sprint with Thirty Slews and by the mid-90's was well established on the West Coast. He was, however, still a relative unknown nationally. Baffert has a lively, often ribald sense of humor and is happy to display it, a refreshing quality in a sport packed with people for whom anything more than two sentences qualifies as a filibuster.

It took a trip to the Kentucky Derby for Baffert to burst onto the national scene. In 1996, he brought his first two Derby runners to Churchill Downs. Once he settled in Louisville, Baffert went about introducing himself to the international press. Derby Week is a media feeding frenzy, rivaled in intensity and pointlessness only by the days leading up to the Super Bowl. In both instances there is an entire week without any real action, leaving reporters with space to fill and looking for anything resembling a story. Once the wisecracking, opinionated Baffert got going, he became a favorite of the media mob in search of something different.

All the positive public relations would be rendered meaningless, however, if his horses ran up the track. The pressure was on, and behind his trademark prescription sunglasses, the former Quarter Horse trainer knew it.

His two-horse entry of Santa Anita Derby winner Cavonnier and the overmatched sprinter Semoran went off as the 5-1 second choice in the wagering, and as the horses came down the Churchill stretch, it seemed that the joker was set to become a hero. Cavonnier had surged to a clear lead and looked home free just 100 yards from the wire. Suddenly, a horse began chewing up ground on the far outside and the two hit the wire at the same time. It was too close to call and the photo-finish sign went up on the tote board. After a long look at the photo, the stewards ruled that Cavonnier had lost, the actual margin no more than an inch. Grindstone, trained by Baffert's role model turned arch-rival, Lukas, had gotten his nose to the finish line first. With no way of knowing if he would ever come that close again, a devastated Baffert returned to his California home base.

It didn't take Baffert long to replace the nightmare with a Derby dream. The very next year, his Silver Charm won a close photo and Baffert made it to the promised land, the Churchill winners' circle. He was suddenly a hot commodity, and his barn increased dramatically in size as owners called from all over, wanting him to train their horses.

The following spring, Silver Charm's owners, Californians Bob and Beverly Lewis, decided to send their champion halfway across the globe for the Dubai World Cup. The 21-hour journey marked the first time a Kentucky Derby winner had raced outside North America since 1962, when '61 winner Carry Back ran in the Prix de l'Arc de Triomphe. Upon their arrival, the Lewises and Baffert received the royal treatment afforded all those willing to fly their horses to Sheikh Mohammed's homeland. They were given camels to ride over sand dunes, Jet Skis to ride in the Persian Gulf, were feted at parties and pampered in five-star hotels. Silver Charm made the long trip worthwhile, beating Sheikh Mohammed's Swain by just a neck in a desperate finish and denying the sheikh victory in his pet race. The manner in which Baffert and his top assistant, Eoin Harty, had prepared Silver Charm to run so well after the long flight and in the desert heat was not lost on Sheikh Mohammed.

Six weeks later, the red-hot Baffert was back in the Churchill Downs winners' circle with Mike Pegram's colt Real Quiet. In addition to their working relationship, the two were good friends who often partied until the wee hours together, celebrating their good fortune. Real Quiet, nicknamed "the Fish" by Baffert because of his narrow build, was bought sight unseen by Pegram for just $17,500. It took the somewhat immature horse seven tries before he got his first win, but once he got going Real Quiet turned into one of the great bargains in racing history, earning more than $3.2 million for Pegram during his career.

That fall, the purchase of Worldly Manner shocked the American racing community because it represented the first time an American Derby hopeful had been bought, yanked out of his trainer's care, and shipped out of the country. And to Dubai, of all places. Longtime California owner-breeders John and Betty Mabee sold Worldly Manner partially because they had another 1999 Derby prospect, General Challenge, with a pedigree even better suited to get the mile and a quarter of the Derby. He, too, was trained by Baffert, and that winter and spring in California, the trainer prepared General Challenge for the Derby, as race fans watched and argued about the methods and results of his decisions. That process, the very public road to the Derby, is one of the great traditions in all of American sports.

At the same time, Sheikh Mohammed was preparing Worldly Manner for exactly the same task, but doing so in private, disdainful of the tradition. Information is the lifeblood of American racing, and a key to the buildup to the Derby, but that mattered not at all to Sheikh Mohammed. For almost 200 years, the Maktoums have done as they please in Dubai. Once the $5 million belonged to the Mabees, Worldly Manner was Sheikh Mohammed's horse, and he was going to get him ready his way.

It turned out that his way involved no official prep races, but rather a pair of informal "trials" against other Maktoum horses. No specific information was given about the results of the trials, and no videotapes were made for public consumption. All that was known was that Sheikh Mohammed and his people were pleased with the progress of Worldly Manner, as well as another colt, a son of the top stallion Storm Cat named Aljabr.

It was a controversial, and many thought ill-advised, way to prepare horses for the toughest test of their young racing lives. No horse had won the Derby without an official prep race as a 3-year-old since Morvich in 1922. In fact, 44 of the previous 45 Derby winners had had at least three official prep races after January 1 of their 3-year-old year.

The mystery he had created about his horses thrust Sheikh Mohammed directly into the media spotlight upon his arrival at the 1999 Kentucky Derby, just as he had planned. He took the opportunity to promote his country and the wonderful training facilities he had built there. He also dismissed those who doubted his ability to ready a horse for the challenge of the Derby by citing the example of Lammtarra. He and his people had indeed trained Lammtarra up to a victory in the 1995 Epsom Derby without the benefit of a prep race. Nobody doubted the power of the accomplishment, but in using that example, Sheikh Mohammed displayed his ignorance of the vital differences between the English and American classic races. As one prominent owner recalled, "He was the definition of arrogance, basically saying he knew better than Lukas and Baffert how to prepare a horse for the Derby, which he'd only seen run one time. I wasn't rooting for him, and I wasn't alone."

Lammtarra had raced only once at 2, winning easily over a weak field, and was trained through the spring of his 3-year-old season in the warm weather of Dubai. He arrived at Epsom in June 1995 as a mystery horse. However, tradition and difficult weather dictate that the European flat-racing season does not begin in earnest until mid-April; that meant that most of the horses Lammtarra was preparing to face had only had one prep race themselves, so they were all fairly equal in terms of fitness or 3-year-old experience. Lammtarra lagged near the back of the pack through the first mile, then unleashed a withering closing kick and passed almost the entire field on his way to a stunning victory.

In America, the situation was almost the exact opposite. Most of Worldly Manner's Derby opponents had run four or five times since January 1, giving them a tremendous fitness and experience advantage over the babied Godolphin colt, who arrived at Churchill Downs just 10 days before the race.

In addition, the early stages of European distance races are run at a much slower pace, meaning a horse need not be in top condition to keep up with the pack. The races often come down to a furious finish, with the winner being the horse who can run the fastest over just the final three furlongs, exactly as Lammtarra had done. Such a strategy has little chance of succeeding in American dirt racing, where tactical speed is paramount.

William Balding is Eoin Harty's top assistant and worked in the same capacity for the prominent European trainer John Gosden for six years before coming to the United States. He summed up the differences between prepping horses in Europe and in America: "In Europe you can fall out of the gate, cruise for the first part of the race, then make one solid late run and still win. In America, you need to have some early speed because if you lose touch with the leaders early on and don't have a strong fitness foundation and experience getting dirt kicked in your face, you simply have no chance to win the race."

A few days before the 1999 Derby, Aljabr was declared out of the race after suffering an ankle injury in his final workout, leaving Worldly Manner to carry the Godolphin hopes alone. When the field rounded the turn and headed for home, however, Derby traditionalists were shaking their heads and Sheikh Mohammed looked like a desert prophet. Unlike Lammtarra, Worldly Manner had excellent early speed and flashed it, staying in third place throughout the first half of the race. At the top of the historic Churchill stretch, the longest in America, Worldly Manner took the lead, and top American jockey Jerry Bailey had the colt in high gear and was driving for the wire.

The Derby is a mile and a quarter, however, and Worldly Manner wanted no part of that last quarter-mile. A Lukas-trained runner named Cat Thief had joined the Godolphin colt on the turn and the two battled furiously for the lead. Cat Thief disposed of the tired Worldly Manner in midstretch, but the heated battle had worn him out as well and he could not hold off the bold late runs of Charismatic and Menifee. Charismatic, Lukas's fourth Derby winner, hit the wire a neck in front, shocking the crowd at 31-1, with Menifee second and Cat Thief third. Worldly Manner ended up a respectable but ultimately well-beaten seventh, while the Baffert-trained General Challenge, bumped early, never got into the race and finished 11th.

Charismatic had run seven times between January 16 and April 18, a grueling 3-year-old prep schedule that was the opposite of the path Worldly Manner had taken. Sheikh Mohammed had done it his way, training Worldly Manner in Dubai without any formal preps, and he had lost in a race that was run almost exactly as his critics had predicted. Interviewed afterward, he promised to return the following year and reiterated his vow to win the race by 2002.

Changes in his program needed to be made, and as usual, Sheikh Mohammed wasted little time. Realizing his chances would increase dramatically if he could pick through 30 horses to find one or two Derby runners, he went to the American yearling sales that summer and fall on a mission. Through his agent, John Ferguson, Sheikh Mohammed spent in excess of $25 million on yearlings, trying for the first time to select those with dirt-favoring pedigrees. In addition to that group of unproven youngsters, who were being pointed for the 2001 Derby, he made another expensive private purchase, seeking a contender for the 2000 Derby from among the proven American-based crop of 2-year-olds. He bought the well-regarded Chief Seattle, a son of 1977 Triple Crown winner Seattle Slew, who had finished a strong second in the 1999 Breeders' Cup Juvenile. The price was thought to be around $3 million.

Sometime in 1998, Sheikh Mohammed had engaged Bob Baffert in a conversation that would have serious long-term implications for both men, and for the Kentucky Derby. Baffert could not recall whether the talk took place in Dubai or in America, but he certainly remembered what was said.

"I guess I should have kept my big mouth shut," he joked. "Sheikh Mo likes to pick people's brains and he asked me what I thought about his facilities in Dubai and his chances of winning the Kentucky Derby. I told him what he'd built over there was amazing, but he'd never win it without running his horses in America first, toughening them up and getting them used to dirt racing. A year later he steals Eoin and now 30 million dollars of 2-year olds are stabled next door to me trying to kick my butt."

What Sheikh Mohammed had done was to have one of his people call the Baffert barn during the 1999 Breeders' Cup at Gulfstream Park in Florida. Eoin Harty picked up the phone, thinking the call was for his boss.

"I'll admit I was pretty shocked when it turned out they really wanted to talk to me," he recalled.

Sheikh Mohammed's representatives made Harty a generous offer, and less than a month later, he agreed to start training the Godolphin 2-year-olds in 2000. Sheikh Mohammed had listened to what Baffert had said, and decided not only to take his advice, but also to hire his top assistant and place his stable in Baffert's backyard, Southern California. Baffert had no choice but to move on.

"It was great for Eoin, but it sucked for me," he cracked, adding in a more serious tone, "I knew Eoin was ready and would make a great trainer on his own, but that doesn't mean I was ready for him to leave. The worst part was losing a good friend, because we'd worked together just about every day for seven years."

As Harty was working with the young horses that spring in Dubai, Sheikh Mohammed and Saeed bin Suroor were trying to get Chief Seattle ready for the Derby. In addition to hiring Harty and implementing Baffert's suggestion that he run his horses in America, Sheikh Mohammed had also formalized a series of prep races in Dubai, copying the American prep structure. Instead of the informal trials he had used with Worldly Manner, he flew top American jockeys to the desert and ran real races, although exclusively with his own horses. The races were taped and timed, giving the whole operation a semblance of openness. However, reports filtered out from the desert about unpublished trials taking place after the United Arab Emirates Derby in late March, which had been run on the same day as the Dubai World Cup. On his home ground, the sheikh still played by his own rules.

Chief Seattle had a few minor ailments that set back his training and did not run in the 2000 Derby. In fact, the $3 million colt never raced again and now stands at stud in Kentucky. Sheikh Mohammed was not about to miss the Derby, however, and he showed up with two horses, China Visit and Curule.

Curule had never raced anywhere but Dubai, so despite running in the formalized preps, he was still an unknown quantity. The other half of the entry, China Visit, had run once in Europe as a 2-year-old, winning a grass sprint in France before heading to the desert. As a 3-year-old he had won his only official start, the 2000 UAE Derby, and since he was by the sire Red Ransom, he was bred to go the mile and a quarter. If Sheikh Mohammed was going to shock the world and win the 2000 Derby from the desert, China Visit figured to be the one to pull it off. Still, most observers felt that his lone 3-year-old prep would leave him short on experience and fitness.

The horse that was the talk of the race, Fusaichi Pegasus, had been the highest-priced yearling sold at Keeneland in all of 1998, fetching $4 million, but not from Sheikh Mohammed. The son of Mr. Prospector was purchased by a ponytailed Japanese businessman named Fusao Sekiguchi. Much as Sheikh Mohammed had been doing for nearly 20 years, Sekiguchi had told his advisors he wanted to buy the horse they felt was the best in the sale, and that money was no object. They identified the horse, he paid top dollar, and a year and a half later, he owned the Derby favorite.

Fusaichi Pegasus romped home in the 2000 Derby. Beautifully prepared by patient trainer Neil Drysdale, he won easily and gave the impression that he had only begun tapping a deep well of potential. As it turned out, he was unable to overcome a series of nagging injuries, and his spectacular Derby run was as good as it got. His victory also marked the first time a million-dollar yearling had made it to the

Churchill Downs winners' circle on the first Saturday in May, a fact that emphasized just how difficult it is to buy the Kentucky Derby.

Both of the colts in the Godolphin entry, sent off at 23-1, had lagged near the rear of the 19-horse field in the early stages. Rounding the final turn, China Visit loomed dangerously on the far outside, but lacked any real kick in the lane. He never threatened the leaders and finished sixth. Curule stayed near the back and made a mild late rally to be seventh, just a head behind his stablemate. While certainly not disgraced, they were never a factor, either. Two years into his prediction, Sheikh Mohammed had been able to do no better than sixth in the Derby, but he had that large, expensive group of 2-year-olds with Harty in California, gearing up for their assault on the 2001 Run for the Roses.

Harty's 32-horse stable included the most expensive yearling purchased at Keeneland in 1999, a $3.9 million son of the stallion Kris S. that Sheikh Mohammed hoped would follow the Derby-winning trail Fusaichi Pegasus had just blazed. It was an expensive group of horses, but one that had been rather hastily assembled. Sheikh Mohammed and Ferguson had bought the yearlings in the summer and fall, but they had nobody in place to work with the young horses. William Balding was the first person they hired.

"I got the job in the middle of November on a Friday, left England for Dubai the next Tuesday, and 30 horses arrived two days later," recalled the tall, lean, soft-spoken Englishman. "It was my job to break them, pre-school them, and get them going. Eoin came over in February and we all left for America in April."

The pressure was on Harty, and he knew it, referring to himself at the time as "the fall guy." He realized that with so many regally bred colts in his care, if he did not shape at least one into a legitimate Derby hopeful, it would reflect poorly on his ability to run a stable. The native of Ireland had served two long apprenticeships since coming to America in his early 20's, and he felt he was ready and desperately wanted to prove it. Before his seven years with Baffert, the wiry, angular Harty had spent seven with transplanted Englishman John Russell, a respected horseman on the Southern California circuit.

The styles of Harty's two mentors could not have been more different, both on and off the track. Baffert had a barn equally weighted between young and older horses, and his workout regimen placed an emphasis on speed, which was not surprising, given his background with Quarter Horses. He wanted his runners fit and on edge when they went to race, like trash-talking 100-meter sprinters. Russell generally trained older, grass-favoring horses, and his workout philosophy was more European, given to long, slow gallops. His charges went to the gate relaxed and with a good foundation, more like quiet long-distance runners. Whereas Baffert was brash and media-friendly, Russell was quiet and private.

Baffert likes to joke that "It took me three years just to train the John Russell out of Eoin," but Harty is far more diplomatic. He knew that the two had worked with different types of horses.

"From John I learned patience and common sense," recalled Harty. "John was also a good businessman and I watched how he handled everything pretty closely. He didn't have very many 2-year-olds, so it was a big shift going to Bob's barn where he had quite a few. It took me a little while to learn what Bob wanted, but the bottom line is that he knows all of his horses and treats them as individuals, just like John had done. Also, we had a mutual respect from the start and I didn't mind his jokes, which made things pretty easy."

One of the hurdles confronting Harty was that he would have to face Baffert on an almost daily basis. The Baffert babies had dominated the 2-year-old races in Southern California the previous three years, and he was loaded again in 2000. The two joked often about what they termed a friendly rivalry. A smiling Baffert commented, "I love to needle Eoin, and what should be fun is that now he'll have a chance to get me back. I'll tell you what, though, if I start whipping that bunch of bluebloods he's got in his barn, I'll be on him every morning."

It is very rare that a coach or trainer stepping out on his own for the first time in any sport does so in his mentor's backyard while that individual is still in his prime. When Pat Riley left the New York Knicks to run the Miami Heat, his trusted assistant, Jeff Van Gundy, took over. The two had been close friends, talking every day for years. Once they became rivals, they stopped speaking entirely, consumed by trying to beat each other and no longer willing to share their insights and troubles with someone with whom they were in direct competition.

Harty and Baffert were in a similarly difficult situation. All Harty had in his barn were 2-year-olds, and every time he entered one in a race, a Baffert horse would be there to test him.

Many of the 2000 Godolphin 2-year-olds were what Harty termed backward. That meant they were immature, physically and/or mentally, and not ready to race early in their 2-year-old year. One of the most backward of the group was the $3.9 million yearling, named Dubai to Dubai. Since forming Godolphin, Sheikh Mohammed has inserted "Dubai" into the names of horses he feels have a chance at greatness, in the hope that their success will put the country in the spotlight. The most successful example of this was Dubai Millenium, whom Sheikh Mohammed called "the best horse I've ever owned or seen." It appeared highly unlikely, however, that the gambit would succeed in 2000.

The first of the Harty horses debuted in early July at Hollywood Park in Los Angeles, where they went winless in six starts, an inauspicious beginning. In late July, they made the 90-mile trek south, down the San Diego Freeway to Del Mar, the picturesque racetrack on the Pacific Coast. Del Mar was created by the late actor and singer Bing Crosby, a horse-racing fan and owner. Crosby maintained a vacation home and horse ranch in Rancho Santa Fe, a hilly community just a few miles east of the Pacific Ocean and 20 miles north of San Diego. Against the advice of his lawyer, Crosby convinced some Hollywood friends to join him in building a racetrack a few miles west of his home. They bought a 350-acre parcel of land adjacent to the beach, and in 1937, Crosby greeted fans at the gate on opening day. A match race between the immensely popular Seabiscuit and Crosby's own Ligaroti the very next year drew more than 20,000 fans and a coast-to-coast radio audience and put the seaside track on the national map to stay.

Harty finally got his first win with one of the Godolphin 2-year-olds on July 29, 2000, courtesy of a $1.3 million yearling purchase named E Dubai. The son of top sire Mr. Prospector displayed tremendous early speed in capturing his debut, beating the Baffert-trained Glorious Bid in the process. It would be the only time in 19 tries at Del Mar that a Harty runner would win a race with a Baffert entrant in the field.

Many young horses struggle with sore shins, the product of putting too much pressure on their still-growing bones. To Harty's dismay, E Dubai was one of them. He raced only once more in 2000, losing a stakes race to a Baffert colt.

There was, however, one other emerging stakes horse in Harty's stable, a colt Sheikh Mohammed had bred in Ireland and named Street Cry. The trainer was high on the colt from the start, and he ran a strong second in his debut at Hollywood Park. A month later at Del Mar, Street Cry won his second start impressively, and Harty entered him in the big 2-year-old race of the meet, the Del Mar Futurity.

Baffert had won the previous four runnings of that event, and had three of the eight horses in the 2000 field, including Flame Thrower, impressive winner of a stakes two weeks earlier. The other top contender was Squirtle Squirt, a $25,000 yearling purchase who had been a front-running winner of three stakes at Hollywood Park.

As the field came down the stretch, Squirtle Squirt was laboring and the Futurity became a Harty-Baffert match race. Flame Thrower was on the inside, with Street Cry right on his shoulder. Flame Thrower had battled furiously for the early lead while Street Cry had rated nicely just off the pace, a scenario that set the race up for the Godolphin colt to ease on by to victory. Street Cry did poke his head in front 20 yards from home, but Flame Thrower battled back and regained the lead at the wire. The teacher had denied the pupil again, as he had done the entire summer. Baffert finished the meet with 33 wins, more than twice as many as the runner-up, and a Del Mar record. The friendly competition had turned into a rout.

The two trainers squared off again three weeks later in the Norfolk Stakes at Santa Anita, the final California prep for the Breeders' Cup Juvenile. The Norfolk is a one-mile race, and Harty believed that his colt, bred for distance, was better suited to the two-turn contest than Flame Thrower. The two once again hooked up at the top of the stretch, raced as a team down the lane, and just as at Del Mar, Street Cry edged in front near the wire. However, the game Flame Thrower dug down, fought back, and beat his rival to the wire by a neck. Said an exasperated Harty after the race, "Apparently, it will take an act of God for my horse to get by Flame Thrower."

Horses are just like people, in that some are inherently more competitive than others. The legendary John Henry, a popular gelding who won 39 races in his remarkable eight-year career, was as fierce a competitor as has ever set foot on a racetrack. If he saw another horse challenging him near the finish, he would immediately fight back, digging in and practically refusing to lose. Others are just the opposite. They are known as hangers, horses that will get right up to another horse, look him in the eye, and then hang, refusing to push on by. Street Cry was racing like a classic hanger.

The rivals faced each other one final time in the 2000 Breeders' Cup Juvenile, run at Churchill Downs. Also in the field was Point Given, whom Baffert had sent out of town near the end of the Del Mar meet in order to get the colt some experience running around two turns. He'd won the mile-and-a-sixteenth Kentucky Cup Juvenile at Turfway Park, then finished second in the prestigious Champagne Stakes in New York, prompting Baffert to say, "He's still pretty clueless, but that horse has so much talent it's scary."

Street Cry was not alone wearing the Godolphin blue in the Juvenile. Sheikh Mohammed had also sent Noverre, a homebred colt out of the same mare that had produced 1991 Breeders' Cup Juvenile winner Arazi, from Europe for a try on American dirt. Under the tutelage of David Loder, Harty's European counterpart, Noverre had won four of six starts on the grass in Europe, but had never run farther than seven furlongs. A Kentucky-bred son of the top U.S. sire Rahy, he figured to handle the dirt, but the tight turns, large field, and extra distance posed other questions for him to answer.

Street Cry finally finished in front of Flame Thrower, who suffered a knee injury in the race, but the best he could do was third. He was beaten by Macho Uno, a gray blur from the powerful Frank Stronach stable, and Point Given, who had made an incredible late run but fell a nose short at the wire. Noverre had trouble handling the first turn and never made an impact, finishing 11th.

Although it might seem surprising, winning the Breeders' Cup Juvenile has not been a springboard to similar success on the first Saturday in May. From its inception in 1984 through 2000, none of the 17 winners of the Juvenile had gone on to win the Kentucky Derby. In fact, none had ever even finished second, and only two had been third. Baffert alluded to that fact in typically blunt fashion the day after the 2000 Juvenile, saying, "Hell, it's probably good we got beat 'cause now at least we can win the Derby."

RECORD OF BREEDERS' CUP JUVENILE WINNERS IN KENTUCKY DERBY

2000	MACHO UNO	DID NOT RUN	
1999	ANEES	13th	
1998	ANSWER LIVELY	10th	
1997	FAVORITE TRICK	8th	
1996	BOSTON HARBOR	DID NOT RUN	
1995	UNBRIDLED'S SONG	5th	
1994	TIMBER COUNTRY	3rd	(Won Preakness)
1993	BROCCO	4th	
1992	GILDED TIME	DID NOT RUN	
1991	ARAZI	8th	
1990	FLY SO FREE	5th	
1989	RHYTHM	DID NOT RUN	
1988	IS IT TRUE	DID NOT RUN	
1987	SUCCESS EXPRESS	DID NOT RUN	
1986	CAPOTE	16th	
1985	TASSO	DID NOT RUN	
1984	CHIEF'S CROWN	3RD	

Harty's first season was disappointing, but Street Cry's third-place finish in the Breeders' Cup made up for a lot, according to the conditioner.

"Well, the goal is simple—find a Kentucky Derby horse. Street Cry is definitely that. He's got class, tactical speed, and his pedigree says he can get the distance. I'm hopeful he continues to develop in Dubai and if so, he'll be back at Churchill next May."

After the Breeders' Cup, the Godolphin 2-year-olds were shut down for the year. They were required to spend 30 days in quarantine in Southern California before being flown back to Dubai in early December. While Street Cry was idle, Baffert ran Point Given in the Hollywood Futurity in mid-December, a race he won easily. The runner-up in that race was Millenium Wind, who was making only his second career start. Also during that period, trainer John Ward sent out a gray colt called Monarchos to run third in a maiden race at Churchill Downs, then shipped him to Florida to prepare for his 3-year-old debut on January 13.

Of the 17 horses that made it to the Kentucky Derby in the spring of 2001, 13 ran at least once during the time the Godolphin colts were in quarantine, gaining valuable experience in doing so. Part of the price Sheikh Mohammed pays for his insistence on flying all his Derby hopefuls back to Dubai is denying them that opportunity. Another part of the price is that when the horses get to Dubai, they change trainers. No matter how capable bin Suroor is, it takes him time to learn their individual habits, likes, and dislikes. Harty can make notes and brief Suroor, but there is still going to be time lost as the trainer and his assistants put the horses through their daily paces in the desert.

Asked his opinion of Sheikh Mohammed's unique and ambitious plan, veteran trainer Jack Van Berg, who won the 1987 Derby with Hall of Famer Alysheba, took off his cowboy hat, rubbed his bald head, and said, "All he's doin' is makin' a pretty darn tough task a lot tougher, but hell, it's his money."

4

Pace Makes the Race

More than 160,000 fans packed into Churchill Downs to watch the 127th running of the Derby on May 5, 2001, but not many people had a clear view of the mile-and-a-quarter race. Half the crowd was in the infield, able to see just a glimpse of the horses as they shot past. The sight lines in the ancient grandstand, especially on either end, are not much better. One person who did have a good spot and was watching intently was Sheikh Mohammed.

None of the 32 regally bred 2-year-olds he had sent to Eoin Harty in the spring of 2000 had made it to the Derby. Street Cry had come close, but like Aljabr two years earlier, he had been scratched a few days before the race due to a nagging ankle injury. His absence made the first full year of Sheikh Mohammed's ambitious, expensive American-based Derby experiment an abject failure. Sheikh Mohammed is not accustomed to failure, especially when it comes from a plan he formulated himself.

Surprisingly, he still had a runner in the race. The previous December, he had purchased a colt named Express Tour from an American couple who had bred him in Florida and raced him there as a 2-year-old, where he won three of four starts, sweeping the Florida Stallion Stakes series. The price was a reported $1 million, pocket change for Sheikh Mohammed but a life-changing sum for Butch and Karen Silva. Longtime farmers and horse people, they were now able to cut back their seven-day-a-week work schedule and put some money in the bank. Having spent upward of $30 million buying and training the 32 Harty horses, the million dollars Sheikh Mohammed spent on Express Tour turned out to be the cost of saving face.

When he bought other people's horses in Europe, Sheikh Mohammed was like a cheetah looking for the weak antelope in the herd, targeting those in need of money in hand instead of hope for the future. For a long time, he would single out a particular horse and have his emissaries make the owners an offer they couldn't refuse. When he bought Worldly Manner and Chief Seattle, he had followed that same plan. Not anymore.

Xavier Moreau is a French horse trader who helped engineer the Express Tour deal and has facilitated many other private purchases for Sheikh Mohammed over the years, mostly for purebred Arabians, but occasionally Thoroughbreds as well.

"Sheikh Mohammed rarely makes any offers anymore because he feels people try to take advantage if they find out he's the potential buyer," said Moreau. "Now he prefers to have his people ask the owner to name a price to find out if they are really willing to sell. If they are willing to do so, as the Silvas were, then he proceeds."

The 2001 Derby had been even more eagerly anticipated than usual by many in the sport because of the presence of the heavy race favorite,

Point Given. The massive chestnut son of '95 Derby winner Thunder Gulch who had just missed in the Breeders' Cup Juvenile had matured nicely and annihilated the competition in his two Derby prep races at 3.

Bob Baffert had made it clear that he felt he had the best horse in the race, and coming from a man who had won two of the last four Derbies, that meant a lot. Point Given's owner, Prince Ahmed Salman, was hoping to one-up Sheikh Mohammed by becoming the first Arab to win the Derby.

By the year 2000, there had been only 11 Triple Crown winners in American racing history, and none since Affirmed in 1978. There have been, however, some close calls in recent years, two of which featured Baffert-trained horses. Both of his Derby winners (Silver Charm in 1997 and Real Quiet in 1998) had won the second leg, the Preakness, only to be denied a hallowed place in equine history in the mile-and-a-half Belmont. Real Quiet had come within a nose, losing a tight photo after having held a seemingly insurmountable lead. The trainer was hoping that for him, the third time would be the charm.

The other close call had come from Charismatic. After springing the upset in the 1999 Derby, he took the Preakness in style, giving Wayne Lukas a shot at the elusive Triple Crown. In the Belmont, clearly beaten but still giving everything he had, Charismatic suffered a broken left foreleg just after crossing the wire. Fortunately, the horse survived, and while he never raced again, he now stands at stud. Lukas has run far more horses (38) in the Derby than any other trainer, and had at least one starter in every race from 1981 through 2000, but his record streak came to an end in 2001.

When the gates opened for the 2001 Derby, there was a mad dash for the early lead. Express Tour, a huge, well-muscled horse, had broken well and his jockey, David Flores, placed him in an excellent position, just behind the early leaders. Point Given had gotten out of the gate well, too, and he was in a good spot, in the clear on the outside and just behind the front-runners.

There were three horses in the first bunch, Balto Star, Congaree, and Millenium Wind, who had attracted a great deal of attention from the bettors. They were the trio that had won the last major prep races, run on the same day, three weeks before the Derby.

The lengthy buildup to the Derby, almost a full year in the making, fosters a level of anticipation unlike that of any other major sporting event. It begins when the 2-year-olds first take to the track in June and reaches another level when the Breeders' Cup is run in late October. The past performances of the Breeders' Cup Juvenile contenders are carefully dissected, pedigrees are analyzed, and predictions are made. Every other 2-year-old that shows promise in November or December is viewed through the same prism. For each owner, trainer, and jockey involved with a young horse that shows real talent, the Derby is the pot of gold at the end of the rainbow.

On January 1, the date when all Thoroughbreds officially become a year older, regardless of their actual date of birth, the excitement goes up a notch and increases exponentially with every prep race from that point on. As of 2002, there were some 40 preps across the country for owners and trainers to pick from on the increasingly packed spring racing schedule. Starting in February, not a week goes by without a prep race with Derby ramifications. As Lukas noted, however, the prep races can create a dilemma for owners and trainers.

"Winning a race like the Blue Grass or Santa Anita Derby now means so much as far as breeding and stud fees that you have to really decide what you're shooting for, winning the prep or having your horse primed for the Derby. You have to be willing to give up something."

One of the last, most important events for Derby hopefuls takes place the first week in April, a month before the big race. It is the Santa Anita Derby, run at gorgeous Santa Anita Park, tucked into the base of California's San Gabriel Mountains, half an hour from downtown Los Angeles.

The following Saturday, three weeks before "My Old Kentucky Home" is played during the post parade at Churchill Downs, three major tracks hold their biggest preps, staggering the starting times so all three can be televised nationally on one show. The tracks are Oaklawn Park in Arkansas, Aqueduct in New York, and Keeneland. Oaklawn hosts the least historically significant of the three, the Arkansas Derby, while Aqueduct's Wood Memorial and Keeneland's Blue Grass Stakes have the longest and most storied traditions and have sent more horses to the Derby than any other preps. Eighteen horses have won the Derby after using the Wood Memorial as their final prep, 10 since 1955. Exactly the same number have used the Santa Anita Derby as a springboard to a Kentucky Derby victory since 1955, and 14 have done so overall.

The Blue Grass, meanwhile, has proven the most powerful path to Derby success, sending 22 horses on to Derby glory, 15 since 1955. Until 1988, the Blue Grass was run on a Thursday, nine days before the Derby, and through the 1950's, it was the final prep of choice for Ben Jones and most top trainers. As an indication of how training methods have shifted since, the Blue Grass gradually fell out of favor because a new generation of horsemen felt it was too close to the big race.

The Derby Trial, another Jones favorite, which was run the Tuesday before the Derby, was moved back three days to a week before the big race, but nobody even considers it a true prep anymore. In the last 46 years, 35 horses have used the Wood, the Santa Anita Derby, or the Blue Grass en route to the winner's circle at Churchill Downs on the first Saturday in May.

Although a relative newcomer to the Derby prep scene, the Arkansas Derby has been productive in the past 20 years. Sunny's Halo won it in 1983 before taking the top spot at Churchill, and Lil E. Tee (1992) and Grindstone (1996) both finished second at Oaklawn before winning the Run for the Roses. Adding Arkansas to the potent trio above, the last 16 Derby winners, starting with Ferdinand in 1986, have prepped in one of the four.

Millenium Wind shot straight to the lead in the 2001 Blue Grass and never surrendered it, and Balto Star had done the same at Oaklawn. It was the Wood, however, that proved to be the key prep for the 2001 Kentucky Derby.

A win in the final pre-Derby start is certainly a positive, but having a horse reach his or her peak on Derby Day is paramount. Silver-haired John Ward, a third-generation Kentucky trainer, believed he had his Derby horse, Monarchos, cranked up perfectly for the big day and thought the odds at race time, 10-1, were a joke. During Derby Week, he had been free with his opinions, especially regarding the training methods of his more highly publicized rivals. Ward felt his main competitors had made some questionable decisions. He thought Baffert

worked his horses too fast in the mornings and was especially disdainful of Sheikh Mohammed's decision to bypass running Express Tour in
any of the traditional U.S. preps.

Monarchos had emerged as a major Derby contender in March,
when he unleashed a powerful late run to blow away the field in the
Florida Derby at Gulfstream Park. Ward played it cool before the colt's
next race, which was the Wood Memorial. The trainer cautioned that
he was not going to have Monarchos in top shape for the Wood, pre-
ferring to use it as a testing ground, much as a track star would use a
warmup race prior to the Olympics. Monarchos's main competition in
the Wood was Congaree, whom Baffert had sent from California in
order to keep with his plan to keep that colt and Point Given apart until
the Derby.

Part of the intrigue surrounding the spring prep races comes from
the different methods the trainers use to prepare their horses for the
challenge of the mile and a quarter of the Derby. Ward was not as concerned with the outcome of the race as he was with getting his horse
to gain experience and learn from it. He was looking for Monarchos to
run the turns smoothly, shifting into high gear once he hit the final
straightaway.

When horses run, they lead with either their right or left front leg.
On a straightaway, horses almost always lead with their right, but when
running around a left-hand turn, which is all American horses ever do,
they shift to their left. It's a natural reaction to compensate for the
1,200 pounds of pressure that is shifted to that side of their body as
they lean into the turns, which on American tracks are often very sharp.

Ward wanted to see his horse make the lead-leg shift as smoothly as
possible, because Monarchos's furious finishing kick only truly began
once he switched leads and was running straight ahead. The trainer
knew that in order to win the Derby, where the long Churchill stretch
favored Monarchos's closing style, his horse would have to switch leads
without missing a beat.

In a prep-type race, there is also the issue of what orders the trainer
has given a jockey. Although bettors might not be aware of it, trainers
are often focused on other things besides winning, and they share those
concerns with the rider. Baffert had gotten a late start with Congaree,

who had taken time to recover from minor surgery on his knee, so he needed jockey Victor Espinoza to ride the horse hard, getting him as good a workout as possible. Feeling that his colt needed both confidence and fitness, he wanted Congaree to win and, if possible, to win big. Ward was more concerned about his horse making a smooth lead change and a strong, extended late run. Winning the race, in his mind, was no more than a well-paying bonus.

Congaree broke alertly and sat in second early on, tracking just behind the leader. Monarchos broke well, too, but faded to a position near the back of the pack. As the field approached the far turn, Espinoza asked Congaree to go, and the talented colt responded and quickly opened up a five-length lead. Monarchos began to pick up the pace on the turn, shifting leads fluidly. His jockey, Jorge Chavez, then guided him to the rail, where Monarchos made a decent late run to gain second, cutting Congaree's margin in half over the final 220 yards without ever threatening the winner. Baffert had gotten just what he wanted. So had Ward.

A week earlier, Point Given had faced only five opponents in the Santa Anita Derby, the last big West Coast prep race. Until 1978, the Santa Anita Derby and West Coast racing in general were not highly regarded by Eastern racing people, who had always felt their product was superior. The results of the Derby to that point had a lot to do with that opinion, although a few West Coast horses had begun to make their presence felt in the Derby in the mid-50's. After Swaps upset Nashua in 1955, Tomy Lee won in 1959, followed by Lucky Debonair in 1965 and Majestic Prince in 1969. Finally, in 1978, came the epic East-West rivalry between Affirmed and Alydar.

Affirmed was a Florida-bred who had spent most of his 2-year-old season on the East Coast. As a 3-year-old, however, his trainer, Laz Barrera, kept him in California. In the eyes of those in the East, that made him a West Coast horse. Alydar was a racing blueblood; bred in Kentucky by the legendary Calumet Farm, he was trained by John Veitch, a third-generation New York horseman. Even though Alydar lost four of six races to Affirmed as a juvenile, the overwhelming feeling on the East Coast was that Alydar was the superior horse and would prove it over the longer distances of the Triple Crown.

Affirmed had better natural sprint speed than Alydar, and his jockey, teenage prodigy Steve Cauthen, used it to advantage in the 1978 Derby. He got the jump on Alydar turning for home and held on for a 1½-length victory. He used the same tactics in the Preakness, holding off a furious finish by Alydar to win by a diminishing neck.

In the mile-and-a-half Belmont, Veitch told jockey Jorge Velasquez not to let Affirmed get away early, and in addition, he had equipped the colt with a set of blinkers in the hope of sharpening his early speed. Following instructions perfectly, Velasquez had Alydar engage Affirmed from the get-go and the two traveled as a team all the way around the huge track. Down the stretch the two warriors battled back and forth, Affirmed on the inside, Alydar right alongside, never more than a head separating them. Just before the finish line, Cauthen and Affirmed gained a narrow advantage and won the photo by a head. Many consider the 1978 Belmont the greatest horse race of all time, and there is no question it helped the image of California racing. Heading into the 2001 Derby, the previous five winners were all West Coast-based horses, three of whom had run in the Santa Anita Derby.

What Baffert wanted from veteran jockey Gary Stevens in the 2001 Santa Anita Derby was to keep Point Given in the clear. He figured he had the best horse in the race and would win easily if the colt encountered no traffic problems. An ultraconfident Baffert had mapped out Point Given's schedule with the intent of winning not only the Kentucky Derby, but also the Triple Crown. Toward that ambitious end, he decided to race the colt just twice before going to Churchill Downs. It was a very light schedule, similar to the training methods popular in the 1920's and 30's, but a strategy that had only produced one Derby winner (Sunny's Halo in 1983) since 1955. Baffert knew it was a gamble, but he figured that since the colt had run six times at 2, finishing his juvenile season in mid-December, he had the foundation to pull it off. Baffert did not want to have his horse come up tired and a nose short in the Belmont, as Real Quiet had.

Point Given tracked the early leader, running trouble-free in second on the outside. When Stevens encouraged him to pick up the pace nearing the turn, he did just that, cruising to a five-length victory. It was exactly the kind of easy win Baffert wanted to see, and he headed to Louisville as confident as he had ever been going into a major race.

By design, Express Tour was the only horse of the 19 entered in the 2001 Derby not to have run in one of the final four important American prep races. Like all the Godolphin Derby hopefuls before him, he had spent the spring training and racing in Dubai, and was flown to Kentucky about three weeks before the race. Although he has made adjustments to other facets of his quest to win America's most prestigious horse race, Sheikh Mohammed has made it very clear that this part of his plan will not change. If and when a Godolphin 3-year-old wins the Derby, he, or she, will have done so coming from the desert.

His stance has been a controversial one from the start. Since he began his quest in earnest in 1999, American horsemen and writers have roundly criticized his decision to prep his horses in Dubai, feeling it leaves them short on toughness and fitness. According to Eoin Harty, his boss uses the criticism as a motivational tool.

"Sheikh Mohammed is the most competitive man I've ever met," said Harty. "When someone tells him he can't do something, it is like showing a red flag to a bull. It just intensifies his desire to prove them wrong."

Sheikh Mohammed has said that if he had won the Derby after sending his horses to an established American trainer and/or running them in the traditional American preps, it would take away from the power of the victory. Intensely proud of his ability as a horseman, he is intimately involved in the training and decision-making regarding his horses, and he wants the credit. He also wants to use a victory in the Derby to capitalize on the tremendous worldwide publicity generated by the race to promote his country, a twist that Matt Winn would have appreciated.

The final Dubai prep race is the UAE Derby, run on Dubai World Cup Day in late March. The prize money for the race is now a staggering $2 million, every cent of which comes straight from the Maktoum coffers. It is a purse that dwarfs those of either the Kentucky or Epsom Derbies, and Sheikh Mohammed has the money poised like bait on a hook, hoping to draw some top American or European owners looking for an early spring payday. Through 2001, no American had taken the challenge.

In the 2001 UAE Derby, Express Tour outfought the hanger, Street Cry, to win by a neck. An hour later, the horses took to the track for the feature event on the multimillion-dollar card, the Dubai World Cup. Racing in Dubai has a surreal quality. The 2001 World Cup started just after the sun had set in the nearby Persian Gulf, and standing in the sparkling new clubhouse, Mike Pegram had watched closely as his horse, Captain Steve, walked to the paddock to be saddled. In between Pegram and his horse was a large group of Muslim men, swaddled in head-to-toe robes known as *dishdashas*, on their knees, praying to Mecca as the sun was setting. Sheikh Mohammed also wears his *dishdasha* when attending Nad Al Sheba, as do all the members of the ruling family.

"It was different, I'll say that," recalled Pegram, adding with a laugh, "racing is racing once the gates open, but as far as the setting, the track, the people, and the desert, it was all pretty exciting and nothing like anything I've ever experienced before."

Due to the oppressively hot weather in Dubai, they only race from November through March, and exclusively at night, under the lights. In accordance with Muslim law, there is no betting on the races, but there is a free "Pick Seven" in which every fan gets to select one horse in each of the seven races. If anyone is lucky enough to pick all seven winners, that person receives a cash prize from Sheikh Mohammed at the end of the race card. There is also a raffle for a new car, but that is the extent of the gambling allowed when one goes racing in Dubai.

Captain Steve, trained by the ubiquitous Baffert, won the 2001 World Cup, giving Pegram the largest winner's purse in racing history, $3.3 million.

"I spent as much of it as I could before I left, I know that," said Pegram, only half kidding.

Baffert, who had already been to the World Cup twice with Silver Charm, brought along his fiancée, Jill Moss, and they made the most of the whole Dubai experience.

"My hotel had everything, and Jill and I were like the Beverly Hillbillies in there. We had a 24-hour butler assigned to us and all you had to do was push a button and his head would pop up on a screen in the room. We were inviting people over and going 'Hey, push this button,' just so we could see the look on their face when his face popped up. I don't know if the butler appreciated us doing it so many times, but who the hell ever heard of anything like that?!"

Baffert doesn't stay in such luxurious accommodations when he runs a horse in the Kentucky Derby.

"Where I stay in Louisville, you have to get your own ice, which is more my speed anyway. Plus, when you come to the Derby, everyone has an opinion about the race, which to me is half the fun. In Dubai, they don't really have a clue about the racing, and you better win if you go over there, because that is one hell of a long flight back if you get your butt kicked."

When the tote board flashed the fractional time for the first half-mile of the 2001 Derby, Baffert showed little emotion, but John Ward shouted "We've got it, we're going to win it!" to Monarchos's owner, John Oxley. The time, 44.86 seconds, indicated that the pace was blistering. Any horse within a few lengths of such a torrid first half-mile had little if any chance to win the grueling mile-and-a-quarter race. The six-furlong time, 1:09.25, was the fastest in the 126-year history of the Derby.

Baffert, meanwhile, was watching Congaree surge toward the lead on the turn, followed closely by Point Given, just as he had planned. Aware of how quickly his horses were going, Baffert was nevertheless hopeful that they were the two best colts in the race and would be able to finish the job. Express Tour had moved into fifth place and was going well.

Heading into the turn, the early leaders were exhausted and backing up quickly, causing serious traffic problems for those trying to close ground from behind. Imagine going 30 miles an hour on a crowded four-lane road, only to have the car in front of you abruptly slow down. Now picture that scenario without the assistance of brake lights. That is the situation facing a rider in the Derby when the speed starts backing up in the large field.

Despite the best efforts of their jockeys, Dollar Bill and another contender, A P Valentine, lost their momentum in the congestion, and with it, any chance to win. As many as 20 horses are allowed in the Derby field, which is another unique aspect of the race. Until the Derby, the maximum number of horses any of the runners has faced is 13, and the large field inevitably leads to traffic trouble of the kind experienced by A P Valentine and Dollar Bill. It also places a premium on a calm, professional ride, which is why the top jockeys have their pick of horses, while many less experienced jocks, who may have ridden a Derby prospect earlier in his career, are left sitting home watching the race on television.

There are three main types of racehorses: front-runners, stalkers, and closers. The front-runner tries to control a race with his or her speed, gaining the lead early on and dictating the pace. If allowed to do so, the front-runner is often able to steal the race. When pressed by other horses in the early stages, however, front-runners have a much more difficult time winning. Thoroughbreds are naturally competitive, and when pressed, tend to push themselves harder, rather than relaxing and saving energy.

The 2001 Derby had a plethora of front-runners, setting up a scenario in which they would all compromise one another by hooking up in a destructive speed duel. That is exactly what happened during the first half-mile. Right behind them was Congaree, who had been a front-runner in his first four races, but was able to rate just off the leaders in the Derby. He was very close to the killing pace, but Baffert was confident the horse was talented enough to go the distance anyway.

Stalkers are horses that possess good tactical speed, but do not need the lead to be successful. This is the type of horse preferred by most trainers, jockeys, and bettors. They are generally able to stay out of traffic trouble, since their jockeys can gain good position in the early stages of a race, just behind the leaders, drafting much as a race car does. Able to settle and relax, they are in excellent striking position for the stretch run. Congaree, Express Tour, and Point Given had all gotten perfect stalking trips, and were poised to make their moves coming out of the turn. At that point, Sheikh Mohammed and Baffert would not have traded their positions with anyone in the race.

Closers are a special breed. They have a strong finishing kick, but are often at the mercy of both racing luck and pace. If they run into traffic trouble, they are all but doomed, and if the early pace is too slow, they have a tough time running down the leaders. What they really need is a hot early pace and clear sailing once they get in gear. Monarchos, a classic closer, had gotten the hottest pace imaginable, inspiring Ward's confident midrace comments. All that remained was good decision-making by his rider, Jorge Chavez, and the race was his for the taking. If, that is, he was good enough.

For a brief moment when the horses reached the head of the stretch, it looked as if Baffert's duo of Point Given and Congaree were going to run one-two. Congaree had inherited the lead from the dead-tired front-runners and Espinoza had him in full gear. Point Given loomed dangerously on his outside, poised to strike, as he had in his two prep races. Express Tour was just inside Point Given, in a perfect spot to make a winning move, but when David Flores asked him to go, he didn't accelerate. Like the three Godolphin Derby colts that had come before him, his gas tank was empty after running a mile.

As Espinoza went to the whip on Congaree, trying to get the inexperienced colt to give him every ounce of energy, Gary Stevens could feel Point Given struggling. It quickly became apparent that the favorite would not win the race. From the back of the pack, Jorge Chavez had Monarchos on the move. The colt had learned his lessons well. He switched leads on cue and was picking off horses one by one as he accelerated powerfully, taking dead aim on Congaree.

In midstretch, Monarchos flew by Congaree and the race was over. He went on to win by two lengths, stopping the clock in 1:59.97, the second-fastest time in Derby history behind Secretariat's track record of 1:59 ⅖ in 1973. Congaree never stopped trying, but he was caught just before the wire by a fast-closing longshot named Invisible Ink. Point Given tired down the lane and finished fifth. Balto Star and Millenium Wind faded badly after their early effort, finishing 14th and 11th, respectively.

Express Tour had wilted in the homestretch, a strip of ground that has ended so many Derby dreams that it has come to be known as Heartbreak Lane, and he finished eighth.

While John Ward hustled down to the winners' circle to live out his dream, Sheikh Mohammed could only sit, watch, and wonder what had gone wrong, as in each of the previous two years. He had run four horses in the Kentucky Derby since making it his top priority and the best any had done was sixth.

His only consolation was that at that very moment, Eoin Harty was at Santa Anita training his second crop of 2-year-olds. The group was significantly larger and more carefully selected than the first, and everyone on the Godolphin team was confident it would yield at least one, if not two, Derby runners. The race for the 2002 Kentucky Derby was about to start, and Sheikh Mohammed had bought more, and better, chances at hitting that particular lottery than anyone in the world.

Eoin Harty

Dubai's Sheikh Mohammed bin Rashid al Maktoum.

The 1915 Kentucky Derby victory of the filly Regret generated nationwide publicity and boosted the race's popularity.

Joe Hickey

The bloodlines of 1964 Derby winner Northern Dancer were prized above all others by the free-spending Maktoum family.

Michael J. Marten/Horsephotos

Two-time horse of the Year Cigar, whose victory in the first Dubai World Cup gave the race instant credibility.

D. Wayne Lukas, who began training Thoroughbreds in the late 1970's, continues to be a dominant force in the Triple Crown and Breeders' Cup races.

Saeed bin Suroor guides Godolphin's 3-year-olds on the Derby trail.

Matt Winn

Godolphin's stable manager, Simon Crisford.

The Coolmore Group, from left to right: Demi O'Byrne, Michael Tabor, and John Magnier.

Sheikh Mohammed exchanges friendly words with top California trainer and arch-rival Bob Baffert.

5

Honoring the Foundation Sires

The 2001 Godolphin 2-year-olds, $35 million worth of horseflesh, left Dubai bound for Los Angeles via private plane in April. Their 18-hour, 11,000-mile journey, with a stop in London, did not go as planned. The group had not been in the air an hour before one of the horses, Dubai Glory, became very ill, suffering from a bout of colic.

"We medicated him, but it didn't take," recalled Harty. "At about the three-hour mark, close to halfway to London, I had to make a decision."

Having failed to respond to the medication, Dubai Glory was getting worse by the minute.

"I decided he had a better chance in Dubai, so we flew the three hours back, dropped him off to go into emergency surgery, refueled, and were back in the air 45 minutes later. If it had been a commercial flight, he'd likely be dead by now."

Thanks to Harty's decision, Dubai Glory survived and began his recovery in Dubai while his 53 stablemates settled in at Santa Anita. Spanish is the first language of any Southern California backstretch, but the Godolphin barn is the exception. The grooms are all male and all Pakistani, sporting Godolphin blue T-shirts and/or jackets.

Seventeen of the horses, a group Harty called "the second string," were sent to Chicago almost immediately. Considered a cut below the rest after having been put through their early paces in Dubai, they would be supervised by David Duggan, who had been Harty's chief assistant in 2000. The hope was that it would be easier for those 17— nine of which had cost a total of $4.6 million as yearlings, eight of which were homebreds—to win some races and learn their lessons against the softer Chicago competition.

The 36 Southern California horses, 26 colts and 9 fillies, consisted of 24 bought at auction and 12 homebreds, horses conceived by mares owned by the Maktoums. Of the 24 bought at auction, 20 were colts, and four were fillies. The colts cost a total of $19.6 million, the fillies $6.4 million. The big-money baby was the $5.3 million colt King's Consul, the second-highest-priced yearling sold in North America in 2000. The high-priced filly was Showlady, a daughter of Theatrical who cost $4 million. Five other colts (Essence Of Dubai, $2.3; Dubai Tiger, $1.8; Dubai Touch, $1.4; Future Minister, $1.3; and Reconnoiter, $1.2) and one other filly (Sweet Arizona, $1.6) cost more than a million dollars. In all, Sheikh Mohammed had paid over $26 million to stock Harty's well-appointed Southern California barn, and nearly $20 million of that total was spent on just seven horses. There was no other barn in America that housed as expensive a group, or had as sharp a focus. The $26 million was spent to win just one race.

THE 2001 GODOLPHIN 2-YEAR-OLDS
STABLED WITH EOIN HARTY IN SOUTHERN CALIFORNIA

YEARLING PURCHASES

COLTS

King's Consul	$5,300,000
Essence Of Dubai	$2,300,000
Dubai Tiger	$1,800,000
Dubai Touch	$1,400,000
Future Minister	$1,300,000
Reconnoiter	$1,200,000
Moonlight Charmer	$950,000
Polish Unity	$850,000
Al Ash Hab	$720,000
Sleeping Weapon	$700,000
Sunray Spirit	$600,000
Classicist	$500,000
Onfowaan	$375,000
Canadian Frontier	$325,000
Wahajj	$250,000
Burnt Ember	$250,000
Stage Show	$200,000
Media Story	$175,000
Shapinsay	$90,000

HOMEBRED COLTS

Dubai Edition
Gloire de Marengo
Ibn Al Haitham
Janadel
Opportunist
Polish
Spillikin

FILLIES

Showlady	$4,000,000
Sweet Arizona	$1,600,000
Election Star	$425,000
Imperial Gesture	$350,000

HOMEBRED FILLIES

Argentina
Ghunwa
Glimmering Bay
High Esteem
Tempera
Zaafira

When one works for Sheikh Mohammed, it is made very clear what is expected of him.

"These are better horses, and they're more precocious," said a relaxed Harty a week before his first 2001 starter ran. "I expect we'll win a few at the end of Hollywood Park and I look for our Del Mar season to be very fruitful. The idea, of course, is to find a Derby horse. Another Street Cry, or two or three if we're lucky. The only thing that can stop us now is me."

It was mid-June, but Harty had been working with this group since January, and felt he already knew what he had regarding precocity and race readiness. Some, such as King's Consul, were still very immature and nowhere near ready to race. Others, such as Dubai Tiger, the colt named for golfer Tiger Woods, were recovering from injuries sustained in Dubai. On the other hand, a select few were well ahead of their peers in terms of ability and professionalism, one of each sex in particular. The colt, a Kentucky-bred named Sleeping Weapon, was a $700,000 yearling purchase. A son of 1988 Breeders' Cup Sprint winner Gulch, he had excellent early speed and was like the student who sits in the front row of a classroom, absorbing everything immediately. Tempera was the name of the filly, and she was bred at Sheikh Mohammed's Darley Stud in Kentucky from a mating between his mare Colour Chart and 1992 Horse of the Year A.P. Indy. Colour Chart had already produced a stakes-winning colt for Godolphin, so they had been hoping for good things from Tempera from the start. Like Sleeping Weapon, Tempera had learned every lesson Harty had taught her, and seemed to be asking for extra homework, so he decided to make her the first horse of the group to race.

On June 10, Harty stood next to Tempera in the Hollywood Park paddock like a nervous father waiting to see his daughter play her first soccer game. Jockey David Flores was unavailable, so he gave the mount to veteran Corey Nakatani. When Nakatani jogged over, Harty told him, "She's a talented filly and she's got a couple of different gears." Pleased to get such a glowing report, Nakatani winked at Harty and the trainer boosted him aboard the precocious filly.

Starting from post 4 in a field of 10, Nakatani and Tempera missed the break slightly, and were immediately crowded by fillies on either side. It was not the start Harty had hoped for. Quickly, two fillies separated themselves from the field and opened up five lengths on the others. Nakatani finally got Tempera in the clear approaching the turn and the filly finished well to be third, well ahead of the rest of the field. Harty was not pleased with the result, but did like the way his inexperienced filly kept to her task despite breaking poorly, being bumped, and having a lot of dirt kicked in her face. He was anxious to get her back to the races.

On June 16, it was Sleeping Weapon's turn. Despite his hefty price tag and a sizzling series of workouts, the Gulch colt did not draw much attention from the bettors that day. The crowd, baking in the hot summer sun, was dazzled by the pedigree and purchase price of a Wayne Lukas-trained first-time starter named Distinction. Fog City Stables, a group that had made a huge splash at the yearling sales in 1999 and 2000, had shelled out $4.2 million for the son of Seattle Slew. The muscular colt looked worth every penny as the dapper Lukas saddled him under the watchful eyes of his Northern California-based owners.

Prince Ahmed Salman's Thoroughbred Corp., looking to find another Point Given, fresh off a 12-length romp in the Belmont Stakes, had a $425,000 yearling in the race as well. Harty himself was a bit taken aback by the potency of the pedigrees in the field, remarking just before the race that "This turned out to be quite the salty spot, but that's Southern California for you."

Sleeping Weapon went off at 6-1 and broke like a shot under jockey Mike Smith. He dueled briefly for the lead, drew away heading into the turn, and was long gone. He won by four lengths, as Distinction, bet down to even money, ran a listless fifth, earning about $1,000 for the race and leaving the Fog City crew still $4,199,000 in the red. Thrilled to have had his high opinion of Sleeping Weapon validated, Harty spoke excitedly about running him three weeks later in the $100,000 Hollywood Juvenile. The 2001 Godolphin colts were off to a flying start.

Harty was enthused about the chances of another filly, Election Star, who had been working well in the mornings, and he ran her one week later. The bettors, always looking for an angle, thought the Harty barn was heating up after Sleeping Weapon's win and made the $425,000 yearling purchase a solid favorite. The filly acted up a little in the gate, missed the break, was pinched by horses on either side, and found herself well behind the leaders. It was almost an exact replay of Tempera's poor break.

Jockey Victor Espinoza rushed Election Star up to contest the pace on the inside and she got as close as third in the middle of the turn before running out of gas. She finished decently, but ended up fifth, more than eight lengths back. Harty was frustrated, and wondered if he needed to be schooling his fillies a bit more in the starting gate.

He wasted little time getting Tempera back on the racetrack, sending her out in front of a big crowd on July 4. The betting public, aware of the trouble she'd had in her debut and impressed by her blazing workouts since, made her the 3-5 choice in a field that was packed with more royal pedigrees. Baffert, who had beaten Harty time after time the previous year, had two well-bred fillies in the race.

David Flores, one of the best gate jocks in the business and Harty's first choice to ride the Godolphin babies, broke Tempera perfectly and went straight for the lead, with only one filly challenging her, the Baffert-trained Western Love. Tempera quickly put her away, opened up by a couple of lengths, and looked home-free. Suddenly, a horse broke from the pack and made a bold move on the outside. Sporting the familiar green-and-white-striped silks of the Thoroughbred Corp., it was the other Baffert filly, a $450,000 first-time starter named Newport Beach. The fans who had emptied their wallets on Tempera thought they were in serious trouble, but Tempera quickly shifted into the "extra gear" that Harty had touted before her debut and the threat was no more. Newport Beach ran on gamely, but never got close to Tempera, who won by three, stopping the clock in a swift 1.03.33 for the 5½ furlongs.

Asked after the race if his filly's performance was even better than he expected, Harty stated firmly, "No. I expected nothing less, actually. She's the best filly I've got." Before and after pausing for the winners'-circle photo, Harty accepted congratulations from friends and co-workers, some in person, others via his cell phone. In answer to a question from one, he said with the growing confidence of a man finally staking his own claim, "Yeah, Baffert had two in and both made a run at us, but she was too good for them." His prize filly had not only won impressively, but also had given him the opportunity to throw a few verbal jabs back at his old boss.

Gary Stevens jogged into the sun-dappled paddock at Hollywood Park on July 8 with a small wad of tobacco stuffed into his lower lip and a grin on his face. The crowd leaning on the white rails surrounding the large, well-manicured walking ring was thin. It was a sultry summer Sunday and this maiden race was only the second of an eight-race card. Maiden events are for horses that have yet to win. Many horses take a long time to win a maiden race, but the Godolphin 2-year-olds were expected to do it fairly quickly, with anything more than three straight losses cause for concern. Everyone likes to say that he or she was there to see greatness in its early stages, and maiden races with expensive, well-bred horses offer exactly that opportunity. This particular event had a field of only seven, but represented just over $7 million of horseflesh.

Stevens was named to ride Future Minister, a $1.3 million colt by top sire Deputy Minister, but only the third-most-expensive horse in the race. His Godolphin entrymate, Essence Of Dubai, was a son of Pulpit, who had finished fourth in the 1997 Derby, and Epitome, who won the 1987 Breeders' Cup Juvenile Fillies. He had brought $2.3 million at auction, and the combined cost of the two Godolphin horses, $3.6 million, was believed to be a Hollywood Park record for an entry in a maiden race. The most expensive runner, however, was Full Mandate, another Lukas trainee. Like Tempera, he was by A.P. Indy and his price tag, $3.2 million, was almost as much as the total for the Godolphin entry.

Harty knew both his colts had talent, but was wary of how the high-strung Essence Of Dubai would react to his first racing experience. Harty's newest assistant, Charlie Vigors, had referred to the colt as a "jack o' the lad. Kind of like a cocky American football player who knows he's good and likes to show off." Future Minister, on the other hand, was all business, and Harty looked for him to streak out of the gate and show the early speed he had been displaying in his workouts.

Alex Solis was Essence Of Dubai's rider, and when he reached the saddling area Harty made sure to let him know what was in store.

"Now, your horse, Alex, he's a real prick, that one. He's genuine, but he's a handful." The jock nodded, then Harty asked Stevens, who had made an off-color joke about the Godolphin name a few minutes earlier, if he knew what "Godolphin" really meant. The Idaho native answered immediately.

"Sure, Godolphin was one of the original Thoroughbreds, way back when."

Stevens was on the right track. Sheikh Mohammed chose Godolphin as the name for the Maktoum family's elite racing stable because it traces back to the origin of the Thoroughbred breed—an origin that has its roots in the Arabian desert. When asked once why he loves Thoroughbreds so much, Sheikh Mohammed responded, "We invented them."

A horse known as the Godolphin Arabian was in fact one of three Arabian stallions credited with founding the modern Thoroughbred. The horse was born in Yemen in 1724, raised in Tunisia, then imported to England. His blood, when crossed with that of mares from England and Ireland, was greatly responsible for creating a breed that now produces the fastest horses in the world over a distance of ground, meaning anywhere from a half-mile to two miles.

The bey, or governor, of Tunis gave the Godolphin Arabian as a gift to King Louis XV of France. The king, and/or his stable master, then made a mistake unequaled in equine history. They banished the horse, who was not looking his best after the arduous journey, from their stables. Legend has it he was soon pulling a water cart in Paris.

While the latter part of that tale is highly unlikely, what is known is that the king and his people were looking to get rid of the horse. That opened the door for a keen-eyed English gent named Edward Coke. Friendly with the duke of Lorraine, an influential member of the French court at the time, Coke arranged the purchase of the horse and brought the Arabian stallion to his farm in England in 1729.

Coke died suddenly a few years later, and all of his horses went to his friend Francis, the second earl of Godolphin. Francis was the son of Sidney, the first earl of Godolphin, a powerful and controversial advisor to both King Charles II and his successor to the throne, Queen Anne, who ruled England from 1680-1711.

The Godolphin family stables were in the Gog Magog hills in Cambridgeshire, less than 15 miles from the racing center of Newmarket. The bay stallion was said to have been a beautiful horse with excellent conformation, and exquisitely proportioned. He never actually raced in England, but sired a succession of phenomenal racehorses. Two of the qualities he passed on to his progeny were brilliant early speed and a hot temperament.

The most significant of his direct offspring, especially in relation to the Kentucky Derby, was named Cade. Born in 1734 from one of Edward Coke's mares, Roxana, Cade was only an average racehorse, but a tremendous sire. Among his sons was Matchem, who became one of the most important influences in breeding history. Matchem is the direct link extending the Godolphin Arabian sire line to the modern era.

One of the best-known direct descendants of the Godolphin Arabian, through Matchem, was the legendary Man o' War. As talented and high-strung as a Thoroughbred could be, Man o' War won nine of his 10 starts at 2, losing only to a horse named Upset. Man o' War's owner, Samuel D. Riddle, believed that asking a 3-year-old to run a mile and a quarter in early May was a mistake. Therefore, Man o' War stayed in his stall as a gelding named Paul Jones won a photo finish over his old nemesis, Upset, in the 1920 Kentucky Derby.

Riddle entered Man o' War 10 days later in the Preakness, which was then run at a mile and an eighth, and the chestnut colt won easily, with Upset second. Three and a half weeks later he won the Belmont by 20 lengths, then reeled off eight more wire-to-wire wins before ending his 3-year-old season. His dominance was such that after the Preakness, no more than three horses ever challenged him in any one race. Riddle then retired Man o' War prematurely, ending his brilliant horse's career with 20 wins from 21 starts. All but unbeaten and untested, Man o' War may have been the greatest racehorse of all time.

In 1937, Sam Riddle found himself the owner of another talented young colt, a fast, hot-tempered son of Man o' War that he named War Admiral. Faced with the same decision about the Kentucky Derby, Riddle entered War Admiral, and was amply rewarded for his change of heart. The colt not only won the Derby, but also the Preakness and Belmont Stakes, completing a sweep of the Triple Crown. The Godolphin Arabian blood had struck again.

The stables that were the home of the Godolphin Arabian are still standing today in Cambridgeshire, and his gravesite is located inside the archway of the stable block. As a final note to the legend of the ultrapotent horse from the desert, every portrait drawn of him finds the bay stallion posed with another animal, a cat named Grimalkin. Grimalkin was the fiery horse's constant companion, the first high-profile example of the practice of placing smaller animals close to Thoroughbreds to keep them calm. In the case of the Godolphin Arabian, however, only Grimalkin would do. After the death of the cat, the Godolphin Arabian was reported to be inconsolable and would have nothing to do with other cats.

The connection between Sheikh Mohammed and the Arabian stallions that founded the Thoroughbred does not end with Godolphin. The Kentucky farm where he bred Tempera and keeps most of his top sires is named Darley Stud, after the Darley Arabian. Of the three foundation sires (the Godolphin Arabian, the Darley Arabian, and the Byerley Turk), the Darley Arabian has had the most lasting influence.

The bay colt caught the eye of a British consul named Thomas Darley, who was in the Syrian coastal town of Aleppo at the beginning of the 18th century. Darley arranged the purchase of the horse from Sheikh Mirza II around 1700. There are varying accounts of exactly what happened after Darley set eyes on the striking colt, the most interesting of which says that the sheikh reneged on the deal and Darley, undaunted, proceeded to sneak the stallion out of the country.

What is known is that by 1704 the stallion was stabled at the farm of Darley's brother, in Yorkshire. His name at the time was Manak, or Manica, a derivation of the famed Muniqui strain of Arabians, known for their speed. Like the Godolphin Arabian, the Darley Arabian never raced in England, but sired many champions. The best of the bunch was the top horse of his time, Flying Childers, who retired unbeaten.

The lasting breeding influence of the Darley Arabian, however, comes from his great-great-grandson Eclipse. Eclipse was foaled on April 1, 1764, a day the sun was almost totally darkened by the moon, hence the name. His dam, Spiletta, was an unraced daughter of the Godolphin Arabian. His owner-breeder, the duke of Cumberland, crossed the two potent strains and came up with a legend, albeit one he never saw race.

A one-time English war hero who had fallen into disgrace after being defeated by the French in 1757 and then signing a treaty with the shady duke of Richelieu, the duke of Cumberland died less than two years after the birth of Eclipse. His horses were sold at a dispersal sale, where a local meat merchant named William Wildman bought the yearling for the meager price of 75 guineas.

Eclipse, like most horses of his generation, did not race until the end of his 5-year-old season. Owners of that era felt that a horse was not physically and mentally mature enough to withstand the rigors of racing until 5. Since they were only racing for sport or the occasional side wager, there was no undue pressure on them to run their young horses. When Eclipse finally set foot on a racecourse, he proved to be a one-of-a-kind animal.

His first race was so impressive that a local gambler, Irishman Dennis O'Kelly, bet anyone within earshot that he could place in exact order the runners in the next heat: "Eclipse first, the rest nowhere." The phrase meant that Eclipse would not only win, but also would do so by at least 200 yards, thereby "distancing" the field and making it impossible to determine the order of the other runners, since they would be too far away. Eclipse did exactly that, establishing himself as one of racing's immortals and making the opportunistic O'Kelly a tidy profit.

Eclipse would retire undefeated after 18 races, and was later purchased by the very same Mr. O'Kelly, who likely used some of the money he made on that shrewd early wager. Eclipse was just as spectacular at stud, siring 344 winners and pushing the blood of the Darley Arabian, in an unbroken sire line, into more than 90 percent of the Thoroughbreds racing today. The power of the legacy of Eclipse can also be found in the annual awards given to the top horses in each division, and the Horse of the Year, in America. They are called, simply, the Eclipse Awards.

The first of the three stallions imported to England from the desert region was the Byerley Turk, a jet-black horse who arrived in 1689, during the horse-friendly reign of Charles II. He was toughened up when he arrived, having been captured by the British in the Battle of Buda, in Hungary, then ridden by Captain Thomas Byerley in the subsequent Battle of the Boyne.

Put to stud at Captain Byerley's farm, his lasting influence comes from his great-grandson Herod. Foaled in 1758, Herod had a decent racing career, but like Eclipse and Matchem, he turned out to be a spectacular stud. He sired 497 winners, far more than the other two. His blood did not, however, stand the test of time. His sire line began to run out in the early 1900's and is now all but extinct.

Back at sunny Hollywood Park, Harty was boosting Stevens and Solis aboard his multimillion-dollar entry while top-class trainer Richard Mandella was tightening the saddle girth on his first-time starter, a bay colt by the speedy Gilded Time named Timely Action. The good-natured Mandella glanced at the $3.6 million worth of Godolphin horses, then looked over at Lukas's $3.2 million Full Mandate.

"My colt's trained pretty good and should run well, but this came up a little tougher spot than I hoped for," he said.

True to Harty's prerace warning, Essence Of Dubai was tough for Solis to handle warming up, but once the gates opened he broke running. He contested the early lead, then backed off and settled into third place. Future Minister was fourth early on, but quickly sprinted up to battle for the lead into the turn while three wide. Future Minister and Timely Action hooked up in a spirited head-and-head battle at the top of the stretch, with Essence Of Dubai quickly gearing up and taking dead aim on the outside.

Timely Action put away Future Minister in midstretch, but before he could draw a deep breath, Solis and Essence Of Dubai were at his throat. The $3.2 million Godolphin tag team was too much for Timely Action. Under a strong, whipping drive from Solis, Essence Of Dubai pulled clear to win going away, a little more than a length in front of Mandella's game colt, with Future Minister third, another two lengths back. Lukas's Full Mandate never threatened the top three and finished fourth, more than eight lengths back of the winner, who stopped the clock in a solid 1:10.24.

Rather than savor his victory, Harty focused his attention on the big-screen monitor in the infield, which showed horses loading into the gate for the feature race from muddy Belmont Park in New York. The colt that got Harty his first win as a trainer, E Dubai, was now 3 and looking to notch his first stakes victory in the Dwyer. His former trainer was transfixed. E Dubai broke in front and blazed through six furlongs in a stunning 1:07.93, continuing on to an easy win in a swift 1:40.38. Harty's cell phone beeped immediately. The first call was from Godolphin racing manager Simon Crisford, followed by a host of other well-wishers from around the country. It had been quite a 15-minute, bicoastal show of strength by what *Daily Racing Form* reporter Steve Andersen called Team Blue.

A $1.35 million son of the brilliant sire Mr. Prospector, E Dubai was proof that the previous year's crop, a bust for the Derby, was not a total washout. Harty felt that the strong debuts of Essence Of Dubai and Future Minister were a sign that this year would be a much different story.

With Essence Of Dubai having joined Sleeping Weapon and Tempera as Hollywood Park winners, Harty's 2001 group was already light years ahead of the 2000 crop, and there were still 24 colts to be unveiled. The Godolphin 2-year-olds were ready for Del Mar.

6

Trouble Where the Turf Meets the Surf

Opening day at Del Mar is one of the best parties in all of horse racing, no matter what your financial status. The Turf Club is packed with trim, tanned folks of both sexes, decked out in Armani, short skirts, and hats of every type imaginable. Outside that cloistered realm is an anything-goes party in the sun. That crowd, mostly dressed in shorts and bikinis, floods into the infield and grandstand as soon as the parking lots open in the morning. Once inside, they plop

down beach chairs and commence handicapping and drinking in anticipation of the 2 P.M. first race. When the horses leave the gate at 2:01,
a roar goes up and the party continues until the last race is run, then
moves to one of the many nearby restaurants and bars that feature
ocean views to enjoy the spectacular sunset.

More than 33,000 flooded the sunny seaside track for opening day
in 2001, the third-largest crowd in the history of the 64-year-old oval,
located just half a mile from the Pacific Ocean. Fans at Del Mar have
grown accustomed to seeing future stars of the sport debut during the
short but classy summer meet. It is a place where many of the big West
Coast owners enjoy spending time, and they want their trainers to have
their top 2-year-olds ready to roll if at all possible. The same has been
true of the big Eastern stables at historic Saratoga since the 1800's.

The opening-day race for well-bred maidens in 2000 had been won
by Bob Baffert's Flame Thrower. The 2001 version went off at 3 P.M.,
as the third race on the card. Harty had spent much of the early part
of the summer setting up his barn to fire on all cylinders at Del Mar,
so opening day was one he had circled for a while. The race was also
Round One of his much-discussed, much-anticipated *mano a mano*
competition with Baffert, and both the teacher and the pupil had a pair
of runners in the five-furlong sprint. Harty had planned on running Ibn
Al Haitham at Hollywood Park, but a minor foot injury set him back
three weeks. He had gotten six workouts into the Maktoum-bred colt
since Ibn Al Haitham returned to regular training, including a blazing
four-furlong move 11 days earlier that was the fastest of 57 works at the
same distance that morning. Ibn Al Haitham was a talented, honest
colt and Harty was happy to have him as one of his opening-day
starters. His entrymate, Sunray Spirit, was a $600,000 yearling buy who
had shown truly exceptional sprint speed in his last four works. He had
top gate jock David Flores aboard, was primed to come out running,
and bred to win early.

Baffert countered with a Mike Pegram-owned colt and a well-
regarded $400,000 Thoroughbred Corp. runner named Ecstatic. The
Fog City-D. Wayne Lukas combo that had bombed out with two
multimillion-dollar colts at Hollywood was back with one named Historic Speech, purchased for the relative bargain-basement price of

$700,000. In contrast to the Godolphin colts, who had been working steadily in the mornings since late April and May, Historic Speech was racing after only three official workouts, and Ecstatic had only had four officially clocked morning works.

At first the betting public ignored the well-bred, lightly worked horses in favor of Shingen Trick, who had run a game second behind Sleeping Weapon a month earlier. A flood of late money did come in on the good-looking Godolphin duo, however, making them co-favorites with Shingen Trick at 2-1.

More than $1 million was bet on the group of maidens, an extraordinarily high figure for that type of race. Betting on maiden races requires relying far more on rumor and hope than on proven form. There are any number of ways to interpret a horse's workouts, and just as many people claiming to be workout analysts happy to charge a fee for what they claim to see in the mornings. In addition, trainers have different ways of working their horses, so the numbers don't tell the whole story. Some, like Baffert, always work their horses fast, while others favor slower, longer works. If a horseplayer is not armed with that knowledge, he or she is starting from a position of weakness. Many bettors choose to rely solely on looks in a maiden race, feeling they have as good a chance of picking a winner with visual clues as they do with the minimal, and often questionable, information available. Finally, there are always people claiming to have inside information about maidens, and it is up to the bettor to determine if and when those whispers are worth a wager.

Sunray Spirit flew out of the gate and won a spirited three-way battle for the early lead, only to find Baffert's Ecstatic glued to his hip and running easily. Ibn Al Haitham broke a bit slowly, settled into stride, and was fifth heading into the turn, in front of Historic Speech, who broke terribly, and was sixth early on but beginning to gather momentum. At the top of the lane, Ecstatic put away Sunray Spirit with ease and opened a commanding two-length lead. Ibn Al Haitham and Historic Speech both found their best stride in midstretch and flew down the lane as a team, passing the tired Sunray Spirit just before the wire, but still two back of the winner. Round One had gone to Baffert, and at the very square price of 10-1.

"He got me today, but this is a long race, not a sprint," said Harty. Many in the crowd who were watching the races rather than partying circled both Ibn Al Haitham and Historic Speech as horses to keep a close eye on, based on their strong finishes.

Round Two took place three days later, in front of a large crowd in for the first weekend of the 43-day meet. Other than opening day, Del Mar only ran races for classy maidens on weekends. There were plenty of maiden-claiming races during the week, but those were anathema to Sheikh Mohammed.

In a claiming race, every horse entered is for sale, for a predetermined price. For maidens—horses that have yet to win—the price range at an upscale track such as Del Mar is $32,000-$62,500. At lesser tracks the price can be as low as $3,000. If someone wants to buy one of the horses entered, he or she drops a claim slip in a box 15 minutes before the race—provided the claim slip has been filled out by a licensed trainer or owner. If nobody else has put in a claim for the horse, that person owns it as soon as the race is over, regardless of the outcome. If the horse gets hurt during the race, it's just tough luck.

Sometimes, owners will get frustrated with a well-bred horse that has not lived up to expectations and will drop him into a claimer. The competition is likely to be easier than what the horse has been facing, and the hope is that he will win, make some money, gain confidence, and not be claimed. Owners Bob and Beverly Lewis and trainer D. Wayne Lukas had done exactly that in February 1999 with Charismatic. Disappointed with his lack of progress, they entered him in a claiming race for a price of $62,500. No one put in a claim for the colt, he won the race, and three months later he won the Kentucky Derby, one of the great stories in racing history. Sheikh Mohammed does not play the claiming game, especially with his expensive Derby prospects.

Left with fewer opportunities than he had hoped for, Harty asked the racing secretary to schedule more contests for classy maidens, but his pleas were ignored. With horses piling up in his jam-packed barn, Harty fielded yet another entry, consisting of the $1.4 million yearling Dubai Touch and homebred Dubai Edition. David Flores was aboard Dubai Touch, a horse Harty had described a few days earlier as being "fast, but full of himself and hard to keep focused, much like Essence Of Dubai and King's Consul." Veteran jockey Eddie Delahoussaye, known for his flying finishes, was up on Dubai Edition, so once again the race shaped up as a Dubai double-team, one gunning for the lead, the other coming on strong in the lane.

Not to be outdone, Baffert showed up with two as well: Saturday's Hero, making career start number two after breaking poorly and running sixth against the Essence Of Dubai-Future Minister tag-team, and a first-time starter named Sugar Babe. Baffert smiled in the paddock when he saw that there was strong betting action on Saturday's Hero, saying with a grin, "They're right, because he's off the rail today and should run real good. He'll let us know if Eoin's two can run or not." Horses that draw the inside post in their first start are often intimidated by being stuck on the rail, and Baffert felt that had happened to Saturday's Hero. For this race, the colt had drawn the far outside, post 9.

As if on cue, Dubai Touch tossed Flores off his back as soon as he got onto the track. The athletic jock managed to hang on to a rein and kept control of the colt, but when he climbed back aboard, Dubai Touch took off running, leaving the lead pony and post parade behind. It was exactly the kind of roguish behavior Harty had feared.

Once the gates opened Flores broke Dubai Touch on top, but Saturday's Hero was right alongside. Delahoussaye and Dubai Edition had broken sideways, bumped with another horse, and were too far back to have any chance to win. Saturday's Hero blew away Dubai Touch on the turn and opened up on the field, a mirror image of the move Ecstatic had used to win on opening day. As one would expect after his prerace antics, Dubai Touch tired badly and finished last, while Dubai Edition made a little late move on the rail in the stretch, finishing fifth.

A smiling Baffert flashed two fingers at Harty as the horses were being unsaddled, meaning he was up 2-0 in their quite-public battle. Harty, meanwhile, went about his postrace business quietly. He was disappointed in the behavior of Dubai Touch, having thought he had done enough preparation with the temperamental youngster. He'd had quite a few hotblooded yearlings like Dubai Touch the previous year, and the only one he was able to turn around in time to do any good on the track before he had to send them back to Dubai had been Street Cry. He had been encouraged at how professional the "jack o' the lad,"

Essence Of Dubai, had been once the gates opened for his debut, but this was a setback. Patience was going to be a key to Harty's summer.

Round Three of the Harty-Baffert battle took place the very next day. This race featured a meeting between the Thoroughbred Corp.-owned, Baffert-trained filly Newport Beach, who had been dusted by Tempera in her debut, and Godolphin's $1.6 million filly, Sweet Arizona. The entire Godolphin training team believed Sweet Arizona was every bit as talented as Tempera and was eager to see her race. The two fillies had been favorites of the professional clockers who regularly watch the morning workouts, and there was an even split among them as to which well-bred filly was faster. Early on the morning of the race, however, Sweet Arizona developed a slight temperature and Harty scratched her. Newport Beach trounced the field, winning for fun.

Asked afterward if she was the best filly in his barn, Baffert said, "I'd say so, she's a real runner." With a sly wink, he added, "Too bad Eoin scratched, but he just didn't want to face my filly today and you saw why." Harty was not around to hear the friendly jibe, as he had jumped on a plane to check on his second string, off to a slow start at Arlington Park in Chicago.

Harty's highly pressurized job required serious time-management skills. He had to plan which of his 36 horses were going to race and when, juggling their morning workouts accordingly. He did the same with the 17 in Chicago, talking with David Duggan every day. His fax machine whirred all morning long, with information going back and forth between his trailer and Chicago, England, and Dubai. He also had to consult daily with veterinarians, then decide if and when to push certain horses who had suffered minor physical setbacks, such as the ankle surgery Dubai Tiger was coming back from and the fever that had prevented Sweet Arizona from making her debut.

Harty gave his assistants, Charlie Vigors and William Balding, a tremendous amount of latitude in carrying their share of the load, much as Baffert had done with him. As Vigors, an eager 28-year-old who was the only member of the training staff to enjoy the Del Mar nightlife, said one morning, "The great thing about Eoin is that he tells us what he wants done, but then lets us go do it without constantly hovering around. He trusts us and that's given me confidence, which I needed because I'm definitely the junior member of the team."

Vigors comes from a racing family in England, and was a top amateur rider before going into the training side of the business. He apprenticed for a brief time in America with Lukas before getting the job offer from Godolphin.

"Coming from Europe as I do, Godolphin is the absolute top, so when they made me the offer I told Wayne and he understood what an opportunity it was for me and let me go with his blessing. The best thing about my job is being around so many high-class horses. These are the best-bred 2-year-olds in the world and as long as they stay sound, we'll win some big races with them."

The importance of early speed and the emphasis that places on getting young horses comfortable in the starting gate was the biggest adjustment Vigors had to make in learning about American dirt racing. He gave Harty full credit for making that a key to their first week or two together.

"Eoin took me out to the gate for schooling just like you would a young horse. He and Bob [Baffert] had quite the juvenile record over the years, so I listened carefully."

The three colts in the barn getting special treatment in late July were Sleeping Weapon, Essence Of Dubai, and Dubai Tiger. The first two were being prepared for the August 15 Best Pal Stakes, a Grade 3, 6 ½-furlong race. The cool, professional Sleeping Weapon handled everything they threw at him like a seasoned pro, but Essence Of Dubai was a completely different story.

"We've got our hands full with that one," noted Vigors with a smile. "Once we get his head on straight, he'll be something. He's bred to run all day, too, so we want to get him going in the right direction now so he'll be ready when the big two-turn races come up."

Dubai Tiger was just beginning to jog lightly, but everyone in the barn agreed he was a special talent. The plan was to get at least one race into him before early November, and they were on track to do just that if he suffered no major setbacks.

Tempera, meanwhile, had clearly established herself as the queen of the stable. She almost always went on the track last in the mornings, and had a special air about her that was noticeable even from a distance. She was being pointed to the August 4 Sorrento Stakes, where she was likely to face the ultraquick Georgia's Storm, impressive winner of the Landaluce Stakes at Hollywood Park, as well as Baffert's diva, Newport Beach. Harty had yet to win a stakes race as a trainer, so he was especially looking forward to the Sorrento.

Del Mar is a speed-favoring racetrack, giving an advantage to horses running on or near the lead. It has a short stretch (919 feet, more than 200 shorter than that of Churchill Downs), making it difficult for closers to get to the wire in time. Every 2-year-old race run at Del Mar through August is one mile or less, not the optimum distance for the majority of the Godolphin colts, whose pedigrees are more slanted toward stamina. Harty structured his stable accordingly, running his sprint types, such as Sunray Spirit, Dubai Touch, and Future Minister, early in the meet. With others—King's Consul, Classicist, and Onfowaan, for example—he was taking his time, waiting for longer races. Harty had executed exactly the same plan for years while working for Baffert, sending out speedballs such as Flame Thrower, Worldly Manner, and Forest Camp at Del Mar, where they figured to thrive, and did. All of them had won the big 2-year-old race of the meet, the seven-furlong Del Mar Futurity.

On July 25, Baffert ran the 2-year-old colt he felt was just as good as those three, if not better. His name was Officer, and the California-bred son of speed sire Bertrando had destroyed a weak field in his debut at Hollywood Park with such ease that Baffert was already looking down the road at the Best Pal, the Futurity, and beyond. Officer lived up to his promise, annihilating another weak field of Cal-breds. Clearly, he was going to give Sleeping Weapon and Essence Of Dubai a stern test on August 15 in the Best Pal.

The most dramatic shift toward the emphasis on speed and precocity in the Thoroughbred occurred in England in the 1770's. Until that time, most races had been four- or eight-mile affairs, run in a best-two-out-of-three format. Durability and stamina were what owners and breeders prized in their horses, and, as in the case of Eclipse, they rarely even raced Thoroughbreds before they turned 5. By the latter part of the 18th century, however, there were far more Thoroughbreds on the scene, thanks to the success of the three Arabian stallions and their progeny. So, while King George III was occupied with putting down the American Revolution, two English noblemen revolutionized the Sport of Kings. Sir Charles Bunbury and Edward Smith Stanley, the 12th earl of Derby, are credited with creating the original English classics. The first was the St. Leger, a two-mile race for 3-year-olds run in 1776. Three years later came the Oaks, a 1½-mile test for 3-year-old fillies, followed the next year by the first English Derby at one mile.

The two men were prominent owners and breeders who decided to introduce and formalize shorter races for the increasing number of younger, more precocious animals. Legend has it that before the Derby, the two flipped a coin to decide whose name the race would bear, and the earl won the toss. If that is true, and the coin had flipped the other way, Sheikh Mohammed would be on a quest to win the Kentucky Bunbury. Although he lost the toss, Bunbury had the honor of breeding the first winner of the Derby, Diomed. Due to the influence of the new races, especially the Derby, English breeders concentrated on finding faster, more quick-to-mature horses.

Not long after the American Revolution, in 1798, the first influential Thoroughbred came to America from England. That horse was Bunbury's 1780 Derby winner, Diomed. At the time of his arrival in the U.S., the stallion, a direct descendant of the Godolphin Arabian, was 21 years old and had fallen out of favor among breeders in his homeland. He was imported by Colonel John Hoomes of Virginia, who stood him for one incomplete season before selling him to Thomas Goode and Miles Selden. Diomed was an immediate success at stud, becoming the leading U.S. sire in 1803, when his first full crop of runners were 3-year-olds. He died at Goode's plantation in Chesterfield, Virginia, in 1808, but had made such an impact that newspapers at the time said his passing rivaled only that of George Washington as a national catastrophe.

In the United States in the 1800's, racing horses was either a rich man's amusement or an outgrowth of an argument, friendly or otherwise, between neighbors. If there was a bet, it was a man-to-man side wager, since there were no bookmakers and no organized form of gambling. Fields were cleared and races were often run from one landmark to another, as when kids challenge each other to a footrace. American racing of that era resembled English racing of a hundred years earlier in regard to distance and rules. Stamina and durability were the order of the day and most of the formal races were four-mile affairs run in the old grueling best-two-out-of-three format.

Until 1821, when the Union Course was built on New York's Long Island, there were no official racetracks in America. The Union Course was the first to be plowed and harrowed, producing a "skinned" dirt surface that resulted in faster times and allowed for more frequent racing than European grass courses. Dr. Elisha Warfield, a prominent Kentucky breeder, was a key force in the creation of the second official U.S. "track." It was built in Lexington, Kentucky, in 1828 and redone in 1832 with a fence surrounding the racing surface, making it, like the Union Course, "enclosed." Before the Civil War, racing was generally done on a local basis. Rarely did an owner take his horse far from home, as purses were minimal and travel difficult, to say the least.

One prominent owner who had more than his share of arguments, about racing or other topics, was "Old Hickory" himself, Andrew Jackson. Before ascending to the presidency, Jackson had been the founding father of the Nashville racecourse and was known as a big bettor who loved wagering on his own runners. The top horse of his era in Tennessee was Haynie's Maria, a daughter of the reinvigorated Diomed. Jackson used nearly every horse he had to beat the local champ but was unsuccessful. Finally, in a move that presaged the private purchases made by Sheikh Mohammed, Jackson attempted to form a partnership with the mare's owner. During his time as president, he raced under an assumed name, but kept a close eye on the stable. After leaving office, Jackson happily resumed his racing and breeding career.

In the pre-Civil War era, the biggest races run in America were a series of North-South match races, spurred by the phenomenal talent of American Eclipse, born in 1814. A grandson of Diomed, he was foaled on Long Island, raced for two years without losing, and was then retired to stud, or so it seemed. He came out of retirement in 1821, and the following year participated in the first North vs. South challenge against the Virginia-based Sir Charles. Eclipse won easily, prompting his New York-based owners to issue their own challenge: Eclipse would race against anyone in the world, for the princely sum of $20,000.

The world was much smaller then, and it was a Virginia group who responded, with a 4-year-old named Sir Henry. The two horses met in 1823 at the Union Course, before a massive and reportedly unruly crowd of some 60,000, including Andrew Jackson and Aaron Burr. It was the largest gathering in America's early history for a sporting event. The 9-year-old Eclipse carried 18 more pounds than his younger rival, and lost the first heat. After a short break, they returned to the track and Eclipse turned the tables, setting the stage for the rubber match, to be held only a few hours later. In racing today, a mile-and-a-quarter race is thought to be a taxing effort, requiring weeks of rest and recuperation. Eclipse and Sir Henry battled through 12 miles in one day, with Eclipse finally finishing off his younger rival in the third heat. Still technically undefeated, he then retired for good as America's first true Thoroughbred champion.

The North-South series continued off and on through the 1840's, when a flying filly named Fashion took center stage. Bred in New Jersey in 1837, she was a daughter of Trustee, who had run third in the 1832 Epsom Derby before being imported to the U.S. First she beat another challenger from Virginia named Boston in 1841, racing near her home in Camden, New Jersey, then she beat him again the following year at the Union Course.

By 1845, Fashion had won 23 of 24 starts. Undaunted, Tennessee native Balie Peyton appeared with a new challenger, named Peytona. She and Fashion met at the Union Course on May 13, and in front of an estimated 90,000 people, the South finally got a winner. The two mares clashed again two weeks later back in Camden, and Fashion got her revenge.

Racing in the Northeast in that era was confined largely to the Union Course, as puritanical forces in the area had risen up against racing, which was too closely associated with gambling for their tastes. It was the same issue that almost stopped the sport a few more times during the 50 years that followed.

Diomed's great-great-grandson Lexington took to the track a few years before the Civil War and is considered the greatest American racehorse of the 19th century. As a young colt, he was named Darley, because his breeder, the aforementioned Dr. Warfield, thought he looked like pictures of the famous Darley Arabian. He made his racing debut as a 3-year-old on May 23, 1853, and won both of his back-to-back heats in front-running fashion. His combination of speed and staying power was so impressive that a syndicate was formed to buy him for a total of $2,500. Although syndication is now a common practice, this was one of the first examples of such an alliance, attesting both to the quality of the colt's performance and the partnerships that rich, powerful men will form in order to get what they want.

The syndicate changed his name to Lexington, took him to New Orleans, and promptly accepted a match race. Lexington, who had four white feet—something that was rarely seen in an era when that was considered bad luck—drew much attention. He won both three-mile heats handily. Next up was the Great State Post Stakes, run at the Metairie Course in New Orleans in front of 20,000 spectators, including former president Millard Fillmore. Lexington easily outdistanced his three rivals, winning both of the four-mile heats, still the preferred distance at that time in America.

Having badly injured his left eye in a freak accident a few months earlier, the brilliant Lexington was losing sight in his right eye as well and close to blind, which soon necessitated his retirement. Like Eclipse, he was even more successful at stud than he was on the track, leading the American sire list for an unprecedented 14 consecutive years (1861 through 1874).

"My horse is better than your horse" was what racing in America was all about in the 1800's. At the highest levels in today's sport, the same is true. Baffert, who trains many horses, including Point Given, for Prince Ahmed Salman, said in late July 2001, "The prince wants to be the first Arab to win the Derby, and so does Sheikh Mo. Let's face it, for those guys, bragging rights are what it all comes down to, because they have more money than they'll ever be able to spend. What they really want is the best horse, and that means winning the Derby."

Asked then for an assessment of the status of his Derby hopefuls, Baffert quickly warmed to the question.

"I've got maybe twenty-five 2-year-olds in my barn at any given time and a couple of them can really run, but you need talent, sound horses, and a lot of luck. Just look at how I blew it with Point Given this year, or whatever happened there. He was the best horse and we knew it six months before the Derby, but you just never know with that race. That Bertrando colt, Officer, he's the one right now. He gives me a hard-on just watching him work."

The same day that Officer smoked the field of Cal-breds, July 25, Saratoga began its summer meet. More than 33,000 fans streamed in, the largest opening-day crowd in the history of "the Spa," which is saying something, considering that it first opened for racing on August 2, 1864. The two men responsible for helping in the building of Saratoga and the rebirth of racing as an officially sanctioned sport in the Northeast were Leonard W. Jerome and August Belmont. What the Reconstruction meant to racing was a shift in power and numbers from south to north. With so much of the South devastated during the war, and its horse population in tatters as well, the evolution of racing in New York and the Northeast was almost inevitable. The biggest obstacle was pushing past the ever-vigilant Puritans, who abhorred all vices, of which gambling was one.

Jerome and Belmont were the same age, and good friends. Both came from well-to-do farming families and had spent time in Europe, which whetted their appetites for formalized horse racing. In fact, Jerome's daughter, Jennie, married Sir Randolph Churchill and moved to England. She soon bore Sir Randolph a son, whom they named Winston. Not only did Sir Winston Churchill become prime minister of England and one of history's great leaders, but he was also a horse owner and once owned the winner of the 1950 Jockey Club Cup.

Jerome bought an estate on Long Island in 1865 and set about building a racetrack on the property. The two also formed the American Jockey Club, a supervisory organization they based on the rules and by-laws of the autocratic, all-powerful English Jockey Club. They did so to impress upon everyone in the area that the racing conducted under their auspices would be above reproach. Having set their foundation, they ran their first races at Jerome Park in 1866, with soon-to-be President Ulysses S. Grant in attendance. The coverage of their race meet was extremely positive, quieting the strong antigambling factions in the area. Soon after, new tracks began popping up all over the place: in Maryland (Pimlico and Timonium), New Jersey (Monmouth), and finally, Louisville, Kentucky, when Churchill Downs opened its doors in 1875.

Like Del Mar, Saratoga annually features the racing and/or stakes debuts of extremely well-bred, highly regarded 2-year-olds. It was where Regret began her career, and where Nashua, Native Dancer, and Secretariat, among others, first established themselves in stakes competition. On opening day 2001, Mayakovsky, racing in the colors of Coolmore partner Michael Tabor, broke a 55-year-old track record, winning his 5½-furlong dash in 1:03.33. The other maiden race was won by the familiar connections of Lukas and jockey Jerry Bailey. Lukas had dominated the 2-year-old scene at Saratoga nearly every year since saddling his first runner there in 1982, and he stood in the winners' circle hopeful that one of the horses in his Saratoga barn would help him start a new Kentucky Derby streak. With Saratoga and Del Mar in full swing, the race toward the 2002 Kentucky Derby was officially underway.

7

Seconditis

August was a pivotal month for the Godolphin 2-year-olds. As confident as he had been entering the meet, Eoin Harty had yet to win a race at Del Mar. He had been sure Future Minister would break through in his second career start, but despite his edge in experience the colt was unable to hold off a first-time starter and finished a disappointing second on July 28. July 29 marked the debut of a $350,000 filly named Imperial Gesture, who had not missed a workout since early May. Imperial Gesture was bred to win early and Harty hoped she would do just that. Instead, she ran as if she were just out for a leisurely jog, finishing a well-beaten fifth as yet another Thoroughbred Corp. prospect crossed the wire in front. This Baffert-trained baby was named Habibti and she displayed such a devastating late kick that many immediately touted her as a possible challenger to Tempera in the Del Mar Debutante at the end of the month.

Harty had horses in two races on August 4, including Tempera's stakes debut in the 6½-furlong Sorrento. Earlier on the card was a maiden event featuring the first start of Janadel, a colt everyone in the barn felt had a chance to become a real force. Joining Janadel would be Godolphin's speed-burner Sunray Spirit, who only figured to improve off his solid debut on July 18.

Sunray Spirit broke like a rocket from his outside post but also broke out toward the middle of the track. He was flying, but just to his inside, first-time starter Roman Dancer was going full tilt as well and he moved down to the rail.

At every racetrack, there are "wise-guy" horses. These are runners that for one reason or another are touted by someone in their barn and/or a respected clocker or two and get bet heavily. If one is privy to the inside information, it can make an otherwise meaningless race quite exciting. If not, it can be maddening. Roman Dancer was a wise-guy horse. He had shown excellent speed in his workouts and his jockey, a young apprentice named Macario Rodriguez, had reportedly told a few people that if he only won one race at the meet, it was going to be on Roman Dancer.

Sure enough, the first-timer was giving Sunray Spirit all he could handle. The two hooked up at the top of the lane and went head to head until, just as Future Minister had done a week earlier, the Godolphin colt cracked. Rodriguez and Roman Dancer went on to win by two lengths, with Sunray Spirit two clear of Janadel, who finished third after being four wide and having trouble changing leads in the stretch. Once again, second was the best the big-money Godolphins could muster.

Two hours later, a field of eight entered the gate for the Sorrento, with Tempera in the far outside post. Harty had been thrilled with the draw, as it gave David Flores the chance to sit outside and track the

Landaluce winner, Georgia's Storm, the entire way. Tempera had continued to put up scintillating workouts, and the bettors made her the solid 4-5 favorite, with Georgia's Storm at 2-1.

A few folks in the paddock scoffed at the odds, noting that despite their breeding and good looks, not a single Godolphin horse had won at Del Mar. As one well-dressed gent took out his wallet to see how much he had to drop on Georgia's Storm, his pal tapped him on the shoulder. Tempera, her coat gleaming, was prancing by.

"You want to bet against that," he said coolly, "you're on your own."

Georgia's Storm popped the gate and went right to the lead, pressed by a 33-1 longshot. Flores had Tempera in perfect stalking position, third and in the open on the outside. On the turn, Georgia's Storm edged clear, but when Flores asked Tempera to shift gears, she cruised to the lead effortlessly. Although the jock never went to the whip, Tempera won by nine lengths, totally outclassing the field. It was a devastating performance, similar to what Officer had been doing to the colts in that it was accomplished with such ease.

In the winners' circle, Harty was joined by his wife, Kathleen, who clutched a bouquet of roses and a bottle of champagne as their picture was taken. Asked how he felt about getting his first stakes win, a relieved Harty replied, "I just wanted to get a win here, period. We've run a few I thought would win. As far as winning a stakes, I hope it's the first of many." The trainer then saw a happy Mike Pegram and his crew waiting at the rail, beckoning him over with promises of a celebratory beer. As he walked over to join them, Harty quipped, "This is good. I thought they'd have water balloons or a squirt gun waiting for me."

A few days later, Harty announced a change in plans.

"We're going to send Sleeping Weapon to New York for the Saratoga Special," he said, the crisp bill of his ever-present New York Yankees hat just inches above the note-filled training sheets in his trailer. "It's a $150,000 race back there and we may as well split him and Essence up at this point."

The presence of Officer, as well as the relatively lackluster quality of the 2-year-olds stabled at Saratoga in 2001, sealed the decision. According to Charlie Vigors, disposition determined which horse they put on the plane.

"Sleeping Weapon has a great mind, so shipping him will be no problem. Essence Of Dubai will stay here with us," said the 28-year-old Brit.

The Essence Of Dubai project was an ongoing one.

"He can be a real prick, no doubt about it," noted Harty with a grin, "so every day we stay on top of him. Some mornings are better than others, but he's got a lot of talent, he's training very well, and the Best Pal will give us a sense of where we stand at this point. I don't know if he can beat Officer right now, especially at six and a half furlongs, but it'll be a good gauge and he's bred to get better as the distances get longer. We're really looking forward to stretching him out around two turns at Santa Anita, but that's a ways off. First things first."

August 11 marked the second starts for Ibn Al Haitham and Dubai Edition, both of whom had made decent late runs in their debuts. This race was a seven-furlong affair, the first maiden event of more than six furlongs all meet, and Harty felt his colts would appreciate the added real estate. Also entered was Lukas's Historic Speech and a Baffert newcomer named High Thunder. Asked before the race if High Thunder was a horse he was particularly high on, Baffert cracked, "Him? He's a chickenshit, hates getting dirt in his face, plus this race is too short for him, he needs two turns. We'll know more this afternoon."

Historic Speech went straight to the lead, with Ibn Al Haitham chasing in second, a length back, and Dubai Edition struggling again in the early stages. Historic Speech kept right on going to the wire, drawing off to win impressively. Ibn Al Haitham faded down the lane and was passed in a flash by the late-charging High Thunder. Near the back early on, Baffert's "chickenshit" had taken plenty of dirt in the face and run right through it, finishing like a future champion and assuming the role of the wise guy's Kentucky Derby dark horse. Dubai Edition never got going at all, checking in eighth and stamping himself as the biggest disappointment of the Godolphin stable so far.

After the August 11 race, the record of the Godolphin colts at Del Mar stood at zero wins in 10 starts, with three seconds and two thirds. It was not at all what Harty had expected, and he was becoming increasingly frustrated, having to rerun every loss over the phone every few days to Simon Crisford. The promise of the Hollywood Park races, especially regarding the colts, looked to be washing out to sea at the beach.

One of the things keeping Harty upbeat was the thought of Sleeping Weapon flying to New York, stomping his opposition, and returning to prepare for bigger and better things. Just a few days before he was scheduled to put Sleeping Weapon on the plane, he noticed the colt favoring one leg after coming back from his daily gallop. The vet was called immediately, and the barn crew held their collective breath.

"It turned out to be a suspensory injury," said a downcast Harty the next day. "The suspensories are ligaments running down the inside of the cannon bone. The X-rays showed they're inflamed, but not torn, so we'll walk him until he's sound. He's likely out for the year unless he gets totally sound quickly. We're certainly not going to rush him, that I can assure you."

Harty had already lost three other colts for the year due to injury, but none hurt the way the news about Sleeping Weapon had.

These types of ups and downs are the norm for most outfits, but the Godolphin situation was anything but normal. There was a $25 million cloud of pressure hanging over the barn, like the early-morning fog over the seaside track. Trainers a notch or two down the class ladder were just out trying to win as many races as possible, hoping one of their horses would get good enough so they could make some real money. Other high-profile trainers such as Bobby Frankel or Bill Mott had a real mix of horses—a few 2-year-olds, older horses, turf specialists, and others just imported from Europe. They had variety in their day, and it kept them fresh. Harty was working under a completely different set of guidelines.

Two-year-old horses are the equivalent of junior-high-school kids. They are capable of doing exactly what they are taught, but rarely do. Their bodies are changing every day, their minds wander, and they require constant supervision. Simply put, being the person in charge of a large number of kids or horses of that type on a daily basis will wear you out. Two-year-olds were all Harty had. There were no old war horses to turn to for solace, veteran campaigners that could almost train themselves and practically knew where the finish line was.

In addition, he had been given what was thought to be the gifted class, the group from which great things were expected. Never before had one trainer had such a large, expensive group of 2-year-olds to prepare for a run at the Triple Crown. With Sleeping Weapon done for the year, there was now even more pressure to unlock the vast potential locked inside the immature minds and bodies of colts such as Essence Of Dubai, Janadel, and King's Consul.

As had been the case since they first sent her out, Tempera continued to be the barn's shining light. They were preparing her for a step up in class and distance in the August 26 Del Mar Debutante and, as usual, she was aggressive in her workouts, doing whatever they asked of her. Baffert was doing the same with Prince Ahmed Salman's talented but less experienced Habibti. The name meant the feminine version of "my love" in Arabic, and everyone on the Thoroughbred Corp. team felt she was a top-class filly.

Baffert and Harty needled each other every morning, either in person or by cell phone, about the upcoming matchup, raising the personal stakes even higher. Baffert was also busy getting his big horse, Point Given, ready for the Grade 1 Travers Stakes at Saratoga on August 25. After his baffling performance in the Derby, Point Given had blown away the field in both the Preakness and the Belmont, then had been given a rest. The plan was to have him fresh for a short, classy fall campaign on the East Coast, starting with the Travers, known as the Midsummer Derby. Baffert wanted him at his best for a Breeders' Cup Classic date with the top older horses in the world in late October. Salman, Baffert, and stable manager Richard Mulhall were shooting for the coveted Horse of the Year award for Point Given, and victory over older horses in the Classic would lock it up.

Greed, the great equalizer, changed those carefully constructed plans, which had been formulated with an eye toward what was best for the horse. Point Given had battled a balky foot the entire spring and was worn out from the debilitating Triple Crown trail. Regardless, the Thoroughbred Corp. team, flying under a self-serving banner of giving race fans a chance to see their new hero, rushed the tired, tender Point Given into the August 4 Haskell Invitational at Monmouth Park in New Jersey.

The Haskell was normally a $1 million race, but track officials had bumped the purse up another $500,000 trying to lure Point Given. Thanks mostly to Mulhall, they succeeded. The former trainer calls the majority of the shots for the Thoroughbred Corp., and once the Monmouth officials sweetened the pot, he pushed hard to go for it. Salman went with what Mulhall thought was best. Baffert was part of the decision-making equation too, but was also aware that Mulhall has a well-deserved reputation for firing those who do not agree with him. With Officer and a large number of other talented Thoroughbred Corp. horses packing his barn, the trainer agreed to go along for the ride.

Baffert had said more than once that Point Given was shy on training going into the Haskell, and before getting on the plane to New Jersey, he said, "The horse should win on class alone." It wasn't much of a field, and Point Given did prevail, but he had to dig to the bottom of his reserve of strength to do so. He had run like a horse with physical problems, and the protective bar shoe he wore on his left rear foot attested to that fact.

Once back in Baffert's Del Mar barn, Point Given resumed serious training to get ready for the Travers, just three weeks away. Deciding how hard to push a top-class horse is a high-wire act, but over time, caution is usually the best way to go. Jack Van Berg, the veteran California trainer, says that whenever he thinks about pushing a horse too hard, he hears the voice of his father, Marion, a top trainer himself. "If you don't wait on a horse," said the elder Van Berg, "he'll make you."

Ahmed Salman is a member of an incredibly wealthy Saudi royal family, and a free-spending, partying one at that. He once booked the entire top floor of a luxury hotel in San Diego, then decided to have all the furniture removed and put it in storage, replaced by the furniture from his nearby ranch. The cost of moving and storage, enough to bankrupt most families, was pocket change to the prince. He wanted his furniture, he got it. To Salman, even the $900,000 winner's share of the Haskell purse was little more than Monopoly money, especially considering the financial windfall that was guaranteed him upon Point Given's retirement to stud. If the horse never ran again, his accomplishments and bloodlines had already made him worth somewhere around $30 million and the most talked-about American horse in training. Every quote from Baffert, Mulhall, or Salman made headlines, which was fine with them.

Salman's comments about making the decision because he wanted to give the New Jersey fans a chance to see his celebrated colt up close were as hard to buy as a hot children's toy on Christmas Eve. Had he and Mulhall stuck to their original plan, any racing fan in New Jersey who wanted to see Point Given would have had at least two, if not three, opportunities to do so at Belmont Park in New York in October.

In the August 15 Best Pal, only three horses, including Essence Of Dubai, challenged Officer. A gorgeous, nearly black colt whose muscles appeared to be ready to burst out of his skin, Essence Of Dubai was on what was for him good behavior in the paddock. As the horses were making their way to the gate, jockey Chris McCarron notified the outrider that his mount, Werblin, felt funny, and a moment later he was declared out of the race. Suddenly, the field for the Best Pal was down to just three; Officer, Essence Of Dubai, and speedy Northern California shipper Metatron.

Metatron broke quickly and went to the lead, with Essence Of Dubai chasing him along the rail. Officer loped along, sitting just to their outside. As the three approached the turn, the special son of Bertrando eased right on by Metatron without being asked, opened up a clear lead, and nonchalantly cantered home with jockey Victor Espinoza sitting motionless on his broad back. Belying the ease with which he ran, the final time was a sizzling 1:15.08, shattering the stakes record. Metatron hung on for second, seven lengths back. Essence Of Dubai quit on the turn and finished 10½ behind the winner.

Afterward, a bubbly Victor Espinoza was unable to contain his excitement.

"I've never ridden a horse like him," he said. "He did it all so easy it was just crazy!"

Baffert, far more experienced with talented young horses, was just as thrilled.

"I told Victor to save as much as he could, just like last time, because we've got the Futurity coming up in three weeks. He's just a freak, this horse. I've had some good 2-year-olds here at Del Mar, but he's the best. He's the chairman of the board right now."

For the sake of perspective, Baffert had won the last five Del Mar Futurities. Officer figured to be odds-on to make it six, and Kentucky

Derby questions were buzzing around the horse like the flies in the track kitchen.

Harty, at a loss to explain his colt's poor effort, said only, "I don't know what happened. We'll check him out tomorrow and go from there."

Jockey Alex Solis was equally perplexed. "He quit running at the three-eighths pole. He just dropped the bit and that was it."

As far as getting a gauge on where Essence Of Dubai stood in relation to Officer, Harty had received a definitive answer, though not the one he wanted.

Four days later, on a gorgeous Sunday, Harty decided to go with his gut and give the quick Sunray Spirit his third start in a month.

"I didn't plan on running him back so quickly, but he was training so well I figured, what the hell?" said Harty. Not surprisingly, he had gravitated toward the Baffert style of training, working his horses hard and fast in the mornings. He and Baffert still worked horses together occasionally as well, sizing up each other's horses in the process. Baffert had a highly regarded pair of Thoroughbred Corp. colts making their racing debuts against Harty's speeding bullet, and the crowd hammered them down under even money in the wagering.

Sunray Spirit broke running and got the lead, with the Baffert horses running second and fourth early on. As the field hit the turn, Sunray Spirit kicked for home, with the Baffert duo flanking him and in hot pursuit. The Godolphin colt won by two lengths, stopping the clock in a swift 1:03⅕, the fastest 5½-furlong clocking posted at the meet.

"I saw Bob's pair make their move, but I knew my horse had a big edge in experience and something left and it was enough, finally," said a relieved Harty after the race. "It felt good to get a colt a win here and it was nice that it was Bob we held off to do it."

Even so, the win did little for Harty's increasingly sour mood. Sitting in his trailer and staring at the high-tech flat screen of his computer, the trainer let out some of the frustration.

"Well, we don't have any Street Cry's, that's for sure. You know, you're given unproven stock and you have to make of it what you can. We're hitting the board, so you know you're doing something right, but I sure thought we'd have quite a few more winners by now. Losing the big horse, Sleeping Weapon, that hurt. "

Asked about the seeming lack of races for his jam-packed barn, Harty answered quickly. "I'm going to be sending horses to Chicago, New York, and up north just to get races into them. It's frustrating, because the guy keeps writing five-and-a-half-furlong maiden races here. He's sure not helping me, that's for sure. He says he's going to write some races at a mile, and at two turns on the turf, but we'll see. I just have to wait and deal with what comes out.

"Imperial Gesture is headed to New York this weekend to get a race in her. There's a plane going to New York to take Point Given to the Travers so I figured why not put her on it? They wrote another sprint race here and that's no good for her. Burnt Ember and Dubai Edition are going too. There's a turf race for Dubai Edition there, and nothing like that here now, so I figured let's do it. Burnt Ember will go six furlongs and I'm hoping he'll like the deeper track back there better."

At the same time Point Given and the Harty 2-year-olds were landing in New York, so was Simon Crisford. The Godolphin racing manager would watch E Dubai go against Point Given in the Travers, then fly immediately to California to see Tempera take on Habibti the next day. It was a weekend of top-class American dirt racing in which Godolphin horses were squarely in the mix, a strong sign that even though the current crop of colts were struggling some, the Harty-led experiment was bearing fruit.

It was also an example of the growing power of the Arab-owned stables at the top level of American racing. The horses the Godolphin pair needed to beat were Point Given and Habibti, both owned by Salman. In Europe, Godolphin was involved in an increasingly serious rivalry with Coolmore, and Travers Weekend foretold a similar situation developing in America between Godolphin and the Thoroughbed Corp.

E Dubai ran the race of his young life in the Travers, but in the end, Point Given was just too much horse and he pushed by the stubborn Godolphin colt late in the race and won comfortably. It was the fourth straight Grade 1 win for Point Given, solidifying his status as the top American horse in training. All that was left were the battles with the older horses, an annual fall rite of passage for top 3-year-olds. Crisford, meanwhile, was thrilled with the game effort by E Dubai, as was Harty, who watched the race on television. Although they had not been able to get the colt over his sore shins in time for the Kentucky Derby, he was clearly a top-class runner with a bright future on the dirt.

Earlier that day at Saratoga, Crisford had watched Burnt Ember win a maiden race by two lengths. The day before, the filly Imperial Gesture had crushed a field of maidens by almost 11 lengths going seven furlongs in her second start. The two easy wins at Saratoga were a double-edged sword for Harty. He was happy the horses had run well, but reminded of just how much damage Sleeping Weapon was likely to have done had he shipped east.

Crisford wasn't the only one catching the red-eye to California. Baffert was on the plane too, looking forward to the Habibti-Tempera duel. Both fillies had been working very well in the mornings, but with her significant edge in experience, Tempera figured to be heavily favored.

The Del Mar Debutante came up fairly light, save for the Arab-owned fillies. The only other threat in the race, Who Loves Aleyna, came from the Bruce Headley barn. Headley, the trainer of the top sprinter in the country, Kona Gold, liked his chances.

"She wants two turns, but she'll make her presence felt today anyway, she's a real runner," said the 66-year-old conditioner in the paddock.

The bettors pounded the odds on Tempera down to 1-2, but only those who watched closely as Harty saddled the filly noticed she was acting up a little more than usual.

In the Sorrento, Tempera had drawn an outside post, but in the Debutante she was toward the inside. When she broke well, Flores put her on the lead, which was not what Harty had wanted. Who Loves Aleyna pressured her all the way down the backstretch, while Habibti dropped down to the rail, just behind the leaders. As the field hit the turn, Espinoza and Habibti had no place to go, only to have Flores and Tempera hand them one. The Godolphin filly, clearly not on top of her game, was tiring and she drifted out, leaving the rail wide open. Despite her inexperience, Habibti shot through the narrow and somewhat intimidating gap. Tempera had nothing left in midstretch, and tired to finish third, as Habibti defeated a game Who Loves Aleyna by a comfortable two lengths. Again, Baffert had beaten Harty, and for the second day in a row, the Thoroughbred Corp. had bested Godolphin.

The next morning, Baffert had a theory about Tempera's lackluster performance.

"I think she was in season," he said. "I saw her on the track the day before the race and she just stopped and looked like she wanted to take a leak and couldn't. She looked uncomfortable to me."

Richard Mulhall was standing nearby, and disputed Baffert's theory.

"Bullshit, she just got beat, that's all." Asked how he felt about the budding rivalry between his stable and Godolphin, Mulhall grunted, "Rivalry? You better find another word, because all we do is whip their ass. That's no rivalry."

When the same question was put to the diplomatic Crisford, he said calmly, "We just look at our own horses, really. I pay no attention to who else is in the race, other than how it relates to the strategy of how the race is run. I think what we all saw were some Group 1-quality horses putting on a very good show. Point Given is clearly quite some horse.

"As far as what happened here at Del Mar, you're always a little more disappointed when you have an odds-on favorite in a Group 1 and don't win, but all of Eoin's horses look marvelous and we're very happy with how everything is coming together. After all, just a year ago, E Dubai was just breaking his maiden here, so we've come a long way in a short time."

Tempera's loss wasn't the only disappointment Harty suffered on August 26. Earlier that day, he had sent out the talented maiden Janadel for his second start, and at the top of the lane it appeared the highly regarded colt was home-free. Only first-time starter Siphonic, from the ice-cold barn of David Hofmans—winless in 23 Del Mar starts—looked to have any chance to catch Harty's horse. The son of multiple Grade 1 winner Siphon switched to the outside in the stretch, engaged Janadel at the quarter pole, and slowly wore him down, winning by three-quarters of a length.

After the race, a jubilant Hofmans compared his colt to his top 3-year-old of 2001, Millennium Wind, the winner of the Blue Grass Stakes.

"He has impressed me as much as Millennium Wind," Hofmans said. "I haven't said much about him because we're not doing well and I didn't want to jinx it."

The end of the losing streak was a relief for Hofmans, one of the nicest men in the sport. It was also a huge lift for good-guy jockey Chris McCarron, in the midst of one of the worst slumps of his Hall of Fame career. The two had shared a much-needed laugh in the winners' circle when Hofmans said to the rider, "Do you remember what this is like?" McCarron smiled and replied, "Do you?"

The close loss was just the latest of a series of losing stretch battles for Harty 2-year-olds, and many fans and touts had picked up on the trend.

"Harty horses just find a way to get beat," said one writer in the press box, adding with a shrug, "I don't see how the guy has his job next year."

A man standing in line to cash at the $50 window echoed the sentiment, albeit from a different perspective.

"The Godolphin horses get overbet and never win, but they sure can run second," he said. "I just put them in the two slot, put a bunch of horses above and below, then pound the exotics around them. It's been my best angle of the meet, so if you see Harty, tell him to keep it up."

No Godolphin 2-year-old had won a tight finish all meet, and Janadel's late fade was the fourth time one of them had lost a closely contested battle. In Harty's first year, the same had been true, as not one horse had won a stretch duel in all of 2000. Street Cry was the best known colt of the group, but not the only Godolphin 2-year-old to hang in the crucial final 50 yards of a race. In fact, Harty horses had lost every photo finish they had been involved in during his tenure, a rather remarkable and troubling development.

Encouraging the "will to win" in a racehorse is a tricky process, and nobody has any concrete answers. Although most Thoroughbreds are naturally competitive, they are nevertheless herd animals, and some seem content merely to run alongside other horses instead of passing them. Harty often works his horses in tandem, as do many trainers, including Baffert. The idea is to get them used to competing, to teach them to give every ounce of effort when asked. The message clearly was not getting through, because when the going got tough in a real race, they folded. Every time.

Michael J. Marten/Horsephotos

Eoin Harty with Street Cry, who was Godolphin's best Derby candidate in 2001 before an injury forced him out of the race.

Michael J. Marten/Horsephotos

Essence Of Dubai was among the 2002 Kentucky Derby nominees.

Michael J. Marten/Horsephotos

Godolphin's $5 million Derby bust, Worldly Manner.

Officer, the 2001 Breeders' Cup Juvenile favorite.

The early 2002 Kentucky Derby favorite, Johannesburg.

Monarchos responded to patient handling and traditional American training methods by winning the 2001 Kentucky Derby.

The top 3-year-old in America in 2001, Point Given.

Godolphin's $5.3 million yearling purchase King's Consul.

Godolphin's prized filly, Tempera, cruises to victory in the 2001 Breeders' Cup at odds of 11/1.

8

Boom Time in Kentucky

On Friday, August 31, Harty finally got the two-turn, one-mile race for maidens he had been asking the Del Mar racing secretary for all meet long, and Ibn Al Haitham was primed for the occasion. After having made an excellent late move in his debut, the muscular black colt had chased a fast pace in his second start and tired a little to be third. Harty felt that with those races under his belt, the regally bred 2-year-old was ready for a top effort and that the mile would suit him perfectly. Baffert felt the same about his entrant, High Thunder, the "chickenshit" colt that had unleashed an impressive late surge down the lane to finish second in his debut and become the maiden everyone was touting as a Derby dark horse. If Ibn Al Haitham was going to get Harty his second Del Mar win by a colt, High Thunder and Baffert were the duo to beat.

Ibn Al Haitham took a bad step at the start, but quickly recovered to be sitting fourth, just behind the leaders as they hit the first turn. On the lead was 21-1 longshot Hawk's Top Gun, a Baffert horse stepping up in class from a $62,500 maiden claiming race. High Thunder was near the back of the seven-horse field, running easily. Moving into the far turn, Ibn Al Haitham made a nice, easy move to engage the leaders while three wide. High Thunder was fifth and beginning to pick up the pace but not showing the kind of acceleration he had in his debut. At the top of the stretch, Ibn Al Haitham appeared poised to cruise by Hawk's Top Gun and roll to an easy victory. He didn't. He hung in the final 50 yards and the Baffert colt, despite having been pressured on the lead every step of the way, dug in and prevailed by a neck, lighting up the tote board.

It was the fifth time a Harty colt had been second at the meet, and including filly races, the fifth time one of his horses had been outfought down the stretch. This one hurt more than most because everything had set up perfectly for Ibn Al Haitham and he still could not get the job done. The close loss also kept Harty's two-year photo-finish losing streak alive, much to the trainer's dismay. High Thunder made a belated move to get third, 2½ lengths back of Ibn Al Haitham, a disappointing showing but yet another example of the inconsistency and unpredictability of 2-year-olds. If he was indeed a Derby hopeful, Baffert still had plenty of work to do.

September 5 was closing day at Del Mar, headlined by the Grade 1 Del Mar Futurity. As a testament to the muddled state of Harty's barn, as well as the brilliance of Officer, not one Godolphin colt was entered. Thirty-four had been nominated to the race months earlier, under the assumption that it would cap off a stellar meet at the beach. Instead, the whole stable had been loaded up and vanned to Santa Anita before the race had even been run. As Harty noted, "They just haven't earned it. Our focus now is on shipping back up to Santa Anita and getting to stretch some of them out around two turns."

Del Mar Futurity Day also represented a symbolic passing of the torch. Earlier in the week, it was announced that Point Given had suffered an injury to his leg and would be retired, leaving Officer to carry the Thoroughbred Corp. colors to further fame. Del Mar officials had persuaded Baffert and Salman to have Point Given come to the track on Futurity Day as a way for fans to say their good-byes, and it was an emotional scene. As usual, Baffert dealt with his emotions through laughter. Standing in the sun-splashed paddock as a huge crowd clapped and snapped pictures of an obviously tranquilized Point Given while he walked around the ring, Baffert said, "Look at the big horse. He walked in the paddock, saw Pie'n'Burger,"—a Baffert-trained claiming horse preparing to run in the next race—"and looked at me like, 'You're not running me for $62,500, now are ya? Things can't be that bad!'"

When Point Given was walked out onto the track he received a rousing ovation that continued as highlights of his fabulous 2001 season were shown on the big-screen television monitor in the infield. The horse was then led to the winners' circle, where the Thoroughbred Corp. team that had worked with him gathered around for a public farewell. As usual, Salman was center stage, kissing the horse, posing for pictures, then dramatically breaking down in tears and being led out of the winners' circle as if he were at a funeral.

The injury suffered by Point Given was similar to the one that forced Sleeping Weapon out of training. He would have recovered and could have raced again in 2002, but Salman decided to take the 40 to 50 million dollars waiting for him in stallion syndication rather than risk a long rehabilitation with no guarantee that the colt would be as good upon his return as when he left. In announcing his decision to retire Point Given, the Saudi prince said, "I'm doing what is best for the horse."

Officer's presence figured to ensure a small field for the Futurity, and it did. Metatron took another shot, as did Historic Speech and Kamsack, both impressive Del Mar maiden winners. Officer sat just off the pace set again by Metatron, effortlessly swooped around the field on the turn, put the race away, and eased past the finish under yet another snug hold from Espinoza. The competition was better, but the race little more than a glorified workout. Kamsack ran on gamely to be second, while Historic Speech, nervous and sweaty in the paddock, was done on the turn and finished last.

"What gets me is how easy he does it," remarked Baffert immediately after the race. The white-haired trainer was beaming the smile of a man who had just won his sixth straight Del Mar Futurity, an unprecedented feat. "I've had some quality colts win this race, but this guy here, he's the best of the bunch. Silver Charm had that tenacity, and Worldly Manner and Forest Camp were extremely fast horses, but this son of a gun is in a different class. I know his pedigree says he's got distance limitations, but honestly, I'm looking forward to testing that out because he hasn't even been asked to run yet and he's just crushing horses."

The pitched battle with Baffert that Harty had spoken so animatedly about before the beginning of the meet never materialized. The two had horses in the same race 11 times, and Harty only managed to beat his former boss once, with Sunray Spirit. Baffert found the winners' circle in five of those head-to-head encounters, en route to 31 wins and yet another Del Mar training title.

Asked about the rivalry, Baffert cracked, "Well, I still call and rag Eoin, but he's not laughing quite as much. The bottom line is we're still great friends and talk every day. His wife is the one I'm worried about, because she really hates to lose. Eoin knows the business and things can change in a hurry, so I'm not too worried about him, especially with the thirty million dollars of horses he's got in his barn."

Next on Harty's agenda was getting those expensive horses settled back at the larger Santa Anita barn and making plans for their final two months in America. After Del Mar, Southern California racing moved to the Pomona Fairgrounds for an 18-day meet that Harty had no interest in. He wanted nothing to do with running his horses at Pomona, a short (five-eighths of a mile), scary track with tight turns. Buoyed by his earlier success at Saratoga, he was planning to send Essence Of Dubai and Imperial Gesture to Belmont Park in New York to run in graded stakes races scheduled for the weekend of September 15.

The other big decision he made was to change Tempera's training and rest her until the Breeders' Cup in late October.

"If it doesn't work, I'm the one to blame," said Harty. "You can lose young horses mentally, especially fillies, and I didn't want to keep pushing her and have that happen. We'll see how it all works out."

Initially he had planned on running her in the next logical spot, the one-mile Oak Leaf Stakes on September 30, but decided she was getting too aggressive in the mornings. He wanted to teach her to relax and have her go slowly in the first part of her workouts, then come on strong down the lane, much as she had done so brilliantly in the Sorrento. Veteran jockeys don't often work many horses in the mornings, but Harty felt that David Flores had an excellent rapport with Tempera and asked if he would make an exception. When the jockey agreed, the experiment began.

The rest of the barn would return to action once Santa Anita reopened on September 26. Harty left the group on September 8 to join the Godolphin bloodstock team at the Keeneland yearling sales, a break he was looking forward to.

"I'll be at the sales helping select next year's crop, and from what I hear, there's an awful lot of quality stock in the first two days, so it should be exciting."

While the American-based Godolphin 2-year-olds were given a brief respite, the Godolphin horses in Europe, including a massive group of 2-year-olds, were kicking into high gear, as the fall is annually the pinnacle of the racing season overseas. The year before he had made the decision to establish a 2-year-old operation in America, Sheikh Mohammed had made a similarly ambitious move in Europe. As usual, his deep pockets were a key to the plan.

A racetrack in France called Evry had closed down, so Sheikh Mohammed bought it. The track, the stables, everything. He installed trainer David Loder there and gave him nearly 100 2-year-olds to train and race. The first year, 1999, was a disaster, as Loder failed to produce even one top-class juvenile. The next year was not much better, with dual stakes winner Noverre the only potential star to emerge from the huge group. After two years and almost nothing to show for the millions he had sunk into the project, a humbled Sheikh Mohammed, who has a strong hand in selecting which horses go to Europe and which ones head to America, scrapped the plan.

In 2001, Loder and the European-based 2-year-olds were back at Godolphin's home base in Newmarket and they had begun the season in spectacular fashion, winning 18 of their first 24 starts. When the competition stiffened in the summer, though, they were unable to keep up with their arch-rivals from Ireland, the Coolmore crew. There was, however, one juvenile colt who was keeping up, and more. His name was Dubai Destination. A $1.5 million Keeneland yearling buy, the son of top turf sire Kingmambo had been second by a head in his June 10 debut, then won his next start impressively in early July. He was scheduled to make his first stakes appearance on September 14 at Doncaster in England, in a Group 2 affair that was certain to have at least one highly regarded Coolmore colt in the field.

The most talked-about horse of any age during the summer of 2001 in Europe had been Galileo, Coolmore's prize 3-year-old colt. Despite Godolphin's supposed winter-training advantage, their stakes horses had gotten off to a slow start in 2001, and Coolmore had taken full advantage, winning nearly every big race on the European calendar. Galileo, a son of Sadler's Wells, the hottest turf sire in the business and Coolmore's pride and joy, was their leader. Undefeated in six career races, the Epsom Derby winner was scheduled to go for his seventh straight on September 8 in the Group 1 Irish Champion Stakes at a mile and a quarter. His main competition was expected to come from Godolphin's fabulous 5-year-old Fantastic Light, who had made a fierce charge at his younger rival in the King George VI and Queen Elizabeth Diamond Stakes, only to be turned back in the final hundred yards.

The night before the Irish Champion, Sheikh Mohammed convened his advisors and proposed a change in race tactics. He wanted jockey Frankie Dettori to make the first move, forcing Galileo to play catch-up. They all agreed that the preemptive strike might catch Coolmore stable jockey Mick Kinane off guard, and Dettori vowed to make it happen. Sure enough, when the horses rounded the final bend, Dettori and Fantastic Light had gotten the jump on their rival. Galileo quickly drew even, but the classy Godolphin horse had enough to hold him off in a furious stretch battle that was as thrilling as any seen in Europe in years.

"The boss" had pulled off a strategic coup, and doing so in Ireland, Coolmore's home turf, only made the victory sweeter for Sheikh

Mohammed. Life in the Godolphin fast lane leaves little time for celebration, however, and immediately after the race, Sheikh Mohammed's private Boeing 747 with the UAE flag on the side was headed for the Keeneland September sale.

Horses have been sold at auction as long as there have been horses, although not all yearlings enter the sales ring. Many of the wealthiest American owners of the early-to-mid-20th century bred exclusively to race, much as the Maktoums do now. The names Vanderbilt, Phipps, DuPont, Whitney, and Mellon were the closest thing to royalty on the American turf. They never would have thought of selling their yearlings, and not just because they didn't need the money; it was simply considered bad form, as longtime Kentucky owner-breeder Alice Chandler recalled.

"Back then, you either bred to race, or bred to sell. Nobody did both because if you did, it was thought that you were selling the culls, the worst of your crop." That stigma has faded over the years, and many owners now both race and sell, although the Phippses still race all their homebreds.

Until the late 1960's, American-born yearlings were sold almost exclusively to American buyers. At that time, Europeans, the English in particular, finally began acknowledging that American Thoroughbreds had become the best of the breed. One of the main reasons for the shift in power had been the purchase and importation of top European stallions to America over the past 70 years. The Hancocks of Claiborne Farm in Kentucky, by way of Virginia, are the family most responsible for bringing the right European blood to America.

After the Civil War, Captain Richard Hancock had gone back to his Virginia farm and begun breeding Thoroughbreds under the name Ellerslie Stud. His son, Arthur, took control of the breeding operation in 1909, a dire time in American racing because of the antigambling movement that would soon shut down all the New York tracks. It was, however, a good time for Arthur Hancock. The very next year he and his wife, the former Nancy Clay, inherited 1,300 acres of prime Kentucky bluegrass near the small town of Paris and gradually began moving their base of operations there, under the banner of Claiborne Farm.

The Thoroughbred population in early 20th-century America was still fairly small, and Arthur Hancock was on the lookout for new blood. He had been successful with the English stallion Wrack, whom he had bought in 1915, and in 1925, he set his sights on French star Sir Gallahad III. After much negotiation, Hancock purchased the 4-year-old colt for $125,000 and brought him to Kentucky. The deal was made on behalf of a four-man ownership group headed by Hancock and featuring three leading breeders of that era. It was the first of what would be many significant 20th-century purchases of top European horses to stand at stud in America, and it did not take long to bear fruit. One of the first mares bred to Sir Gallahad III was Marguerite, and the mating produced the brilliant Gallant Fox, winner of the 1930 Triple Crown.

Eleven years after he bought Sir Gallahad III, who had continued to thrive as a stallion, Hancock went after Blenheim II, an Epsom Derby winner owned by the Aga Khan. The 49th in line of descent from the prophet Mohammed, the Aga Khan was the hereditary and spiritual leader of millions of Shia Muslims. A very large man with large appetites, he was also a sportsman who began buying horses around 1920 and quickly became one of the most powerful owner-breeders in Europe. Unlike almost all other European owners of that time, he did not mind selling his stallions to American interests, if the price was right. When Arthur Hancock upped his offer to $250,000, the Aga Khan sold him Blenheim II, a transaction that some in Europe still point to as the beginning of the end of their reign as the preeminent source of quality Thoroughbreds.

During Blenheim II's time at Claiborne, one owner-breeder who sent many mares to him was Calumet Farm boss Warren Wright. Wright was rewarded handsomely for his decision, as the combination was responsible for three of his Kentucky Derby winners: Blenheim II sired 1941 Triple Crown winner Whirlaway, and was the maternal grandsire of both Ponder (1949) and Hill Gail (1952). In addition, Blenheim II also sired the 1947 Derby winner, Jet Pilot, a chestnut colt owned by cosmetics queen Elizabeth Arden Graham and trained by Tom Smith of Seabiscuit fame.

Blenheim II, known for imparting high speed and a hot temper to his progeny, was not the only top-class European horse the Aga Khan sold to American breeders. In 1940, having escaped from France just before it fell to Hitler's blitzkrieg, the Aga Khan found himself in exile in Switzerland. Short of ready cash, he sold the 1935 English Triple Crown winner, Bahram, and the 1936 Epsom Derby winner, Mahmoud, to American buyers. Bahram did not amount to much in the breeding shed, but Mahmoud proved to be a tremendous sire, and his exportation is still lamented by old-time European bloodstock experts.

In 1948, the Hancock legacy was handed to Arthur Boyd Hancock Jr., known as Bull. A large, imposing man, the six-foot-two Bull took over the Claiborne operation just after World War II and, like his father, turned to Europe for some of his most important stallion purchases. Noting that there were no stallions in America with the blood of the potent Nearco line, he made up his mind to acquire it.

At the small Dormello stud some 40 miles outside Milan, an eccentric Italian named Federico Tesio had been breeding talented horses since 1900. He cemented his reputation as a breeding genius by producing not one, but two undefeated colts that would leave lasting footprints on the Thoroughbred breed. Nearco, born in 1935, was the first Tesio colt to stamp himself one of the all-time greats, winning all 14 lifetime starts and finishing his career with a victory in the mile-and-a-half Grand Prix de Paris. Ribot, born in 1952, was next, but sadly, Tesio never saw his second masterpiece race. He died on May 1, 1954, just two months before Ribot won the first of his 16 career starts, which included back-to-back triumphs in Europe's top race, the Prix de l'Arc de Triomphe. Both colts were sold to British breeders immediately after their racing careers and proved to be two of the most powerful stallion influences of the 20th century.

Bull Hancock wanted some Nearco blood at Claiborne and he focused on purchasing Nasrullah, an accomplished, if a bit temperamental, son of Nearco. Racing for the Aga Khan, the colt had won top-class events at distances ranging from five furlongs to a mile and a quarter. It took six years for Hancock to get the deal done, but in 1950, Nasrullah finally arrived at Claiborne. His first crop of 3-year-olds included the superb colt Nashua, second to Swaps in the 1955 Derby and subsequent winner of the Preakness, Belmont, and a highly publicized match race with Swaps later in the year. Nasrullah became the leading American sire five times, with his legacy extended gloriously by his son Bold Ruler, owned and bred by the Wheatley Stable of Mrs. Henry Carnegie Phipps.

Fourth in the 1957 Kentucky Derby as the 6-5 favorite, Bold Ruler came back to win the Preakness, then finished third in the Belmont. He ended his 3-year-old season beating older horses in the big fall races and was named Horse of the Year. He won five more major races at 4 before an injury forced him to retire with 23 wins from 33 starts, but the best was still in front of him. Bold Ruler rose right to the top of the list of sires of winners in 1963, and stayed atop that perch for seven straight years. He was known as a sire of extremely precocious, fast horses, and the only thing lacking in his stud career was that none of his offspring had ever won a Triple Crown race. In 1971, the 17-year-old stallion contracted cancer and eventually had to be euthanized, just a year before his greatest son took to the track.

Secretariat burst upon the 2-year-old scene in 1972, winning eight of his nine starts, the only loss coming in his debut. He was the champion of his division and the first 2-year-old ever to be voted Horse of the Year. Secretariat was such a hot stallion prospect that he was syndicated for a record $6 million before he had even raced at 3. Bull Hancock's 23-year-old son Seth, stepping in after his father's death the previous fall, put the deal together and arranged for Secretariat to stand at Claiborne, as Bold Ruler had.

Despite all that, many doubted Secretariat's ability to go the Derby distance of a mile and a quarter because he was a son of Bold Ruler. Secretariat not only went the distance, but he also ran it faster than any horse before him, breaking the track record by almost a full second. He would have done the same in the Preakness if not for a clock malfunction, then headed for his date with Triple Crown destiny in the Belmont.

Again, there were those who questioned whether he could get the grueling mile and a half. It had been 25 years since the previous Triple Crown winner, Calumet Farm's Citation, so many wondered if there would ever be another. There was, and then some. Secretariat's 1973 Belmont was the greatest performance in American Thoroughbred history. He won the race by a staggering 31½ lengths, shattering the track and world records for the distance.

From the international bloodstock wheeling and dealing done by the Hancock family, the fresh, potent Nearco blood of Nasrullah had led to Bold Ruler, and finally to Secretariat, who captured the attention of the racing world. His exploits, in combination with the presence of far more international buyers at American sales, had given the breeding industry a big boost by the early 1970's.

In 1967, a chestnut son of the stallion Raise a Native had brought a record price of $250,000. Named Majestic Prince, the colt won the 1969 Kentucky Derby and Preakness, and when his full brother was offered at sale in 1970, he sold for a new record, $510,000. Named Crowned Prince, he was taken to England and proved so precocious that he became the champion 2-year-old colt. Finally, in 1973, a Japanese group paid $600,000 for a yearling they called Wajima. Again, top dollar brought top returns. Wajima won the 1975 Eclipse Award as best American 3-year-old on the strength of a pair of photo-finish victories over Horse of the Year Forego. All of that escalation, however, was just setting the table for a coldblooded, single-minded assault on the sales that lined many a Kentuckian's wallet and reinvented the bloodstock business.

In July 1975, three men—John Magnier, Robert Sangster, and Vincent O'Brien—flew from Ireland to Keeneland with a huge bankroll and a risky plan. They intended to buy top-class American yearlings, race them in Europe, turn as many as possible into champions, then sell them back to American breeders. If that ambitious undertaking went well, they also planned to keep some top stallion prospects in Ireland, at their Coolmore Stud in County Tipperary.

The three men complemented one another beautifully. Magnier had the business savvy, the gambling instincts, and the ambition, but he was not a trainer. He needed someone to turn the yearlings into champions. That man, the hands-on key to the operation, was his father-in-law, Vincent O'Brien, who had installed Magnier as the head of Coolmore Stud in 1973. The greatest trainer in Irish history, O'Brien was a small, soft-spoken fellow with an uncanny knack for spotting yearlings that was topped only by his ability to bring out the best in young horses. His skill as a horseman was such that he had earned the moniker Master of Ballydoyle. His genius was also exactly what one brash young Englishman was counting on.

Born into a wealthy family in 1936, Robert Sangster was an aggressive, competitive kid. Introduced to the sport of boxing at age 10, he took to it right away. Upon entering the service, the cocky 18-year-old volunteered for boxing as his main sports activity, but immediately got under the skin of his instructor, who quickly placed him in the ring with one of the biggest men in the regiment. Giving away some 40 pounds, Sangster knocked his opponent cold with one perfectly thrown right hand to the jaw.

After doing his time in the service, Sangster entered the family business, which was operating a "pools" betting company. He also began buying horses and quickly became entranced with the action of the racecourse and the betting coups that often accompanied a big win. He soon figured out a way to combine his growing love of Thoroughbreds, risk-taking nature, and the killer instinct he had developed in the ring. After meeting Magnier and O'Brien in the mid-1970's, Sangster sought out a select group of other wealthy men willing to invest and formed a syndicate.

On the advice of Magnier and O'Brien, they focused on sons of 1964 Kentucky Derby winner Northern Dancer. "The Dancer" was not a large horse, but he had heart, stamina, and impeccable grass bloodlines, exactly what Magnier and O'Brien valued most. It was a high-profile, expensive gamble, which made it the perfect power play for Robert Sangster.

The group arrived in Kentucky, without fanfare, in July 1975. When they left three days later they were the talk of the breeding industry. In those 72 hours, they spent a stunning $1.8 million for 12 carefully selected horses, including one smallish Northern Dancer colt with four white feet that had caught Vincent O'Brien's well-trained eye. The little chestnut cost $200,000 and they named him The Minstrel.

A year later, they were back, but this time the men from Europe were the center of attention. None of the yearlings they had purchased in 1975 had debuted on the racetrack yet, but the Coolmore crew stuck to their guns, buying 12 more colts, plus three fillies, at a cost of $2,419,000. In all, they were into the American yearlings for close to $5 million, counting transport, insurance, and fees, before a single one of their horses had gone into a starting gate.

When they returned to Ireland, the pressure shifted to the racecourses of Europe, and the training acumen of Vincent O'Brien. It is the curious nature of the bloodstock world that nearly every breeder in Kentucky was rooting for the Coolmore younsters as hard as Sangster and his partners were. Simply put, if the Kentucky-bred horses swept to classic victories on the European turf, everyone in the business figured to continue to share in the wealth, and for quite a while, too.

It didn't take long for the Coolmore colts, who ran in Sangster's name and colors, to make their mark. The Minstrel, the Northern Dancer colt with four white feet, won all three of his starts as a 2-year-old, capping off the run with a four-length romp in the season-ending, Group 1 Dewhurst Stakes at Newmarket.

Forced to run over soft, rain-soaked ground in his first two attempts at winning a classic at 3, The Minstrel lost both times. Hall of Fame jockey Lester Piggott was the stable's contract rider, and when he told them the colt would be fine over firmer ground, they entered The Minstrel in the Epsom Derby and prayed for the rain to stay away. The weatherman complied, and in one of the greatest finishes in Epsom Derby history, Piggott drove The Minstrel home in front by a head, gaining the lead only in the final 20 yards. The whoops and hollers of Kentucky breeders could almost be heard all the way across the Atlantic, and soon after, The Minstrel was syndicated for a record $9 million.

Sangster's money, Magnier's management, and O'Brien's magic touch forever changed Thoroughbred racing. They relentlessly pursued the Northern Dancer yearlings at the sales, and continued to score their share of classic victories. Their no-nonsense approach to the business of bloodstock, racing, and syndication drove the prices of yearlings and breeding shares to heights Kentucky breeders never dared to dream of. Their arrival also coincided with the attention-getting Triple Crown heroics of two more American superstars, Seattle Slew (1977) and Affirmed (1978). The potent combination made horse racing a hot investment, and the industry was flush with cash and new blood.

One of the Coolmore trademarks, hotly debated to this day, was retiring their best horses early. They almost never kept a horse in training after the age of 3, and often looked to sell or syndicate colts based on what they had accomplished as 2-year-olds. Although Secretariat had been syndicated early in his 3-year-old season, that had been a matter of economic necessity for his owner. With Coolmore, such deals were routine, and they pushed the breeding envelope farther in the direction of precocity than ever before.

One example of this was the brilliant Storm Bird. Purchased at the 1980 Keeneland sales for $1 million, the son of Northern Dancer won his first four starts, all in Ireland. He then journeyed to Newmarket for a showdown with English juvenile sensation To-Agori-Mou in the Dewhurst. The two colts hooked up in an epic duel over the seven furlongs, and as they drove up the hill to the finish, they were noses apart. Piggott had been replaced on the Coolmore horses by Irishman Pat Eddery, and when Eddery cracked Storm Bird with the whip, the colt responded and seized a short lead a hundred yards from the wire. To-Agori-Mou never quit, but Storm Bird held his advantage and won by half a length.

That winter, as the trio dreamed about the Epsom Derby, a disgruntled stable lad, fired from Ballydoyle, snuck into Storm Bird's stall and hacked off his mane and most of his tail. His connections believed the horse never recovered from the extraordinary trauma caused by the incident. He raced only once at 3, lost, and was promptly retired. Nevertheless, the interest in the fast, tough, royally bred colt as a stallion prospect was high. Sitting in the bar at the Hyatt hotel in Lexington after having spent $9 million at the 1981 Keeneland sales, Magnier received an offer for Storm Bird. Two days later, the colt was sold to an Oklahoma oilman named Robert Hefner for the jaw-dropping price of $28 million.

Within a year of that sale, Magnier had masterminded the syndication of three more classic-winning sons of Northern Dancer: Kings Lake at $16 million, Assert at $24 million, and Golden Fleece at $28 million. The total for the four colts was close to $100 million, and while the money was not all cash up front, Coolmore had certainly made their point. After decades of watching the best European-bred horses being bought by American breeders, they had given the cycle a new twist. First, they bought the cream of the Kentucky yearling crop, and O'Brien made them into racing superstars. To complete the cycle, they then sold some of the same precocious colts they had bought on speculation just two years earlier, none of whom ever ran after age 3, back to American breeders at a massive profit. In addition, a precious few were kept to stand at Coolmore Stud in Ireland in an attempt to keep some of the best blood in Europe and stem the tide of all the top European horses going to America as stallions. By 1981, Magnier, Sangster, and O'Brien had accomplished almost everything they had set out to do. Little did they know that three men from the desert were about to cut them off at the knees.

The Maktoum brothers ran their first horses in England in 1977, but didn't show up at Keeneland until 1980. When they did arrive, nobody quite knew what to make of the tight-lipped Arabs from the tiny country no one had heard of. The Maktoums do not do anything halfway, and when they did get to the sales, they needed not only to stock their stables with runners, but also to simultaneously build up a band of broodmares so they could begin breeding their own horses. Either task on its own is an expensive one, but together they figured to require a titanic amount of money. The Maktoums had it, and to the delight of everyone in the industry other than Coolmore, they spent it freely. They were advised, in the first four years, by a large group of British bloodstock agents and top trainers, all of whom profited handsomely from the Maktoums' entrance into the sport.

Everyone at a yearling sale is a gambler, with the Coolmore crew a perfect example. Everyone, that is, except the Maktoums, and that is their trump card. When any other prospective buyer stops bidding on a horse, he does so with a sense of foreboding. The Maktoum brothers, on the other hand, had no feelings of doubt, that nagging sense of what might have been. Like the first person in line at a sumptuous buffet, they simply took what they wanted and left the rest for everyone else to fight over. English racing is what the Maktoums knew and loved, so it came as no surprise that the horses they were most interested in were the sons of Northern Dancer. That meant that there was a new player at the ultra-high-stakes poker table, and if the Coolmore crew wanted to stay in the game, they were going to have to pay. And pay.

The Maktoum brothers spent $2,425,000 on eight horses at Keeneland in 1980, second only to the Coolmore crew, but the determined newcomers were just getting warmed up. From 1981 through 1984, the bidding wars between the Arabs and Coolmore pushed yearling prices so high that Keeneland had to add another zero to the electronic board that showed the bidding. It was a problem they were more than happy to address.

The brothers struck gold right away. They had paid $325,000, the highest price at the 1980 July sale run by Fasig-Tipton, Keeneland's competitor, for a filly they named Awaasif. In 1982, she won the Grade 1 Yorkshire Oaks and was named champion filly in England. To the delight of the Maktoums, Awaasif proved even better as a broodmare, producing, among others, the Group 1 winner Snow Bride. Just a few years later Snow Bride gave them the undefeated Epsom Derby-Arc de Triomphe winner Lammtarra. Not all their purchases worked out nearly as well, but their percentage of hits to misses was about average. The difference, of course, was that they were about to start swinging their well-oiled bats far more often than anyone else in the game.

In 1981, the Maktoums upped the ante considerably, buying 15 horses for $9.7 million at Keeneland alone and supplanting the Coolmore crew as the biggest spenders at the sale. Included in that group was a $3.3 million Northern Dancer colt they had gotten by outbidding Coolmore. They named him Shareef Dancer, and his pedigree (Northern Dancer — Sweet Alliance, by Sir Ivor) traced back on both sides to the foundation stallions, a fact not lost on Sheikh Mohammed. Northern Dancer traces back directly to the great Eclipse, making him a direct descendant of the Darley Arabian. Sir Ivor traces back through Man o' War to Matchem, meaning he comes straight from the Godolphin Arabian. Sheikh Mohammed had bought his way back in time, to the stallions that had come from his part of the world to found the Thoroughbred. Trained by top English conditioner Sir Michael Stoute and racing in the colors of Sheikh Maktoum, Shareef Dancer won the Group 1 Irish Derby and was later syndicated for a record $40 million.

In 1983, the rivalry with Coolmore reached new heights. Pushed every step of the way by Sangster and company, Sheikh Mohammed paid a record $10.2 million for a Northern Dancer colt he named Snaafi Dancer. This roll of the breeding dice came up craps. The colt never made it to the races, and when sent to the breeding shed, proved a dud, unable to impregnate any mares. For anyone else, a mistake of that magnitude, even with some help from fertility insurance, would likely cripple an operation. For Sheikh Mohammed it was merely a speed bump on his road to total dominance of the sales and the establishment of the largest Thoroughbred operation in equine history.

The Maktoum brothers' biggest spending spree occurred the very next year, in 1984. They put down a staggering $51 million at Keeneland alone, accounting for almost one-third of the total spent at the entire auction. Sheikh Mohammed was responsible for $41.5 million, by far the most one man had ever spent at a single sale. Of the 29 horses that fetched over a million dollars that year at Keeneland, 21 went to either the Maktoums or Coolmore.

"In the beginning," Sheikh Mohammed said in 1989, "we had no horses, so we needed to buy as many as possible and we spent whatever it took, sometimes too much. We needed to set a foundation, and we did."

The impact the Coolmore crew and the Maktoums had on the Keeneland yearlings was astounding. In 1974, the year before Sangster, Magnier, and O'Brien first showed up, the gross for the July sale was $17.1 million, an average of $53,489 per yearling. In 1979, the year before the Maktoums arrived, the gross had jumped to $42.4 million, and the average leaped to $155,567. The best was yet to come. The sale peaked in 1984, when the gross hit $175.9 million, an average of $544,681 per horse.

Even the ridiculously wealthy don't like paying more for something than they know it is worth, and Sheikh Mohammed was no exception. The era that British journalist Jamie Reid referred to as "the magic carpet ride" was over. For four years the Maktoums had been a soft touch for everyone in the European Thoroughbred industry, hit up by ex-jockeys looking for work as exercise riders, all sorts of trainers, and a series of bloodstock advisors that ranged from military men of honor to street hustlers. Once he felt comfortable enough to manage his own affairs, Sheikh Mohammed streamlined his operation from the top down, installing a young up-and-comer in the European bloodstock world, Anthony Stroud, as the one person in charge of that part of his operation.

Likewise, Sheikh Mohammed was tired of being run up in the sales ring by Sangster, Magnier, and O'Brien. In the spring of 1985, he extended an invitation to the Coolmore triumvirate and their families, asking them to come to a meeting at his palace in Dubai.

Sitting pretty at the peak of an unexpected, unprecedented 10-year boom created in large part by those two foreign entities, the thought of the two sides meeting sent shivers down the collective spine of the Kentucky breeders.

9

Small World

There were, of course, no minutes kept at that momentous meeting in the Maktoum mansion. Word eventually leaked out that Sheikh Mohammed had given his guests an example of his mastery of falconry and that they were duly impressed when his well-trained predators swooped down on their desert prey. None of that mattered to the Kentucky breeders, desperate to find out what would happen when the two sides flew to the 1985 sales that summer to do their own hunting.

When the July sale began, both groups were as active as ever, but, coincidentally, no longer bid on the same horses. Exactly what understanding had been reached will never be known, but after the desert summit, the Maktoum-Coolmore bidding wars were over.

It was at the 1985 Keeneland July sale that the feisty Robert Sangster made his last stand. The one-time pugilist had been the king of the sales ring for going on a decade, and though Sheikh Mohammed had knocked him from that lofty perch, he was not going to go quietly. A pact had obviously been made with the Maktoums, but Sangster was as determined as ever to buy the horses on his now shorter hot list.

The one he wanted most was a colt by the great European turf star Nijinsky II out of the mare My Charmer, who had already produced Triple Crown winner Seattle Slew. As agreed, Sheikh Mohammed sat quietly on the sidelines, but Sangster found himself being driven into the stratosphere by a D. Wayne Lukas-led American ownership group. In a karmic twist, Lukas's contingent was fueled by the two sources of money that had propelled the Maktoums and Coolmore to the top of the sales charts. The primary investors were Texas oilman L. R. French and former San Diego Chargers owner Eugene Klein, who had recently won the Preakness with the Lukas-trained Tank's Prospect.

"We had a few oil guys in our group, plus we had just made some serious money syndicating Saratoga Six [$12 million], Tank's Prospect [$10 million], and Pancho Villa [$8 million]," recalled the trainer. Sangster was not alone either, as he had convinced sometime partner Stavros Niarchos, one of the richest men in the world, to come in for about a third of the Coolmore action.

As the two sides went back and forth in $100,000 increments, the price quickly passed the $10.2 million record Sheikh Mohammed set when he bought Snaafi Dancer in 1983. According to Lukas, there had been some seismic shifts in his group during the bidding.

"When we got to about $9 million, Gene Klein dropped out, then I got a note passed down the row to me from Lew French saying, 'Go to $15 million,' but he didn't know that his percentage had just gone way up. I knew mine had, and I was in for my entire net worth at that point so I made a judgment call."

Sangster took the bid to $12.5 million, more than $2 million above the record, at which point Lukas tried to put him away with a devastating $500,000 raise, making the bid a mind-boggling $13 million. Past the point of no return, Sangster reraised another $100,000, and as Lukas recalled with a sigh, "In those situations your adrenaline gets flowing and you want to win, but I decided $13 million was it so I went for the kill and when he reraised me, we lost the horse."

At a ridiculous cost, Sangster had won his final battle, but the war belonged to Sheikh Mohammed.

Despite the $13.1 million Sangster paid for the one colt, the overall figures for the sale had plunged. The gross fell by 17 percent, the average dropped more than $60,000, and there were nine fewer million-dollar purchases. The bubble had burst, leaving the American breeding industry wondering just how low things would ultimately go. The 10-year Coolmore run was ending as well, and to hasten their departure from the top, a virus wreaked havoc with Vincent O'Brien's barn that summer, and Sangster was having trouble keeping his finances in order. John Magnier, in the game for the long haul, hunkered down and focused his energies on the promotion and expansion of Coolmore Stud, which had grown tremendously since the audacious plan was hatched a decade earlier.

It was a new dawn in the Thoroughbred industry, and it had blown in on the warm desert winds. On the English turf, it brought about a dramatic change. Sangster had been the leading owner in England from 1982 through 1984, but Sheikh Mohammed took over the top spot in 1985 and, with his stable growing to epic proportions, showed no sign of giving it up.

The Maktoums were not the only Arabs making noise in European racing in the early 80's. The big horse in Europe in 1986 was Dancing Brave, owned and bred by the Saudi prince Khalid Abdullah. He won the 2000 Guineas, lost a photo in the Epsom Derby, won the King George and the Arc de Triomphe, and was retired after a fourth-place finish in the Breeders' Cup Turf. It was syndication time, and Sheikh Mohammed was the major buyer, proving that if there was a top horse for sale either before or after his or her career, Sheikh Mohammed was likely to own it. The deal solidified a growing resentment on both sides of the Atlantic about the increasing dominance of the Arab owners, both in the sales ring and on the racetrack.

Aware he needed to smooth some feathers, the savvy sheikh executed another bold political power play. Before the 1986 sales, he chartered a Concorde and flew a group of Kentucky business leaders and government officials, including Governor Martha Layne Collins, to Dubai. Sufficiently impressed with what they saw and the generosity of their hosts, the contingent flew back much more comfortable with the Maktoums and what they were doing. Their goodwill mission accomplished, the Maktoums continued pumping money into the Bluegrass economy.

In 1986, with Sangster, Magnier, and company no longer a threat, the three eldest Maktoum brothers ranked one-two-three in money spent at Keeneland, buying a staggering total of 57 yearlings for just under $40 million, but the overall picture was bad and getting worse. The gross for the sale dropped another $33 million, meaning it had gone down almost a third in two years, signaling the death knell for many of the major Kentucky players who had mortgaged themselves to the hilt during the boom. Farms were lost, stud fees began dropping, longtime personal and professional relationships frayed and broke and an industry that just two years earlier was flying high fell to earth with a resounding thud.

Like Sheikh Mohammed, Lukas was just finding his stride in 1986, and spotted the first of his four Kentucky Derby winners, Winning Colors, at that sale. He was looking for horses with high speed who could win on American dirt, while the men from Dubai were still focused on the horses that would run well on European grass, so the two rarely locked horns over the same yearling. Using the open bankbook of Eugene Klein, Lukas spent more than $14 million on yearlings in 1986, including $575,000 for the large, muscular roan filly out of the French-bred sire Caro.

While the overall sales numbers continued to slump in Kentucky and Saratoga, the titanic spending of the Maktoum brothers proceeded unabated and mostly unopposed. For three consecutive years (1989 through 1991), Dubai's royal family spent more money at Keeneland than all North American buyers combined, a testament to the depth of their desire to overwhelm the competition with sheer numbers. It was also a sign of just how large an operation they were building, one that would dwarf any that came before it. Only Lukas, who happily spent in excess of $100 million on more than 330 horses for his various owners from 1985 through 1990, was anywhere near their level.

The strategy had worked wonders in the smaller arena of English racing. After rising to the top of the owners' list in 1985, Sheikh Mohammed won the title every year but two from 1985 through 1999, breaking every record in the history of the English turf. The only man to top him was his older brother Hamdan, who also gave the family its first Epsom Derby triumph in 1989 with Nashwan.

During that period, the Maktoums, who had continued to buy broodmare prospects at every sale, also expanded their breeding operations in Europe and America. In 1982, Sheikh Hamdan began the expensive process of building a breeding farm from the ground up on a gorgeous 2,700-acre spread just outside Lexington, Kentucky. Hamdan named the place Shadwell Farm, and over the years it became home to his burgeoning broodmare band as well as a select group of stallions. Although he is an infrequent visitor to his Kentucky farm, Hamdan is known for his uncanny ability to recognize older horses on sight after having seen them only briefly as yearlings.

Over the years he added six more stud farms in Europe to the mix. Five of the six, including the 1,200-acre Shadwell Stud 20 miles north of Newmarket, are in England, and one, the 1,700-acre Derrinstown Stud, is in Ireland.

In 1984, Sheikh Maktoum also bought a Kentucky farm, Gainsborough Stud, located only 12 miles from Shadwell. Originally a cattle and tobacco farm, it stretches out over some 1,800 acres of choice land, and was where Lammtarra and Fantastic Light were bred, along with numerous other champions. In addition, Sheikh Maktoum owns the smaller Gainsborough Stud in England, and two farms in Ireland, one of which came as a gift from Sheikh Mohammed. Sheikh Maktoum chose Gainsborough as the name of his racing and breeding operation to honor the 1918 English Triple Crown winner, who later was the sire of Hyperion, one of the most influential European sires of the 20th century.

Sheikh Mohammed bought his big farm, Dalham Hall Stud in New-market, in 1981, and it remains the centerpiece of his extensive and expensive English breeding operation. He also owns seven other smaller stud farms in and around Newmarket, making his Darley Stud Management the largest landowner in that historic area, other than the Jockey Club itself. He also has three stud farms in Ireland, including a luxuriously appointed 1,450-acre property known as Kildangan in County Kildare, not far from the ancestral home of Irish racing, The Curragh.

In 1998, Sheikh Mohammed finally bought his first Kentucky farm, Raceland, a 650-acre parcel that had belonged to the Hancocks' Claiborne Farm. When Jonabell Farm went on the market in the summer of 2001, Sheikh Mohammed decided to add the 790-acre spread to his Bluegrass holdings, for a price in the $15 million neighborhood. Jonabell, which is adjacent to Bluegrass Field airport and just a stone's throw from Keeneland, is next door to Shadwell. Until his death early in 2001, it was where Triple Crown winner Affirmed had spent the last years of his stud career.

The purchase of Jonabell meant that by 2002, the Maktoum family owned more than 5,500 acres of Kentucky bluegrass in and around Lexington, and those holdings were valued at close to $100 million. The sheikhs are classic absentee owners, sometimes going years without visiting the Kentucky farms, which employ nearly 500 people full-time, and hundreds more on a part-time basis.

The year 1994 marked the official formation of Godolphin, as well as a turning point for Coolmore. After 43 years as the unquestioned master of the Irish turf, 77-year-old Vincent O'Brien finally retired. The winner of 16 English classics, including six Derbies, he was also the first Irishman to train a St. Leger winner: Ballymoss, in 1957. The very next year, Ballymoss, a horse so beloved by Irish racing fans that his likeness was put on a postage stamp in 1981, became the first ever Irish-trained winner of the Prix de l'Arc de Triomphe as well. It was O'Brien's work with 1970 English Triple Crown winner Nijinsky II, a son of Northern Dancer and the last horse to win the 2,000 Guineas, Epsom Derby, and St. Leger in the same year, that solidified his fame. It also cemented his love of "the Dancer's" pedigree and led directly to the Coolmore assault on the Keeneland sales. On his home turf, O'Brien won an astounding 27 Irish classics, a number many in the land of green consider as sacred as Jack Nicklaus's 18 wins in golf's professional majors.

Wasting no time, Magnier replaced him immediately with 24-year-old Aidan O'Brien (no relation), the top steeplechase trainer in Ireland at the time as well as the top amateur jump jockey. O'Brien put away his jockey silks once given the plum assignment and, working alongside Magnier, went about rebuilding the Coolmore racing dynasty.

Known for his attention to detail, the baby-faced O'Brien walks every racecourse the morning of a race, checking the ground and looking for any edge, much as caddies do for professional golfers. His record indicates that he has found more than a few. In less than 10 years he had shattered every Irish and English single-season record for money won by a trainer, and set a standard previously thought unattainable. Especially adept at developing young horses, O'Brien reached a new level in 2000, when he sent out Giant's Causeway to five straight Group 1 wins in Europe, then pointed the son of Storm Cat to the Breeders' Cup Classic, on dirt. Despite drawing the far outside post and losing ground every step of the race, the ultragame colt known as the Iron Horse made American Horse of the Year Tiznow run the race of his life to beat him by a short head.

In 2001, the trainer was even better. An O'Brien horse won the first six Group 1 races for 2-year-old colts contested in Europe, led by two wins from the American-bred Johannesburg. Normally modest to a fault, O'Brien did admit, "I'd like to win all 10 Group 1's for colts this year, that would be quite an accomplishment." It is a record that can be equaled, but never broken, and with O'Brien just entering his prime, the only one with any shot is the fuzzy-cheeked O'Brien himself. His dominance has been such that he has already earned the nickname the Boy-King.

Robert Sangster's role as the money man in the operation was ably filled by Englishman Michael Tabor, who made his millions in the bookmaking business, much as Sangster's family had. Tabor, an East London native, joined forces with Magnier and company in the mid-90's.

"My role?" he responded when asked how he fits into the operation. "I pay the money, mostly." In 1995, the bald, trim Tabor sold his Arthur

Prince bookmaking business for a reported $50 million and jumped into Thoroughbred racing with both feet.

"I woke up one day far more affluent than I'd ever been, and decided to stop dabbling in horses and really have some fun," he said with the easy smile of a man who is getting exactly what he wants out of life. Tabor's official residence is in the tax-free haven of Monaco, but he also maintains a home in Florida and loves American racing. The first horse he ever bought specifically to race in America was a son of Gulch he purchased privately on the recommendation of Demi O'Byrne. He named the colt Thunder Gulch and gave him to D. Wayne Lukas to train. On May 3, 1995, the two were in the winners' circle at Churchill Downs.

"I've always loved America," Tabor said with a smile, "especially the vitality of the country and the people, and to me the Derby is the greatest race of them all. The atmosphere is just absolutely electric. To win it like that, right out of the box, was far more than I ever dreamed of, but I'll tell you, I'd kill to win it again."

Tabor's infusion of cash, combined with the success of Coolmore's stallions, gave them the push they needed to become a major international player at the yearling sales once again in the late 1990's.

Of the Coolmore principals, only Magnier is actively involved with the day-to-day operations. Partial to expensive fedoras that match perfectly with his hand-tailored suits, Magnier cuts quite a figure in the paddock and knows it. He has proven so adept at the deal-making that is essential to success at the highest levels of the volatile, worldwide breeding industry that he is, at present, the most influential stud master in the business.

Many top stallions, such as Europe's champion sire, Sadler's Wells, stand at Coolmore Stud deep in County Tipperary in Ireland, just as Magnier, O'Brien, and Sangster planned some 25 years ago. The success of the Coolmore breeding operation is due in part to the tax breaks given breeders by the Irish government. Magnier has made the most of the opportunity given him, and is considered a national treasure as a result. Other Coolmore stallions, such as Thunder Gulch, Fusaichi Pegasus, and Giant's Causeway, are at Ashford, the Kentucky stud farm Coolmore took over from Robert Hefner after he was unable to keep up the payments on the $28 million Storm Bird deal. Still others are in their ever-expanding Australian satellite operation.

Magnier is consistently one step ahead of the game, and his most recent money-making innovation was to have some of his stallions do double duty. In 2001, 13 of Coolmore's Kentucky-based stallions covered a full book of mares (50 to 125 each, depending on the quality of the stallion) in the spring, spent most of July in quarantine, then were flown halfway across the world to service a whole new set of mares. Eight of them, including Derby winners Fusaichi Pegasus and Thunder Gulch, went to Australia, the others to the Southern Hemisphere. The aggressive approach, considered unthinkable just a few years ago, greatly increases the on-hand cash for Coolmore. Thunder Gulch alone was bred to a record 216 mares in 2001, and another 10 Coolmore-owned stallions covered between 125 and 175 mares as well.

Ric Waldman is a consultant to Overbrook Farm, home of the most expensive stallion ($500,000 per mating) in the world: Storm Cat, a Lukas-trained son of Storm Bird. As he recalled, "When J. T. Lundy at Calumet had a few of his stallions breed to 50 or 60 mares in a season in the mid-70's, people were aghast at what they considered reckless overbreeding. A lot of people are aghast at this, too, but frankly, we're all swept up in the tide to some extent. The yearling market the past nine years has been extremely strong and there's a lot of money out there."

Magnier had also bought shares in Storm Cat in the late 1990's. Waldman would not say just how many, but did volunteer that Coolmore was the largest private owner of shares in the stallion other than W. T. Young, who owns Overbrook and bred and raced Storm Cat. The savvy purchase put Coolmore in a win-win situation at the sales. Since buying in, every time the Coolmore crew bid up another buyer or paid top dollar themselves for a Storm Cat yearling, they were not only getting a potential champion and/or stallion prospect, but also helping his reputation as a top sire and increasing his worth. They are many such multifaceted deals in the breeding industry, as well as under-the-table agreements that make determining what really happened at a given sale next to impossible to judge.

As for the Maktoum brothers, they cut back dramatically on their yearling purchases in the early 1990's. They bought 25 horses for $9.1

million in 1993, only eight horses for $3.1 million in 1994, and just seven for $1.9 million in 1995. The $500 million or so they had spent in the previous 13 years had established their broodmare bands and provided them with a number of top stallions as well, setting them up to be self-sufficient owner-breeders. They formed Godolphin during that time and took aim on the major races around the world from their new home base in Dubai. It was only when Sheikh Mohammed decided he had to have the Kentucky Derby that they returned with a vengeance to the American sales, where they were welcomed with open arms by an industry that had slowly been rebuilding through the 1990's. Sheikh Mohammed alone dropped over $25 million at Keeneland in 1999, and returned in 2000 to spend just under $41 million, narrowly missing his own 1984 record.

The 2001 Keeneland September sale, interrupted for that one day by the attacks on New York City and Washington, D.C., continued for 11 days after the major players had gone, but the middle and bottom of the market did not hold up nearly as well as the very top had the emotional day after the staggering events.

"A lot of the folks we count on from places like Montana, Wyoming, and Idaho to buy a bunch of horses in the last week of the sale just never showed up," noted Kentucky breeder Bob Courtney. Travel disruptions at the nation's airports were partly to blame, but there were other factors at work; the uncertainty surrounding what the government referred to as the war on terrorism was unsettling to an industry that feeds off a strong economy.

When Eoin Harty finally got a flight back to California, he had to dramatically alter his plans for Essence Of Dubai and Imperial Gesture. Their stakes races, scheduled for the weekend of September 15 at Belmont Park, had been canceled, so he looked instead to the September 29 weekend at Santa Anita. Essence Of Dubai would get a chance to redeem himself against the best in the West in the one-mile Norfolk, while Imperial Gesture would make her stakes debut the next day in the Oak Leaf, substituting for Tempera.

On September 20, Harty sent the well-regarded Classicist to Bay Meadows in Northern California to make his debut. Classicist never showed the blazing speed in the mornings that many in the barn had, but he wasn't supposed to. A son of 1990 Derby winner Unbridled out of a mare named Classy Cathy who won a long-distance Grade 1 race, he was the Godolphin colt best bred to get the mile and a quarter of the Derby. He was also the poster colt for the shift to buying horses bred specifically to run in the Derby.

As *Daily Racing Form* pedigree expert Lauren Stich noted, "You look at what they bought at Keeneland in 1999 and 2000 and they still seem stuck on horses whose best future is on the turf. To me, Classicist is the type they should be focused on, bred to run all day and best suited for the dirt."

Harty was cautiously optimistic. "He hasn't quite figured everything out yet," he said about the $500,000 yearling purchase, "but he needs to get his feet wet and they have a mile race carded up there, so he'll make the trip with Media Story and hopefully they can run one-two."

The Northern California circuit is 400 miles above the Southern California circuit, but light years below it in class, so Harty had a right to believe he would run one-two if his horses ran to their breeding and works. Media Story, who had been third in his debut a month earlier at Bay Meadows, won the maiden race by two lengths, but Classicist lost a photo for the place, so Harty didn't get his one-two. What he did get was a glimpse of what Classicist was capable of, as the immature but clearly talented horse made a very nice run over the final half-mile after breaking slowly.

Racing in Europe was unaffected by the attacks, and the September 14 stakes debut of Godolphin's prize European juvenile, Dubai Destination, went off as scheduled. The result was exactly what Sheikh Mohammed, David Loder, and the Godolphin contingent had hoped for. The striking colt assumed the lead halfway through the race and was in such control of the seven-furlong affair that jockey Frankie Dettori eased him up at the finish. The official margin of victory was one length over Coolmore's well-regarded Rock of Gibraltar, and plans were made for Dubai Destination to make one more start before being put away for the season.

The next top-class race in Europe was the Queen Elizabeth II Stakes, the fall showcase race at famed Ascot racecourse in England that annually crowns the country's champion miler. Built in 1711 at the behest of equine enthusiast Queen Anne, Ascot and its lush grass have

been a staple of Thoroughbred racing ever since and provide the setting for the most elegant meet in all of racing, Royal Ascot. It is held
in mid-June, and the dress code for those in the "Members' Enclosure,"
the English version of an American "Turf Club," is as follows. "Ladies
are asked to wear formal dress with a hat covering the crown of the
head. Gentlemen are reminded that only black or grey morning dress
with top hat, or service dress, is acceptable." One gains admission to
the area where the queen sits, the "Royal Enclosure," by invitation only.

As racegoers approach the course the five-story grandstand looms
high above, but first they must pass through an old, imposing, red-brick
façade. In a somewhat surreal touch, elderly men in formal dress and
bowler hats straight out of a Merchant-Ivory period film man the iron
entrance gates. Once inside and facing the course, there is nary a building in sight, only the grass of the courses themselves and the hundreds
of mature trees that surround the massive plot of land.

Ascot has two intersecting courses for "flat" racing. The "round"
course is massive, stretching out almost two miles in circumference,
with a demanding uphill finish. An undulating one-mile straightaway
joins the round course some 2½ furlongs from the finish line. All races
up to a mile are run on the straightaway, but no matter where the horses
start, they must still tackle the uphill, or as the British refer to it, "stiff"
finish.

As is the case with the majority of European tracks, the horses run
clockwise, finishing from right to left, the opposite of American racing.
Inside the flat course is the "hunt" course, where the best steeple-
chasers face off in tests of stamina, speed, and agility, and inside that
is a nine-hole golf course and a cricket field.

In long-distance races at Ascot, the field runs away from the grandstand for the first half-mile, seemingly bound for points unknown. It is
a stunning sight to an American visitor, used to always being able to track
the action around a single oval. Due to the size and shape of the course
it is difficult to see any European race with perspective until the final
hundred yards. Even at that crucial juncture it is often next to impossible, especially in sprint races, where the large fields often split into two
distinct groups, one on each side of the course. Gauging which horse has
actually hit the wire first when they are 50 yards apart is no easy task.

Oddly, as formal as the dress and atmosphere are at Ascot, the pre-race activities of the horses are far more random, which is the case throughout England. There are no set places for horses to be saddled in the paddock, making it a real adventure to try to view a particular horse or two as they walk around. When the horses leave the paddock to go onto the track, they do so in no given order, and there is no for-mal post parade to watch them warm up. They trot from the paddock to the track without the steadying presence of lead ponies, immediately break into a strong gallop down the hill to warm up, and head out of sight en route to the distant starting gate.

"We have all the rules you Yanks do," one Englishman noted, "we just don't follow many of them."

The field for the September 29th QE II lacked both substance and depth. Not surprisingly, Godolphin was poised to take full advantage of the situation, running two horses. The talented Noverre, winner of four of eight lifetime starts, was the solid 2-1 favorite. His stablemate Sum-moner was entered solely to go to the front and set a solid early pace, setting up Noverre's powerful late kick.

The use of such "pacemakers" is far more common in Europe than it is in the United States, though few stables have enough depth to sac-rifice talented horses in such a role. Godolphin, of course, is one of the select few. For those who believed in history repeating itself, Sum-moner was to be ridden by Richard Hills, who had been aboard a pace-maker in the 1994 QE II—a 66-1 shot named Maroof—and had stolen the race. Those who bet with "the Tote," England's parimutuel system, got exactly half of that, 33-1, on Summoner.

The odds, however, varied depending on how and where one placed his or her bet. Betting is akin to a religion in England, and taken just about as seriously. English bookmakers will give a prospective bettor, or "punter," odds on just about anything. Some had Summoner as low as 25-1, while one enterprising bookie had the horse at a fat 40-1. A few years ago, a man called up Corals, the bookmaking operation formerly owned by Michael Tabor, and asked what odds they would give him that his son, then 9, would graduate from high school with straight A's. Nonplussed, the Corals bookie asked the gent to send him the child's most recent grades, and after a quick perusal, named a price. One would have to surmise that the child has not stopped studying since.

One of the most famous scores made by a bettor concerned, of all things, the American space program. In 1963, President John F. Kennedy announced that America would put a man on the moon before the end of the decade. Soon after, an enterprising Englishman called a few bookmakers and asked what odds they would give on Kennedy's prediction coming true. He shopped around, found the best price he could, sat back, and waited. Six years later, and just a few months before the deadline, Neil Armstrong made his famous walk. One small step for a man, one sweet score for the patient gambler.

Bookmakers set up shop at the racecourses in England in the large open space between the grandstand and the track. There are usually about 30 to choose from, and they work the crowd, shouting out their odds, and writing and erasing furiously on blackboards as said odds shift. It is free enterprise at work, and savvy bettors prowl the area like Wal-Mart shoppers, their eyes constantly scanning the boards in search of a bargain. The odds do not vary dramatically, but you can often get 8-1 on a horse offered elsewhere at 5-1 or 6-1, a significant advantage.

There is parimutuel wagering as well, just as in America, but very little money is bet that way. Having grown up with the bookmaking system, hardly any of the big bettors bother with the windows. "Exotic" wagers such as exactas or trifectas, extremely popular in America, are only offered through the Tote and attract very little action.

As Noverre and Summoner lined up to run the QE II mile on Ascot's straightaway, another pair of Godolphin runners was preparing to attack the dirt oval at Santa Anita, some 6,000 miles away. Harty had entered both Essence Of Dubai and the hard-trying maiden Ibn Al Haitham in the Grade 2 Norfolk, the final big Breeders' Cup prep race for 2-year-olds on the West Coast. The day was the best example yet of the ever-widening scope of the Godolphin operation, and its depth as well. In two top-class races run the same day in England and California, the Maktoum brothers not only owned the race favorite, but a talented stablemate to boot.

In light of the travel problems that ensued as a result of the September 11 attacks, Baffert had said he would keep Officer in California, rather than fly him to New York for the Grade 1 Champagne Stakes on October 6. Salman quickly overruled him, declaring that Officer would indeed skip the Norfolk in favor of the Champagne; the prince said he wanted the people of New York to have an opportunity to see his sensational colt run, even though Officer had yet to even contest a Grade 1 race, let alone win one.

That surprise announcement meant that the undefeated Came Home, back at his California home base after a successful raid on the Hopeful Stakes at Saratoga, was the likely favorite in the Norfolk. As so often happens, however, especially with young horses, a minor injury was discovered 48 hours before the race and forced Came Home's owners to scratch the speedy colt. Kamsack, who had been impressive chasing Officer home in the Del Mar Futurity, was the next-best West Coast juvenile, but his connections had wanted to avoid a confrontation with either Officer or Came Home and had already arranged his training schedule around the $400,000 Breeders' Futurity at Keeneland on October 6.

That left the Godolphin entry, neither of whom had lived up to expectations, as the even-money favorite. Their main competition figured to come from Ecstatic and Roman Dancer, a pair of speedsters who had defeated Godolphin colts in their debuts at Del Mar. Neither one was likely to relish the two-turn mile, however, while Godolphin's colts were bred to run all day.

The early stages of the Norfolk featured a spirited three-way fight for the lead. Roman Dancer, the wise-guy horse from the Chris Paasch stable, had the rail. Ecstatic, who had won the maiden race on opening day at Del Mar for Baffert, was between horses, and Ibn Al Haitham was on the outside. The trio battled through moderate fractions, while jockey Alex Solis positioned the unpredictable Essence Of Dubai in a perfect spot, just behind the lead group.

As the field approached the turn, an exhausted Roman Dancer drifted toward the middle of the track, carrying his two rivals with him. Despite being pushed out at least six wide, Ibn Al Haitham was running hard and began to pull away from his tiring fellow pacesetters. At the same time, a gaping hole opened on the rail for Essence Of Dubai, and when Solis saw it, he pushed the go button and the son of Pulpit accelerated into the wide-open space.

Ibn Al Haitham was clear of his pace rivals by midstretch, but he was no match for Essence Of Dubai. The $2.3 million colt felt Solis's whip quite a few times and finished strongly, flashing past the wire three lengths in front. Ibn Al Haitham was a clear second. Roman Dancer finished third, but was disqualified and placed fourth for his failure to maintain a straight course in the lane.

The one-two finish for Godolphin and Harty, unimaginable just a few days earlier in the huge shadows of Officer and Came Home, was a much-needed boost for the trainer as he looked to put his Del Mar struggles behind him.

"We all knew Essence had talent, but the way he ran in the Best Pal shook my confidence," the trainer told reporters, adding, "Clearly this wasn't one of the tougher Norfolks in quite a while, but all the same, it was a great result."

The win also meant that Harty would have a runner, or two, in the Breeders' Cup Juvenile, which, given his short window of opportunity, was his personal Derby. The good news was bolstered by the fact that Sleeping Weapon continued to make excellent progress in his comeback from the suspensory injury, recording his first official workout the next day. He only went three furlongs, but did it easily and came back healthy.

Harty was also pleased with the progress of Dubai Tiger, who was in full-time training and moving forward with each workout. It now appeared likely the much-hyped colt would be able to get in one race before being sent back to Dubai, thereby avoiding the "Apollo jinx." Apollo was the last horse to have won the Kentucky Derby without having started at least once as a 2-year-old. In 1882. As for King's Consul, the $5.3 million colt was beginning to shake his Del Mar doldrums. He was much more focused and aggressive in his first two Santa Anita works, giving Harty hope that he, too, would get in that one all-important start in America.

Meanwhile, on the rain-soaked grass of Ascot, Hills had done as instructed and sent Summoner right to the front. The other riders were aware of what he was doing, but not wanting to push their horses early, they left him all alone on the lead. Noverre was sitting in midpack, being confidently handled by Frankie Dettori, while just off his shoulder was Coolmore's QE II hope, Hawkeye.

Before the QE II, the two superpowers, as they are known overseas, had won 26 Group 1 races between them. Despite having far fewer horses, the Irish-based crew held a convincing 17-9 advantage in the races that really counted. The numbers were especially galling to Godolphin because the supposed key to their plan was having their horses spend the winter and early spring training in the temperate climate of Dubai, ready to roll when the racing resumed in April. That had not proven to be the case. Despite the handicap of having prepared his string in the wet, windy hills of Ireland, Aidan O'Brien's Coolmore horses were ones crossing the line first as soon as the big races began.

As the QE II field rounded the bend and headed up the steep grade to Ascot's finish, a very relaxed Summoner was a good five lengths in front. When Hills asked him for more, the 4-year-old answered and kicked on strongly for the wire. Sensing the upset, the large crowd gasped audibly. Dettori had Noverre in high gear, but despite giving the colt some serious urging with the whip, an activity frowned upon and closely monitored in Europe, they were making little headway.

The morning of the QE II, Ascot executives had unveiled a statue of Dettori, and for good reason. In 1996, the jockey had ridden into racing's history books by sweeping all seven events on the ultraclassy QE II card, a feat known in Europe as "the Magnificent Seven," and one that cost bookmakers an estimated 40 million pounds, or about $60 million. The remarkable achievement, along with his role as Godolphin's stable jockey, made the handsome, charismatic, well-spoken Dettori a superstar.

The son of a champion jockey, Dettori has achieved a level of fame that transcends racing in Europe, especially after his brush with death in a plane crash. On June 1, 2000, Dettori and fellow jockey Ray Cochrane got in a small plane to fly from Newmarket to Goodwood to ride that afternoon, a fairly normal part of the weekly routine of top European jockeys. The plane nosedived shortly after taking off, however, and crashed in the Devil's Dyke area of Newmarket racecourse, killing the pilot instantly. Incredibly, both jockeys survived, although Dettori sustained a fracture to his right ankle and Cochrane had relatively minor head injuries, with burns to his face and hair.

Dettori recovered quickly, and resumed his hectic, high-profile lifestyle. He appears regularly on television game shows, does countless interviews, and is without question the most recognizable face in the game to casual observers of racing in Europe. Every year on QE II day, punters all over England bet his every mount heavily, hoping for a repeat of his 1996 sweep, so having lost with his first four mounts leading up to the 2001 QE II, the pressure on the jock was mounting. Known for his acrobatic flying dismount from the saddle in the winners' enclosure, a move he copied from Hall of Famer Angel Cordero Jr., Dettori knew that Noverre now represented his best opportunity to execute the crowd-pleasing maneuver.

Unfortunately for Dettori and his many backers, Summoner, the supposed pacemaker and lesser half of the Godolphin team, was long gone. He reached the wire a length and a half in front, with Noverre a clear second and Hawkeye third. In the winners' enclosure, the Godolphin contingent was almost embarrassed by the result. After accepting the trophy, Sheikh Maktoum turned to Simon Crisford and whispered, "Who would have believed that?"

Not only had Godolphin horses contested two major stakes races on separate continents in the same day, one on dirt, the other on grass, they had run one-two in both. Sheikh Mohammed talked often of the world becoming smaller as a result of easier travel and communication, and September 29 was the best example yet of how he had proven to be the man best suited to take advantage of the new era. If one expects to be the top outfit in racing, one must have his horses perform at a high level in the most important races. Godolphin's runners had done exactly that on September 29, but those races paled in comparison to what was scheduled for a month later, the Breeders' Cup World Thoroughbred Championships, to be held October 27 at Belmont Park.

10

Hallowed Ground

Tempera had already punched her ticket to the Breeders' Cup with her nine-length win in the Sorrento, but Imperial Gesture was still a major question mark going into the one-mile Oak Leaf on September 30. Harty wanted to put another Godolphin graded stakes win on top of Essence Of Dubai's Norfolk score, and his hopes were bolstered when, once again, his top opponents fell by the wayside before the race.

Baffert's Habibti figured to be the prohibitive favorite, but she came down with a fever the morning of the Oak Leaf and was scratched, joining the injured Who Loves Aleyna on the sidelines. Their absence meant that Imperial Gesture, coming off her 10¾-length maiden win at Saratoga, was favored in the watered-down six-horse field. Imperial Gesture was a half-sister to the brilliant Sardula, who fell just a head short in the 1993 Breeders' Cup Juvenile Fillies race. Harty was hopeful the late-developing filly, the last horse to have been taught her early racing lessons in Dubai, would earn herself an opportunity to avenge the family name in the 2001 Juvenile Fillies.

Stuck on the inside, Imperial Gesture was taken back early and struggled to find her footing, running a bit awkwardly in fifth. By the time she found her stride, longshot Tali'sluckybusride had made a pre-emptive strike on the turn for home and bolted to an insurmountable lead. Imperial Gesture ran decently down the lane to be second, but finished 4½ lengths back of the surprising winner. Although it was not another brutal photo-finish loss, it was yet another second-place finish for a Harty horse, continuing the unhealthy trend that had begun at Del Mar.

Four days later, Harty sent two of his colts out to go a mile on the turf. Spillikin was first up, and Sheikh Mohammed's homebred made a strong late run in the middle of the course, but came up half a length short, losing to a 35-1 shot. An hour later, Dubai Edition, a son of Sheikh Maktoum's Eclipse Award-winning turf mare Hatoof, and therefore bred to love the surface, was sent off as the 2-1 favorite in his race. In tight quarters on the turn, the best he could do was, of course, second. Whether they were running on dirt or grass, Harty's horses were plagued by the "seconditis" disease that had seeped into the barn at Del Mar and had turned into a full-fledged epidemic at Santa Anita.

Racing is conducted almost exclusively on grass in England, which forces the sport to move from course to course every few days, as the grass can only withstand so much racing at once. A country roughly the size of California, England has 59 racecourses, every one of them unique. Of the 59, Newmarket is king. It is to English horse racing what Chicago's Wrigley Field or New York's Yankee Stadium is to baseball, a place fairly dripping with the history of the sport.

A tiny town of 4,000, located 40 miles or so from London but just 10 miles from where the Maktoums were educated at Cambridge, Newmarket is the only community in the world where horses have the right of way. Stables are scattered throughout the area, and horses and their stable lads beat the sun up every morning and take to the streets on their way to work out over the hundreds of acres of windswept gallops, a tradition that dates back more than 300 years to the reign of Charles II. It is common to see strings of 40 racehorses trotting slowly across a busy street, with a long line of cars stacked up at the red light, waiting calmly for them to pass. The jockeys are able to control the traffic flow by using their whips to press a button on the stoplights, changing them instantly so they can cross. Many of the Newmarket roads, especially those on the outskirts of town, have two separate sidewalks: a wide one for horses, and a thin one for people.

In European racing, horses, who are creatures of habit, stay in their home stable all year. Only the top horses ever travel by plane, so when a European horse goes to race, the experience is like a two-day field trip. He is loaded into a horse van, driven to the racecourse, runs, and either stays the night or comes straight back to his stable. In America, trainers and their horses are more nomadic, moving from track to track every few months. Some New York-based horses winter at Gulfsteam Park in Florida, move north to Keeneland in the spring, then go to Belmont in May, up to Saratoga in late July, and back to Belmont in September before starting the cycle all over again. In England, almost all the major stables are in and around Newmarket, as has been the case since the sport took hold in the early 18th century.

The Godolphin horses, as well as much of the staff, make their home at historic Moulton Paddocks, a 150-year-old, 1,300-acre estate tucked well back from any public road. The horses stay in stalls with gold plates on the doors, commemorating the Group 1 victories scored by the runners that used them in previous years. Needless to say, some of the plates have quite a bit of inscription. A gorgeous facility, Moulton Paddocks has housed many top trainers and horses in its illustrious history, including those of Jim Joel, who won numerous classics in the early 1900's. The house itself, which has some 20 bedrooms, also has a wing that was built especially for King Edward VII, a horse lover who stayed there often when visiting his good friend Sir Ernest Cassel around the turn of the 20th century.

In European racing, workouts are informal exercises known only to those intimately involved with the stable. In America, every formal workout is judged and timed, with the information then going into a database available to every bettor, usually through *Daily Racing Form*. There are a few scribes whose job it is to watch the gallops at Newmarket and report what they see, but again, it is far more informal. For three years, Simon Crisford was one of those who covered the gallops.

"It's certainly not as you do it in the States," he said, getting out of his Lexus and walking up a hill in his heavy boots to observe the Godolphin string on a wet, cold October morning. "After a little while you learn how different trainers work their horses and get a sense of who is doing what, but even then it is from a distance and we just watch, we don't time them."

At that moment, the blue saddlecloths of the Godolphin horses appeared over the crest of the Limekilns gallops, the very same hills where Charles II rode his horses.

"This is my favorite time and place," said Crisford, his hands wrapped around a cup of hot coffee. "It's just as it was 300 years ago, same trees, same hills, same beautiful animals."

Indeed, the wide-open, windy, rolling greenery as far as the eye could see did have a sense of timelessness. A few feet away, an aging sign that read "One mile" was nailed to a weather-beaten post. Crisford explained that in this particular area, a horse could work anywhere from half a mile to two miles, from a starting point down near a clump of trees a mile away, thus the sign.

Just then Saeed bin Suroor appeared, riding high in the saddle, bundled up in a heavy blue Godolphin jacket, overseeing his horses. Quickly they streamed by at a high gallop. First in line was Sakhee, getting in a final tuneup before his trip to France for the Prix de l'Arc de Triomphe. Right behind him was Fantastic Light, prepping for the Breeders' Cup. Next came Noverre, then Slickly, both Group 1 winners. Twenty more classy horses followed before bin Suroor nodded to Crisford and rode off to monitor the rest of the morning's activities.

Crisford hopped back in the Lexus, reversed his field, and a minute later parked by the side of a steep hill that was populated by horses trained by two of England's finest, Sir Michael Stoute and Henry Cecil. Crisford pointed out that many trainers often had their horses run full tilt up the hill twice as a final workout about a week before a race, a very serious work to be sure. As if to prove his point, a horse came chugging by, halfway up the hill and already beginning to labor.

"Wouldn't fancy a bet on that one with your money," remarked Crisford.

In England, horses had been raced seemingly forever, as was the case in Ireland, but formal racing truly took root during the reign of Henry VIII (1509-47). An avid hunter, Henry also loved racing horses and was the first English leader to keep a stable of paid riders employed for his amusement. Racing was held primarily at Greenwich, the home of the king's stables, and consisted of either long-distance races (8 to 12 miles), contested by "hunting horses" owned and bred by the king and other nobles, or sprints, featuring the speedy "Irish hobby" horses that he began importing. The War of the Roses had taken a tremendous toll on the horse population in England, as wars of that era were wont to do, and Henry embarked on a dedicated mission to bring them back, aggressively importing as many fine horses as he could get from around the world.

In the early 17th century, racing prospered around England and Scotland, with towns all over sprouting makeshift racecourses. The sprints, much like Quarter Horse races of today, were contested at distances of a quarter-mile to a half-mile. Open to anyone with a horse and the willingness to run him, they were very popular because everyone could see the action-packed race from start to finish, unlike the meandering "hunting-horse" races favored by the nobility. The "Irish hobbies" had been running in Ireland, mostly at The Curragh, still the top racecourse in Ireland today, since the first century A.D. There is evidence to support the argument that their blood, which has survived through the female line, has as much to do with the Thoroughbred's natural speed as the blood of the three Arabian foundation stallions.

King James I (1603-25) was also influential in continuing to drive the breeding of horses closer to the creation of the Thoroughbred. He loved the sprint races, and bred the hobbies at his Tutbury royal stud, as well as English "running-horses," the other type of fast horse that contested the short, exciting dashes that so captured the imagination of common race fans of that era.

Before Charles II (1660-85), English monarchs had availed themselves of Barbary Coast horses through the spoils of war, dating back to the time of the Crusades (1076-1270). A horseman from birth, Charles II, often referred to as the Jockey-King, took a different tack, gaining access to a host of stallions by marrying a Portuguese princess. During his rule, known as the Restoration, Charles II both popularized and standardized horse racing in England. In 1665, he established the King's Plates, four-mile races that were contested in multiple heats. He also rode in many of the races himself at Newmarket, winning the Newmarket Town Plate twice on his mount Old Rowley.

His genuine love of horses and devotion to the sport gave Newmarket its identity and drove interest in horse racing to an all-time high, but self-preservation was an equally strong motivation for his desire to race horses and improve the breed. Having seen his father, Charles I, beheaded after being overrun by Oliver Cromwell's bigger, faster cavalry, he wanted to create a strain of even faster, more powerful horses, ensuring that his head would stay on his neck. The standardization of the four-mile races and the set of rules that accompanied them was the first pivotal step toward giving English breeders something definitive to shoot for, turning what had been quite a haphazard enterprise into a much more selective, focused endeavor. Less than 100 years after the reign of Charles II, the foundation stallions had done their duty, the three original English classics had been created, and the Sport of Kings was firmly established.

Every fall, English racing returns to Newmarket for the five-day Cambridgeshire meet, and it is a unique and busy week. There are five days of top-class racing combined with three days of high-class yearling sales, which commence an hour after the weekday races have ended. The meeting features three Group 1 races, one of which is the Middle Park Stakes for 2-year-old colts. The "Houghton" sales take place at the Tattersalls sales pavilion right near the center of town, and directly across from the headquarters of the Jockey Club, the group that has ruled racing in England with an iron hand since its formation in 1751.

The 2001 Middle Park was seen as little more than a coronation for Johannesburg, Coolmore's brilliant son of the American sire Hennessy. They had purchased the colt for the relatively minor sum, for them, of $200,000 at the Keeneland September sale in 2000 and he had more than earned the money back, easily winning his first five career starts, the last two of which were Group 1 affairs. In his previous race he had defeated Zipping, an aptly named French colt who was back for another go, but the rest of the field was fairly nondescript. To ensure a rapid early pace, Coolmore entered a pacemaker named Line Rider.

Sheikhs Hamdan and Maktoum were present to root on their juvenile duo, the David Loder-trained Farqad and Official Flame. On a day when a brisk wind blew white, puffy clouds across the bright blue sky, the sheikhs and their large, all-male entourage stood stiffly in their blocky dark suits, just a few yards from John and Sue Magnier, Michael Tabor, and their friends in the large paddock. Of the seven runners entered, the two superpowers were responsible for four.

As the colts paraded around the large, mature trees in the recently reconstructed paddock, Johannesburg's neck was noticeably wet, often a sign of nervousness. Coolmore stable jockey Mick Kinane, unconcerned, used his whip to gently wipe a bit of the sweat off as the horses headed through the crowd and onto the track. As they left the scene, the respective ownership groups and trainers went inside and up to the top floors of the brand-new Millenium Grandstand to watch the six-furlong race.

There are two separate courses at Newmarket: the July course, used exclusively for summer racing, and the Rowley mile. The Middle Park was to be contested over the Rowley course, an undulating 10-furlong straightaway with a significant dip about 300 yards from the finish.

"I consider it the truest test in racing," said Michael Tabor the night before the race. "The horses can stride out freely, they never really get hemmed in, and you've got to be able to maintain your momentum up the hill to the wire."

The bookies feverishly adjusted their odds as the horses jogged to the gate, but Johannesburg was so well regarded that very few were even offering win odds on the Coolmore juvenile, choosing instead to make punters wager on who would finish second. The few that did have odds on the Kentucky-bred sensation made him 30-100, right in between 1-5 and 2-5.

The pacemaker, Line Rider, broke well and went straight to the front while Kinane kept Johannesburg held up in midpack until the horses neared the dip. At that point, Kinane roused his colt and he assumed command immediately. Only Zipping mounted any kind of a challenge, but he never threatened Johannesburg, who won as he pleased. The two Godolphin colts made little impression and finished well up the track.

Despite recording the facile win, Kinane kept Johannesburg to his task past the wire. One of the unique and quite beautiful quirks of the Rowley course is that after the horses cross the finish line, they canter up a slight hill. As they reach the crest, anyone standing at ground level and looking in that direction sees only the horses silhouetted against the horizon, the variety of silks making a colorful collage against the afternoon sky.

Asked after the race if he had instructed Kinane to ride Johannesburg past the winning post, O'Brien acted as if he had been caught cheating on a test.

"He's bred for dirt and we've had our eye on the Breeders' Cup with him for a little while. I told Mick if it all went well to ask him for a little after the finish to see how he'd handle it. He said he liked it just fine."

The day before, the meticulous trainer had been at Southwell, an all-weather track that closely approximates the American dirt surface, some 50 miles from Newmarket. He had gone there to test multiple Group 1 winners Galileo, Mozart, and Black Minnaloushe before taking all three to Belmont for the Breeders' Cup. O'Brien had done the same thing with Giant's Causeway in preparation for the 2000 Breeders' Cup Classic, in which the colt put in a brilliant run and battled Tiznow the length of the Churchill stretch, losing by just a head. Southwell is a counterclockwise track, so the horses had also gotten a chance to experience a fairly tight left-hand turn, something they had yet to encounter in their careers. Asked if Johannesburg was likely to join the American-bound trio, O'Brien plunged his hands into the pockets of his full-length, undertaker-like black coat and mumbled, "Yes, if he stays sound he'll go in the Juvenile. He's already had a long season, and I understand Officer is quite a good colt, but we're looking forward to a good run."

Two minutes after hearing O'Brien's comments, Corals bookmaker Simon Clare made Johannesburg the 5-1 second choice in the Juvenile, with Officer favored at 2-1.

"I thought about making them 5-2 co-favorites," said the well-coiffed Clare, "but then I got off my rooting chair and went a little more conservatively. I think we'll likely get good action on him at fives."

After the last race, everyone headed to Tattersalls for the sales. Some stopped for a pint on the way, but by the time the first colt entered the sales ring, the steep, small, circular pavilion was packed. The auctioneers at Tattersalls are a theatrical crew. Since only about 50 horses are sold in one session, as opposed to Keeneland's 200, there is less time pressure, allowing the auctioneers to dictate the pace, and they milk it for all it's worth. Once a Tattersalls auctioneer narrows down a sale to two potential buyers, the show truly begins. He slows the pace dramatically and point his remarks directly at the combatants, at which point the crowd resembles that at a tennis match, heads shifting from side to side to follow the action. An English yearling sale is commerce as theater and plays quite well, finishing with a sweeping bang of the gavel, often accompanied by an acknowledgment of the buyer: "I'm bid three hundred, do I hear three-twenty? Three-twenty? I put it to you, sir, three-twenty or I sell to the rail. No? And I thank you sir, sold to the rail for three hundred, well done, Mr. Goodbody."

Outside the pavilion, things also move at a much more comfortable pace. Unlike Keeneland, there are no televisions outside, only speakers to relay the well-modulated voice of the auctioneer. There are TV's in the two smoky bars and plush restaurant in the surrounding buildings, where, as at Keeneland, much business is done over many drinks.

The horses walk around a circular paddock at Tattersalls, and until they enter the sales ring, at no time are they put into tight quarters or under a roof, as they are at Keeneland and other big auctions. As a result, they are far better behaved than their American counterparts before being led through a large wooden door and into the pavilion. The grounds at Tattersalls, where they have been selling horses for more than 200 years, are lush and hilly. As at the racecourse and the gallops, one can feel the weight of history with every prancing step the young, spirited horses take.

Most expected the usual Godolphin-Coolmore top-end battle in the sales ring, and they were not disappointed. John Ferguson, still in his Godolphin winter jacket, had been out at the barns for some final check-ups and was ready for action, as were Sheikhs Hamdan and Maktoum, dressed casually in khakis and windbreakers. Sheikh Mohammed was rumored to be flying in later that night. John Magnier, Demi O'Byrne (attired much more conservatively than at Keeneland, where he had sported an outfit of pink pants, a tricolored shirt, and no socks), and Tabor stood high in one corner, while Ferguson staked out a spot on the floor directly below his friendly adversaries, where they could not see him.

As expected, the two superpowers were the major buyers, accounting for the four highest-priced horses and nine of the top 10 on the first night, but it was not Ferguson who did the bulk of the buying for the men from the Middle East. Sheikh Mohammed's bloodstock man was the underbidder on the sales topper, a $2 million son of the Shadwell stallion Green Desert who went to Coolmore, but Sheikhs Maktoum and Hamdan were the big-spending Maktoum brothers on Day One. Sheikh Maktoum's Gainsborough Stud outbid Coolmore for the second-most-expensive colt at the session, a $1.6 million son of European sire Grand Lodge. He again beat back the Irish for the next-most-expensive horse sold, a Sadler's Wells colt that went for just over a million. Sheikh Hamdan, meanwhile, dominated the upper middle of the market, buying four colts in the $300,000 to $750,000 range.

Standing just outside the walking ring, wearing pressed slacks and a long-sleeved polo shirt, Saeed bin Suroor watched the proceedings from a distance, interrupted every two minutes or so by the beeping of his high-tech cell phone but happy to talk about his job.

"I've watched the Kentucky Derby since I was a child. That was always the big race," he said. "We've failed so far in the Derby and that is difficult for us. We understand people thinking we're not doing it the right way but we disagree and are confident."

The soft-spoken bin Suroor became more animated when asked if he believed he could train a Derby winner from Dubai.

"We can win for sure coming from Dubai. We've done it everywhere else and for the Breeders' Cup in the U.S., so it's not a problem for me at all," he said. "The Derby is a very important goal for Sheikh Mohammed as well as our whole team. We're learning every year, and didn't expect to win the first year of the new plan with Eoin and David Loder. I understand much is expected of us but people must be patient. We'll win it. I hope this year, but if not we'll just keep trying until we do."

Told Sheikh Mohammed predicted a Godolphin Derby victory within four years and that 2002 would be Year Four, the slim, relaxed trainer laughed out loud.

"He said that, not me! He takes a lot of pressure off me, which I like. I can just do my job, and he can tell people when we will accomplish our goals."

When the conversation turned to the Arc de Triomphe, Europe's fall classic to be run two days hence, bin Suroor broke into a grin.

"Sakhee is doing extremely well right now. We gave him plenty of time earlier in the year but people must remember it's a long season and we have many nice horses. I think a mile and a quarter is his best distance, but he stayed the mile and a half last year,"—he was a strong second behind the Aga Khan's remarkable Sinndar in the 2000 Epsom Derby—"so I have no problem with the Arc."

After the midweek sales were over, the Godolphin team focused their attention across the English Channel, to Arc de Triomphe weekend. Going racing in France is like traveling back in time. Their betting windows are still segregated by price, and not every type of bet is taken at every window. On Arc Day, there were not nearly enough clerks manning the windows to handle the betting volume, but nobody seemed too bothered, other than the thousands of English punters who had made the trek across the channel. The event was paramount, the particulars secondary.

French racing, while highly competitive, is conducted on a rather small scale, and the purse money, far below American standards, is even well below the purses for big races in England. There is not much 2-year-old racing in France, and seeing how little money is offered, that comes as no surprise. Many horses are sent to America after beginning their careers in France and they do extremely well on the firm American turf, especially on the lucrative Southern California circuit.

"They have less mileage on their legs," said Simon Crisford when asked why he believes that to be so. "The French love cycling, right?

Well, their horse racing is very similar, a long, slow beginning in single file, then a furious sprint to the finish."

It is also instructive to understand that sending a horse from England to France is, in Crisford's words, "Like going from Santa Anita to Golden Gate. It's just not that long a trip, so we put them in the horse box the day before, drive 'em over, and they wake up the next day at the course, go out for a walk in the morning, run in the afternoon, and are home the next night."

A crowd of 36,000 showed up at Longchamp racecourse for the 80th running of the Arc on a cool, cloudy October 7. The French have style, and they exhibited it in abundance on Arc Day. Their clothes were magnificent, the champagne and wine were flowing freely, and the racing was top class. The Arc Day card featured no less than five Group 1 races, the centerpiece of which was the Arc itself, a testing mile-and-a-half event that is the most important race open to horses of all ages in Europe.

Longchamp is France's most famous racecourse, a massive facility built in 1856 on the banks of the river Seine in Paris's Bois de Boulogne district. The first races at Longchamp were run on an April Sunday in 1857, with Emperor Napoleon III in attendance, having arrived after sailing down the Seine in his private yacht. France's first major race, the Grand Prix de Paris, began soon after in 1863, and by 1914 was the richest race in the world. Due to the outbreak of WW I, however, all French racecourses were requisitioned for the war effort and did not reopen until 1919. Although the Thoroughbred population had dropped severely as a result of the war, the Prix de l'Arc de Triomphe came into being in 1920, the race and its title a tribute to the French soldiers who had served in the war.

Longchamp has three courses that all finish over the same long straightaway, and the Arc is run over the longest course, which measures a mile and three-quarters around. From the enormous grandstand, one can see the Eiffel Tower in the distance as the horses navigate the huge, undulating right-handed course, which features a fairly severe downhill run leading into the seemingly endless 500-meter homestretch.

Sakhee was the solid race favorite despite a poor outside draw (post 15). Bred by Sheikh Hamdan and trained by John Dunlop at 2 and 3, he had run second in the Epsom Derby, but had battled foot problems ever since. After being transferred to the Godolphin stable under the care of bin Suroor, he had only run twice as a 4-year-old, his most recent race a stunning seven-length romp in the Group 1 Juddmonte International Stakes at York. That performance, one a proud bin Suroor called "even more than we had hoped for," had earned him the highest statistical ranking of the year in Europe.

As usual, Godolphin and Coolmore were well represented throughout the day. Aidan O'Brien captured his 19th Group 1 race of 2001, winning the Grand Criterium for 2-year-old colts with Rock of Gibraltar. The result only served to further flatter Dubai Destination, who had beaten him so easily three weeks earlier.

O'Brien saddled the St. Leger winner, Milan, in the Arc, and the crowd hammered him down to 4-1, second favorite behind Sakhee. Plenty of rain had fallen in the previous 48 hours, making the going quite heavy, and many felt that would hinder Sakhee's chances of repeating his monstrous performance at York. Placed forwardly throughout the early stages of the race, Sakhee blew that theory to bits when Frankie Dettori asked him to turn on the jets entering the stretch. He quickly drew away from the field and was never threatened, winning by six lengths, one of the three largest margins in the history of the race. The formerly unbeaten French filly Aquarelliste was a game second, while Milan made a belated late move to finish a distant fifth.

The win, the third Arc triumph by a Maktoum-owned horse, capped a phenomenal weekend for the Dubai contingent, who had won the final three Group 2 races the day before, turning the awarding of trophies after each race into something resembling a Maktoum family outing. The ceremony after the Arc was the most elaborate of all, and took place in the historic paddock, under the massive horse chestnut trees that have provided shade to horses and their owners at Longchamp for well over a century. The camera-happy Dettori planted himself in between bin Suroor and the three brothers, and there were smiles all around as shutters clicked away. After leaving the paddock, Dettori and Crisford were led into a media tent for interviews, but none of the Maktoum brothers came with them. A few perfunctory questions were asked and answered, at which point Dettori announced that the Arc had been his 100th Group 1 victory and that if there were no more questions, the drinks were on him. That was the end of the press conference and champagne was poured liberally in the sauna-like tent.

Outside, however, word filtered through that the American bombing of Afghanistan had commenced. Racetrack security then accompanied the ruling family of Dubai, their personal security men, and their large entourage out of the racecourse, headed for their private planes. The time for celebration had ended and the group returned back to Dubai to deal with far more serious matters.

The United Arab Emirates' rather precarious position in relation to the "war on terrorism" had put the Maktoums, three of the most high-profile Arab leaders in the Persian Gulf, on the hot seat. Three weeks after the September 11 attacks, six Palestinians were killed in the ongoing conflict with Israel, an incident that prompted a stern statement from Sheikh Abdullah bin Zaid al-Nahayan, information minister of the UAE. Speaking in regard to the UAE's role in the U.S.-led coalition against terrorism, he said, "These killings put us all in a very awkward position. If this continues, most of us will have to reconsider our role." His comments came only days after the revelation that 10 of the 19 hijackers responsible for the attacks began their journeys to the United States from Dubai.

The Maktoums crave a strong business relationship with the Western world, especially the United States, and let U.S. Naval ships berth in their harbor, yet they strongly support Palestine in its struggle with Israel, staying true to the pro-Arab position their father took after the 1973 war. They were also directly responsible for the decision that saw the UAE formally recognize Afghanistan's oppressive Taliban regime, which provided a haven for the Al Qaeda terrorist organization and its leader, Osama bin Laden. It was a stance the Maktoums renounced only after the Taliban leaders failed to agree to turn bin Laden over to the American-led coalition. In addition, the money that was funneled to Mohammed Atta, the leader of the hijacking operation, came directly from banks in Dubai, a place where no law was even on the books addressing money-laundering.

As a front-page story in the *Los Angeles Times* pointed out, "Millions in Al Qaeda funds cascaded through the free-wheeling financial institutions of Dubai." The *Times* article also noted that "Despite quiet but persistent prodding by U.S. and other Western diplomats, the emirates' ruling elite was hesitant to reckon with the growing terrorist populace. Regulations that would target terrorists would also interfere with a laissez-faire economy that has bolstered the wealth of their entwined desert kingdoms."

The man in charge of that banking industry is Sheikh Hamdan, who politely but firmly refused to answer any questions about the situation when asked at Longchamp.

Back in America, the October 6 weekend was a busy one across the country for 2-year-olds. Officer was at Belmont for the Champagne Stakes, while Harty had Burnt Ember going at Keeneland in the Grade 2 Breeders' Futurity, Janadel and Classicist in maiden races at Santa Anita, and Sunray Spirit making his stakes debut at Belmont in the Grade 3 Cowdin Stakes.

Siphonic, the colt who had outfought Janadel down the lane at Del Mar, demolished Burnt Ember and the rest of the Breeders' Futurity field and won by six. David Hofmans had been high on Siphonic from the get-go, and the colt now looked like a legitimate challenger to Officer in the Breeders' Cup Juvenile. More importantly, he figured to be even better suited to the mile and a quarter of the Derby. Officer kept his own record perfect by cruising to yet another easy win in the Champagne, dusting off Wayne Lukas's top Derby prospect, Jump Start, in the process. He also gained the advantage of having had a race over the Belmont strip in anticipation of a spirited Breeders' Cup battle with Johannesburg, Siphonic, and a host of others, including Essence Of Dubai.

Validating Harty's lofty opinion of him, Janadel put it all together in his race, settling nicely in the early stages, then coming up the rail to win by a length in a solid time. Harty had high hopes for Sheikh Maktoum's Irish homebred and planned on getting him a fourth start, in a two-turn race, before his time in America was up.

The next day at Belmont, Sunray Spirit hit the gate at the start of the Cowdin, dropped back to last, then unleashed a powerful run down the lane to win going away, albeit in a very slow time. Harty was not concerned with the time, focusing instead on getting his third graded stakes win and hoping the barn had turned a corner just in time. It was the third win by a colt in a week, and he was hoping for another the next day from Classicist. Unfortunately, the Unbridled colt again suffered from a poor start, fell back to last in a five-horse field, went wide on the far turn, and could do no better than third, more than five lengths back. The winner, Striking Song, was one of the many big-money Fog City yearling buys who had done little running early in their careers. Fog City's other trainer, Bob Hess Jr., planned on sending the immature but talented colt to the Breeders' Cup if he stayed sound and kept improving in the mornings.

The Breeders' Cup is the year-end goal for all top-class American horses, and over the years, has become much the same for European Thoroughbreds as well. The 2001 version promised to be a truly international affair, with huge contingents coming from the two superpowers, complemented by the best of the rest of Europe. As always, the $4 million Classic was the most talked-about race. The horse to beat was the Bobby Frankel-trained Aptitude, coming off a smashing victory in the Jockey Club Gold Cup over the Belmont surface. His top American challenger was the defending champion in the race, California-bred Tiznow, a horse who had battled back problems all summer and could do no better than third in his two preps for the big race.

In Europe, all the prerace discussion focused on the rubber match between Godolphin's Fantastic Light and Coolmore's Galileo, both of whom were being pointed for the Classic, rather than the Turf. Galileo was going to the dirt for purely financial reasons. He had proven his ability on the grass, so to try and increase his value as a stallion, John Magnier wanted to give him a shot at proving he could run just as well on the dirt. Fantastic Light trained on the dirt often in Dubai, and the Godolphin brain trust had said they felt a mile and a quarter was his best distance, so he was bound for the Classic too.

Harty had at least three, and maybe four horses ready to take their shots at the day he had been pointing to all year. Essence Of Dubai was set to battle Officer, Siphonic, Came Home, and Johannesburg in the Juvenile, and the maiden, Ibn Al Haitham, was going to join him after his strong run in the Norfolk. Tempera was primed for the Juvenile Fillies, coming off the forced vacation and change in training pattern Harty had imposed on her after the loss in the Del Mar Debutante.

Imperial Gesture was going on the plane to New York as well, but Harty was unsure if she would join Tempera or run in a lesser stakes race the day after the Breeders' Cup.

In addition, the Maktoums had at least eight more horses entered, including the likely favorites in the Filly and Mare Turf (Sheikh Maktoum's Lailani) and Mile (Noverre). Coolmore was coming with everything they had, too, with Bach (Mile) and Sophisticat (Juvenile Fillies) joining Galileo, Johannesburg, Mozart (Sprint), Black Minnaloushe (Classic), and Milan in what was by far the deepest and most talented Irish raiding party ever to go racing in America.

In the wake of the terrorist attacks, there were many who wondered whether or not the Breeders' Cup would even take place. As Breeders' Cup President D. G. Van Clief recalled, many phone calls were made and meetings called to tackle the topic.

"Our main concern was if and how we would secure the event, so we got input from the New York Racing Association, the Nassau County Police, the NYPD in Queens, the FBI, and Governor Pataki's office to make that determination."

Fairly quickly, all parties agreed it was possible to secure what would be the first international sporting event held in the New York metropolitan area since September 11. At that point, Van Clief turned his attention to congressional and senatorial contacts, as well as the State Department.

"There had been a lot of public discussion about the appropriateness of certain individuals attending, so we checked up and were told that the individuals and their countries, like Dubai and Saudi Arabia, were in lock-step with the U.S. and the coalition against terrorism, so that was that. We didn't know at that point if any of them would come, but that's actually normal as a lot of major owners are busy people and don't finalize plans until the last minute."

Asked about his plans just before the running of the Arc, Sheikh Mohammed had said, "We are very much looking forward to the Breeders' Cup, it is a wonderful day for horse racing."

It was a typically cryptic response that left the sheikh with his options open and everyone in the business waiting for him to make a decision.

11

Center of Attention

In the two weeks leading up to the Breeders' Cup, Godolphin was in the spotlight, due mostly to the fact that when the pre-entries came out on Wednesday, October 17, they had listed the Classic as "first preference" for their two superstars, Sakhee and Fantastic Light. Both horses had been pre-entered in two races, the Classic and the Turf, but it was thought to be a given that Fantastic Light would run in the Classic and Sakhee would go in the Turf. As usual, the sheikhs were keeping everyone guessing.

They had exactly a week to make their decision, as entries would be made final on October 24 at 9 A.M., just before the draw for post positions. Both horses galloped or worked every morning on the Belmont dirt, and again, the consensus among those watching was that Fantastic Light handled the unfamiliar surface better. The Godolphin folks on the scene, Saeed bin Suroor and assistant trainer Tom Albertrani, said only that they were pleased with how both horses were coming up to the big day.

The sheikhs weren't talking. Still in Dubai, they were also keeping their travel plans a mystery. When asked about it on a conference call, Simon Crisford made sure to leave the door just a bit ajar.

"Sheikh Mohammed never tells me in advance about his travel plans," he said. "He'll call me as he's getting on his plane and we just go from there."

That Crisford himself was not around to handle the media crush early in the week was odd as well. It is a huge part of his job and he is quite adept at it. Bin Suroor, still struggling a bit with English, is rather uncomfortable when asked to do too much talking.

Watching the horses work in the mornings and walking around the barn area during Breeders' Cup Week is a unique experience. It is the only time all year that horses and horsemen from around the globe come together and work side by side for almost a week, leading Harty to compare the atmosphere to an Olympic village. Conversations were being conducted in Japanese, French, Spanish, and a variety of heavily accented English as the horses were put through their respective paces.

The only constant is the quality of the horseflesh. About 100 of the best Thoroughbreds in the world are gathered together, and to an equine enthusiast it is like going to the Louvre or the Met. As they come onto the track to jog in the early-morning sun, each horse seems more beautiful than the previous one. Coats gleam, muscles ripple, and the exercise riders often have their hands full keeping the finely tuned athletes focused on the task at hand.

Just before the 9 A.M. entry deadline on October 24, Godolphin finalized their plans. They put the decision up on their website, a democratic, if rather impersonal, method of disseminating such hotly anticipated information. Jon Lees, chief racing writer for *The Racing Post,* the top turf daily in England, was not surprised.

"They do that all the time. At home, I'll ring up Simon with a question and he'll ask me to call him back in an hour or so, then 45 minutes later someone in the office will tell me they saw the answer to my question on the website. It's a bit frustrating, but there's not much we can do, now is there?"

The decision was front-page news all over the sports world. The sheikhs had pulled a switch. Sakhee would run in the Classic, and Fantastic Light in the Turf, a risky move with a monumental upside. If Sakhee could follow up his smashing run in the Arc with a victory in the Classic, he would make racing history. If he failed, they could say he didn't like the dirt, and that would be that. Being a son of Bahri, a turf sire, his bloodlines said the dirt was not likely to be kind to the Arc winner. Fantastic Light, on the other hand, was a son of American sire Rahy, bred to handle the dirt just fine. Regardless, the decision was final.

The about-face devastated the European press and fans, who had been salivating over the chance to witness a rubber match between Fantastic Light and Galileo in the Classic ever since the Godolphin horse had handed Coolmore's champion his only career defeat seven weeks earlier. They were even, one win apiece, and the plan was that the Classic would break the tie, but it was not to be. Asked how he felt, Galileo's trainer, Aidan O'Brien, said quietly, "I'm disappointed, but I've learned not to be surprised by anything in racing."

There was much discussion about how the Sakhee-Fantastic Light decision had been made, but the principals were shedding no light on the situation. Sheikh Hamdan had bred Sakhee, and had called the shots regarding the colt's career at 2 and 3. Once Sakhee became a member of the Godolphin team, however, it meant that he was trained officially by bin Suroor and that Sheikh Mohammed, never wanting for an opinion, was firmly in the decision-making mix. To further complicate matters, Hamdan also owned and raced Mutamam, who was coming off his first Grade 1 win and was expected to be one of the favorites in the Turf.

Regardless of how it had been reached, the decision ensured that Godolphin had already achieved one of their major goals. They are always conscious of getting Dubai into the headlines at major events, and going for broke with Sakhee guaranteed that they would remain the focus of tremendous attention from the worldwide media until the Classic was over. In addition, Sheikh Mohammed had told John Ferguson to let Breeders' Cup President D. G. Van Clief know that Godolphin would donate all the purse money it won to the NTRA Charities-New York Heroes Fund, created to assist the families of rescue workers and other victims of the terrorist attacks. A press release to that effect went out on the afternoon of October 23.

The post-position draw was held just after the entry deadline on Wednesday the 24th, in a massive tent, just inside the main gate at Belmont Park. It seemed a shame for everyone to be inside on such a beautiful Indian summer day, but plans are plans. Everybody ate the free breakfast, but most nibbled their fingernails as well. The Breeders' Cup draw is crucial, both because of the enormity of the event and the presence of the large fields.

To determine who would start in what spot, post positions and horses' names were drawn at random, then relayed to the crowd by track announcer Tom Durkin, a large man with a deep, booming voice. The races are drawn in order, so the Juvenile Fillies was the second race to be called. When Durkin announced that Bob Baffert's Habibti would start from the rail, the trainer pounded his fist on the table and anyone within 15 feet was easily able to hear the "Fuck!" he spit out to go with it.

Eoin Harty, on the other hand, was all smiles after hearing Durkin intone that Tempera would begin from post 9, on the far outside.

"Of all four horses I'm running, I was begging she'd draw the outside. Somebody was looking out for me," he joked. When Tempera had drawn outside in the Sorrento, she relaxed early and romped late. Drawn inside three weeks later in the Debutante, she had dueled for the early lead on the rail and tired in the stretch to finish third. Harty's other potential runner, Imperial Gesture, also drew well, getting post 7. Still undecided about whether he would run her, Harty was at least leaning.

"My owners are sportsmen who love a challenge, and especially love million-dollar races. They'd like to try it if she continues to look well," he said.

The Breeders' Cup races for 2-year-olds are run at a mile and a sixteenth. At any American track other than Belmont, drawing an outside post going that distance is asking for trouble because the race is run around two turns and there is a short run to the first one. Horses drawn outside are likely to go very wide early and lose tons of precious ground. Going a mile and a sixteenth at Belmont, however, means running around only one turn, making the outside the place to be. With the only turn more than half a mile away, horses starting from the outside encounter little traffic trouble, and their jockeys have time to let their mounts, and the race shape, determine strategy organically.

Post position is even more important with younger horses, who are often intimidated if stuck inside, on or near the rail. An inside draw forces the jockey to make an immediate decision. He must either gun his horse hard to maintain a good position early, risking getting caught in a speed duel, or take back and hope he will be able to weave his way through traffic when it counts. If he does neither, the horse can get pinned on the rail, have dirt kicked in its face, get bumped around, and never get a chance to show what it can do. Victor Espinoza, on Habibti, and Gary Stevens, stuck in post 2 aboard Michael Tabor's undefeated Bella Bellucci, would be under the gun.

Bobby Frankel allowed a thin smile to form on his lips when his filly, You, drew post 5. Looking to break a career-long winless streak in the Breeders' Cup that had mushroomed to 36 straight, Frankel ranked her as having the best chance among his six starters on the day.

Four races later they drew for the Juvenile, which featured a full field of 12, making post positions even more important. The news was not good for David Hofmans. His precocious Siphonic, undefeated in two career starts, had drawn the dreaded rail. A minute later, the connections of Came Home were all smiles after hearing Durkin say "Came Home, number 11." Jockey Chris McCarron, who had chosen to ride Came Home over Siphonic, grinned like a man who had just filled an inside straight. The undefeated European challenger, Johannesburg, drew number 3. It wasn't a horrible spot, but not what trainer Aidan O'Brien, fresh off the plane from Ireland, wanted to hear. The Godolphin colts, Essence Of Dubai and Ibn Al Haitham, fared better. Essence, who figured to come from midpack, drew post 4. Ibn, the maiden, had more tactical speed and drew the number 8 post. Again, Harty was all smiles.

Finally, only two horses remained: Officer and longshot French Assault. One would get post 7, the other, post 2. Painfully aware that his fate was now a fifty-fifty proposition, Baffert drew a deep breath as Durkin was given the information on the podium.

"Officer, number 2," said the announcer, and again, the trainer reacted as if he had been punched in the stomach. The heaviest favorite on the card was pinned on the inside with speed all around him, just about the worst spot imaginable for the sensational son of Bertrando. Usually happy to talk to anyone about his horses, especially the international press, Baffert bolted out the side door immediately after hearing Officer's draw. An hour later, having calmed down some, he said, "He's usually the stalker, now he's going to be the stalkee. Now that he drew the number 2, he better be the real deal. Victor's going to have to let him run away from there a little bit."

Already facing the most pressure-packed ride of his life, jockey Victor Espinoza was now squarely on the spot. A relative newcomer to the top echelon of riders, Espinoza was unfamiliar with having a bull's-eye on his back in a race of this magnitude. All the other riders would be looking for his green-and-white silks, and if they could find a way to bump, trap, or jostle him, they would. A happy-go-lucky type, Espinoza had had little more to do in Officer's first five races than make sure he didn't fall off. Suddenly, his split-second decision-making would go a long way toward determining the fate of the most talked-about American 2-year-old of 2001, a 2-year-old unfamiliar with racing in a large field, having never faced more than six horses in his short, brilliant career.

Before the Del Mar Futurity, there had been talk that Gary Stevens would replace Espinoza aboard Officer. Stevens had been the pilot for Point Given throughout his stellar 3-year-old campaign, has ridden many top Thoroughbred Corp. horses, and is considered one of the top best-race riders in the world. Espinoza, on the other hand, had only won his first Grade 1 race, a 30-1 upset aboard Early Pioneer in the 2000 Hollywood Gold Cup, 15 months earlier. He followed that up with an even bigger surprise in the 2000 Breeders' Cup Distaff, piloting the D. Wayne Lukas-trained Spain to victory at 55-1 for the Thoroughbred Corp.

In the end, Richard Mulhall, Ahmed Salman, and Baffert decided to allow Espinoza to keep the mount. The trio was about to find out if the 29-year-old Mexico City native was up to the task.

Once the draw was over, a Breeders' Cup representative asked bin Suroor if he would consent to be interviewed by the assembled media regarding the Sakhee-Fantastic Light switch. The trainer agreed, but was anything but happy about it. After some negotiation, he stood up, smoothed out his slacks, and said politely, "I'll talk to them, but I won't say anything."

Albertrani, on the other hand, was eager to talk, partly because he felt the press had been hasty in their earlier judgments. A native New Yorker, the one-time assistant to Bill Mott, who trained inaugural Dubai World Cup winner Cigar, was happy to be back home and did one interview after another. He repeated over and over that he and bin Suroor knew the two horses intimately, while everyone else had only seen them gallop around the track for a few days.

"You guys all form opinions pretty quickly, but we know the horses, so we really don't pay any attention to what you guys say." His comments, of course, indicated that the well-respected horseman, the lone American on the Godolphin team, paid a lot of attention, but his point was made nonetheless.

Later that gorgeous fall afternoon at Belmont, Dubai Tiger made his long-awaited racing debut for Harty. Handling the much-hyped $1.8 million yearling had required a lot of patience and it was a tribute to the trainer and his staff that they were going to get him to the races before their time with him was through. He had been sizzling in his morning drills and Harty was looking forward to seeing him race.

"He's finally ready to compete, and this will be it until next year, so I'm looking for a good run out of him today," he said. That Dubai Tiger was running on the day of the draw, when practically every member of the world's racing media was at Belmont, was no coincidence.

David Flores was aboard for the six-furlong sprint, and the two had an eventful journey. They were bumped hard at the start, and Flores had just gotten the colt back on track when he was roughed up again entering the turn. Forced to steady his mount, Flores finally swung wide into the stretch, and once in the clear, Dubai Tiger made a threatening run at the leader before tiring late to finish third.

"That was frustrating to watch because he never got a chance to show what he can do, and it was his only chance until Dubai. Funny game, this," said Harty. Asked his opinion the next day, Flores said, "He's a good one. We had so much trouble I was never able to get him into a rhythm, but he tried really hard and came back fine. He's got a chance to be a really good horse next year."

Friday afternoon marked the debut of King's Consul, whose size and gleaming coat made an impressive appearance, just as at the yearling sales.

"I'm looking forward to seeing him race," Harty had said on Wednesday. "Mentally, he's really come around in the last month, and you can see it just by looking at his workout times. He's still a big, backward horse, but he started to figure the game out at Santa Anita and I'm expecting big things from him."

Crisford, who had arrived on Thursday, was equally confident when asked about the big-money yearling Friday morning, saying with a wink, "We expect him to win."

The entire Godolphin team was milling around in the paddock before the race, admiring the striking $5.3 million colt. Harty, whose normal race-day attire consists of slacks and a button-down shirt, had on a suit and tie, indicating the importance of the occasion and his expectations of having his picture taken in the winners' circle.

Flores was up for this ride as well, a seven-furlong sprint. In midpack early on, King's Consul quickly advanced to be second entering the turn, and assumed the lead as the field headed for home. He was on the inside rail, the worst place to be at Belmont, but held on to the lead into deep stretch. Flores kept the big bay to his task, but the inexperienced colt seemed to be looking around, waiting for a challenge, which finally came in the last 50 yards. Unlike every Godolphin colt before him, King's Consul did just enough to win the photo by his long, expensive neck.

Sixteen months after running his first Godolphin 2-year-old, Harty had won a photo finish, and it seemed somehow fitting that it fell to the most expensive horse he had ever trained to turn the trick. One does not often get what one pays for in racing, especially in the yearling game, but for Harty, the purchase of King's Consul was worth every penny that Sheikh Mohammed had spent.

"Oh, he's one of the ones," said a still pumped-up Flores an hour later. "After the break he put himself into the race on his own. When he did that I said to myself, 'ooh, good.' He's still a little green, but when he saw the other horse right before the wire he responded and never let him get by, even when we were galloping out afterward. Eoin did a good job with this horse, taking it easy with him over the summer and letting him figure things out slowly. I worked him once last month at Santa Anita and he did everything on his own, I never had to move my hands at all. He's very strong. If he sticks together I think he'll be back in May."

Asked how the colt compared to the two running in Saturday's million-dollar Juvenile, Flores seemed almost insulted by the question.

"He's better," the Tijuana, Mexico, native stated firmly, adjusting his ever-present cowboy hat. "Like I said, if he sticks together physically and matures in the head a little more, you'll see him at the Derby."

Three races later, Harty saddled the ultraquick Sunray Spirit in the day's feature race, the Grade 3, one-mile Nashua Stakes for 2-year-olds. The colt that had given him his only head-to-head win over Baffert at Del Mar never got into the race and finished well up the track, denying Harty his first two-win day.

Before leaving the racetrack, Crisford told a few reporters that Sheikh Mohammed would not be flying in for the Breeders' Cup, choosing to stay in Dubai and watch the races via satellite. Salman had been the first to declare himself a no-show, and Khalid Abdullah had decided to stay home as well, meaning none of the three high-profile Arab owners would be at Belmont Park to see their horses compete against the best in the world.

The idea for the Breeders' Cup sprang from the mind of John Gaines, whose family's Gainesway Farm just outside Lexington had long been one of the top breeding operations in the business. In the spring of 1982, Gaines convinced other big breeders, flush with the millions of dollars being pumped into their business by the bidding wars of recent years, that a championship day at the end of the fall racing season would be a fine way to promote their product. The only time Americans saw horse racing on television in that era was during the Triple Crown, and Gaines knew that if the sport was to prosper, more people needed to see it. He convinced a select group of influential fellow Kentuckians such as Seth Hancock, Brereton C. Jones, and Leslie Combs that if they put on seven championship races worth more than a million dollars each and held the event at a different major racetrack every year, someone would televise the annual showcase, which would help attract new fans and new buyers for their bloodstock.

Gaines proposed that the unheard-of amount of prize money, the key to the plan, would come from the breeders themselves. After all, the mint juleps had been flowing freely for going on a decade at that point, and with the Maktoum brothers having just jumped in, there appeared to be no end in sight. Gaines figured that if breeders were required to pay annual stallion and foal nomination fees to keep their horses eligible to run in the rich new races, a percentage of those payments would be more than enough to cover the $10 million or so needed for purses. An old breeding axiom says "Breed the best to the best, and hope for the best." Gaines's idea was to have the best race against the best, which would help create clear-cut champions for the public, and future Thoroughbred buyers, to follow. It was simple, and it was brilliant.

Aware of the importance of attracting the Arabs and Europeans who had been lining the breeders' pockets to the new venture, he included two races to be run on the grass. The majority of the European racing power structure, led by the all-powerful English Jockey Club, still was not impressed. There was a great deal of discussion, much of it rather forceful, regarding the late date of the proposed races and the use of medication. European horses had always been trained to peak for the summer and early fall, and it was felt they would be nowhere near their best in late October or early November. Also, horses are not allowed the use of drugs of any kind in Europe. At the time, the only racing jurisdictions in North America with a similar policy were New York and Canada, and European owners and trainers feared they would be at a distinct disadvantage facing American horses that routinely raced or trained on medication. There was also the different weather and all the travel to be considered.

Gaines knew that he was offering far more purse money than anyone had ever seen before, and was counting on that simple fact to carry the day. It did, and was exactly the formula Sheikh Mohammed would follow a decade later when creating the Dubai World Cup. If you put up enough money, people will send their horses wherever and whenever you tell them.

Gaines's dream became a reality on Saturday, November 10, 1984, at sunny Hollywood Park in Los Angeles, California. Pouring through the gates were 64,254 excited fans, betting a titanic $8,443,070 to boot. In the first Breeders' Cup race, 2-year-old Chief's Crown, the heavy favorite in the Juvenile, won nicely to start the day off on a classy, formful note, but that changed in a hurry. The Juvenile Fillies was next, and 74-1 shot Fran's Valentine crossed the wire a half-length in front but was judged to have impeded a horse on the turn for home, disqualified, and placed 10th. Second-place finisher Outstandingly went to the winners' circle, and the Breeders' Cup had survived controversy number 1. There would be more.

Appropriately, the first grass race, the Mile, went to a Robert Sangster-owned horse, the Irish-bred, California-based mare Royal Heroine. The Aga Khan's Lashkari, dismissed at 53-1 in the $2 million Turf, made it a grass sweep by European owners when he outfinished France's All Along, America's 1983 Horse of the Year, by a long neck.

Finally, it was time for the richest horse race ever run at the time, the $3 million Classic. Slew o' Gold was made the 3-5 favorite off his strong victories in the prestigious New York fall races. Preakness winner Gate Dancer was in the field too, as were California heroes Desert Wine and Precisionist. The speedy Precisionist went right to the lead, but was quickly joined, then put away, by 31-1 longshot Wild Again, ridden by Pat Day. Slew o' Gold, under Angel Cordero Jr., tracked the leaders all the way and looked as if he would go right by Wild Again when the field turned for home. He didn't. Day had plenty of horse left, and the two battled head and head down the lane, bumping each other as they ran.

From the back of the pack, Laffit Pincay Jr. and the unpredictable Gate Dancer made a huge run, and they joined the fray in the final furlong. The three staged a furious finish that featured quite a bit of contact, most of it initiated by Gate Dancer, with Slew o' Gold getting the worst of it in between horses. Day managed to get Wild Again to the wire just in front of Gate Dancer, with Slew o' Gold squeezed about half a length back. Immediately, the stewards lit the inquiry sign. After a lengthy delay, they decided that Gate Dancer was the main culprit and moved him from second to third. It was as fantastic a finish as anyone, including John Gaines, could have dreamt.

The Maktoum brothers did not run any horses in the first Breeders' Cup, but they showed up in force the following year at Aqueduct racetrack in New York. Sheikh Mohammed paid $240,000 to supplement his sensational filly, Pebbles, in the mile-and-a-half Turf. Boxed in around the final turn, jockey Pat Eddery found a hole at the rail and Pebbles burst through the opening, got the lead, and held on gamely to win by a head, breaking the course record in the process. The blaze-faced chestnut, trained by the canny Clive Brittain, had captured the fancy of many fans when Brittain admitted that he supplemented her feed with a pint of Guinness each day. She ran in the maroon-and-white colors of Sheikh Mohammed, and those colors were victorious again five years later when Gary Stevens piloted In The Wings home first in the 1990 Turf at Belmont Park.

The 1990 Breeders' Cup also found a Maktoum horse involved in one of the most shocking finishes in racing history. A $1.65 million Keeneland yearling, Dayjur proved to be the fastest sprinter in Europe in 1990, so the Maktoums flew him to New York that fall to contest the six-furlong Breeders' Cup Sprint, a race that would mark his first start on dirt. Dayjur and the brilliant filly Safely Kept left the rest of the field in their wake and headed for home as a team. Slowly, Dayjur wore the filly down and began inching clear in the final stages, only to see a shadow on the track just yards from the wire. Spooked, he jumped the shadow, losing his momentum and the race. It was the most dramatic and unexpected Sprint finish in Breeders' Cup history, and the Maktoums have not come as close in a Breeders' Cup race on the dirt since.

Their next winner came in the 1994 Mile, courtesy of the Sadler's Wells colt Barathea, co-owned by Sheikh Mohammed and his breeder, Englishman Gerald Leigh. He had run in the 1993 Mile, but blew the first turn badly, impeding a number of horses, and finished fifth. In preparation for a return trip to America, trainer Luca Cumani installed a special left-handed turn at a Newmarket gallop to teach Barathea how to handle the unfamiliar bend. The move paid dividends when the colt smoothly tracked the early pace and romped home by three lengths under Frankie Dettori. Despite having 27 starters since, far more than any other owner, only Daylami, running for Godolphin in the 2000 Turf, has crossed the wire in front.

Horses earn their way into the Breeders' Cup in one of two ways. Points are awarded in selected graded races over the course of the year. Fields are limited to 14 runners, so when more than 14 pre-enter a race, the top eight point-earners get in automatically. After that, a selection committee then ranks the rest, in order of preference. Whatever the flaws in the system, it works. Rarely does a properly nominated, truly worthwhile horse fail to make it into the starting gate.

The Breeders' Cup nomination system, however, is a different story. Each year, owners are given the opportunity to pay a nominal fee for young horses and their sires, making the horses Breeders' Cup eligible. If they fail to do so, and the horse matures and runs his or her way into Breeders' Cup contention, a large supplementary fee is required. Every year, quite a few owners are faced with the difficult decision of whether or not to pay the penalty.

In that 1984 Classic, the Black Chip Stable paid $360,000 to supplement Wild Again into the race, a move universally derided at the time. After the race was over, the winning owners left with a profit of nearly a million dollars. Most expensive supplemental gambles have not worked out nearly as well. In 2000, Aaron Jones paid $400,000 to supplement Riboletta into the $2 million Distaff. The heaviest Breeders' Cup favorite of the day, she ran the worst race of her career, finishing a well-beaten seventh.

In 2001, there were quite a few owners who did pay the penalty, the stiffest of which was levied on the owners of Distaff contender Miss Linda. They coughed up $400,000 to get their improving 4-year-old filly into the competitive race, $310,000 more than the $90,000 that television producer David Milch (*Hill Street Blues, NYPD Blue*) paid for his Val Royal to be able to run in the $1 million Mile. The connections of 4-year-old handicap star Lido Palace, however, decided not to pay the $800,000 it would have taken to get their horse into the gate for the $4 million Classic.

"When the numbers say you will only break even if you run second in the toughest race of the year, to me, it becomes an easy business decision," said owner John Amerman, who also owned Siphonic. The former chairman of Mattel Toys had bought Lido Palace from associates in South America, much as Aaron Jones had done with Riboletta. Rarely do owners and breeders in South America nominate their horses for the Breeders' Cup, and both Amerman and Jones were caught in the supplementary-fee dilemma as a result.

The Breeders' Cup represents an opportunity for some American horsemen from smaller circuits to take on the larger outfits and shoot for the big money. Keith Desormeaux, older brother of two-time Kentucky Derby-winning jockey Kent, was one such individual. His horse, French Assault, had drawn the number 7 post Baffert was hoping for in the Juvenile. A Louisiana native, Desormeaux graduated with a degree in animal science from Louisiana Tech before going into training full-time. He was only too happy to adjust the chaw of tobacco in his lower lip and talk about his prize colt, a Kentucky-bred son of the sire French Deputy.

"Twenty grand, that's what we paid for him at the Keeneland September sale last year," he said. Asked what attracted him to the colt, he smiled and spat a brown stream into the dirt. "He was well-balanced, correct, and had that air about him. With good horses, you know pretty quickly and he was like that. I knew as soon as I looked at this guy that he was special. It's the other horses, the ones you end up trying to convince yourself about that are a little more difficult. Just like women. The more you gotta keep convincing yourself, the more trouble you get into."

While it is a million-dollar race, the Juvenile was just a stepping-stone in Desormeaux's starry eyes.

"Where I grew up, in the bushes, racing was part of the fabric of our community. We saw the Derby on TV every year and the glamour, excitement, and the tradition got all of us. That's always been the big one, the biggest in the world and the one I think everyone wants to win. My brother's won it twice"—with Real Quiet in 1998 and Fusaichi Pegasus in 2000—"and we'll be there in 2002 as long as everything works out. We'll take the Louisiana Derby route."

Told that he would likely be facing a couple of Godolphin colts on Derby Day, just as he would in the Breeders' Cup, the cocky Cajun conditioner's eyes lit up.

"Tell you what, my $20,000 horse is going to beat both of their blue-bloods on Saturday. As far as the Derby goes, I'll be happy to knock 'em off next May, too. They spent what, 20 million at Keeneland? If they let me spend half a million every year there and train what I bought, I'd win the Derby for 'em within 10 years. Guaranteed. Hell, write that down and I'll sign it."

Another subplot to the 2001 Breeders' Cup was the unprecedented number of Arab-owned horses entered in the day's eight races. (In 1999, the $1 million Filly and Mare Turf joined the original seven events.) The Maktoum brothers, of course, led the way, with 14 horses pre-entered. The Saudi princes, Ahmed Salman (Thoroughbred Corp.) and Khalid Abdullah (Juddmonte Farms), had three apiece, and Mohammed Jumah al-Nobouda, a Maktoum family friend, had one. In all, 21 of the 104 pre-entered, or just over 20 percent, were Arab-owned.

The quality of the horses owned by the Middle East royalty is what really shone the spotlight on the situation. They were responsible for an incredible six of the eight morning-line favorites: Officer (Juvenile), Aptitude (Classic), Flute (Distaff), Lailani (Filly and Mare Turf), Fantastic Light (Turf), and Noverre (Mile). It was a tribute to the quality of their massive breeding and racing operations, as well as the size of their respective bank accounts. Trainers like Keith Desormeaux go to a yearling sale with owners that have $100,000 to spend and want four or five horses. Sheikh Mohammed goes to the same sale with unlimited funds and resources, looking for whatever regally bred horse catches his eye, caring not at all if the horse's career earnings do not amount to one-tenth of his purchase price. Most American breeders need to sell some of their yearlings to keep the business afloat. The Maktoums, Abdullah, and Salman breed only to race.

Racing began as the Sport of Kings, supported by the only people who could afford the luxury of breeding and racing horses at the time, the English nobility. In America, the descendants of industrial barons who built fortunes from enterprises such as oil, steel, shipping, and railroads occupied that position throughout much of the 20th century. In the 21st century, the "kings" that support the high end of the sport come from the Arabian desert.

12

International Racing at Its Best

No Arab owners showed up for the Breeders' Cup World Thoroughbred Championships, but 52,987 fans did, showing their support for the sport on the sunny but cold Saturday. D. G. Van Clief had said providing security for everyone at Belmont Park that day was the subject of much discussion and planning, and that part of the decision was to "have a show of force." As a testament to his words, machine-gun-toting Marines in full camouflage dress patrolled the plant in addition to the hundreds of uniformed police roaming the massive grounds. Having gone through so much over the preceding six weeks, everyone in attendance seemed to take the extra security in stride, and the day began on schedule and without incident.

Temperatures in New York had risen into the 70's during the week, but the mercury had dropped significantly on Friday and the wind had picked up. Breeders' Cup Day was colder and windier still. It wasn't bad if you were in the sun, but in the shade the wind chill was in the 30's. The wind, gusting over 20 miles an hour, blew directly into the faces of the horses as they raced down the backside, then pushed at their backs down the stretch.

Before the first race, there was an emotional ceremony featuring all the jockeys parading onto the racetrack holding flags of the different nations represented on the day, followed by a rousing version of the national anthem. As had been the case in the New York area since the attacks, there was a patriotic feeling in the air, formalized by the huge number of American flags worn and/or carried by the sizable crowd.

The Distaff is the opening race on the Breeders' Cup card, and as the horses were leaving the paddock to walk onto the track, tragedy struck. Exogenous, a 3-year-old filly who was one of the race favorites, reared up and fell awkwardly, hitting her head on the ground and getting her leg caught in a gate as well. It took 10 minutes to get the dazed, scared filly untangled and into an ambulance, where veterinarians worked feverishly to keep her calm and deal with her injuries. Although they initially felt Exogenous would recover, she did not, and had to be euthanized a few days later.

Flute, owned by Prince Khalid Abdullah's Juddmonte Farms and trained by Bobby Frankel, was the even-money favorite in the Distaff, but it was another Arab-owned horse, the Thoroughbred Corp.'s Spain, who opened up a clear lead at the top of the stretch. The defending Distaff winner seemed headed for an easy win, but jockey Pat Day got 12-1 shot Unbridled Elaine into high gear and to the wire just in time. The loss did not sit well with Spain's trainer, D. Wayne Lukas.

"I spent 10 minutes this morning telling Victor [Espinoza] to wait before making his move with her. I even told him, 'Look, when you think it's time to go, that means wait,' then he takes off with her at the three-eighths pole like our conversation never happened. Losing is never easy, but when it's a two-million-dollar race, you have your horse dead fit and ready to run, and the kid does something like that, boy oh boy."

The furious finish set the stage for the Juvenile Fillies, the acid test for Harty's decision to change Tempera's training and have her sit out the Oak Leaf. The bettors only had eyes for You, Frankel's filly, making her the 4/5 choice in the nine-horse field. Bella Bellucci, owned by Michael Tabor, was the second choice at 4-1, and Baffert's Habibti, running for the Thoroughbred Corp. and ridden by Espinoza, was next on the board at 7-1. Those two were bucking 17 years of history, as both had only two career starts, and no horse with that little experience had ever won the Juvenile Fillies. In addition, they were stuck on the inside, with Habibti on the rail and Bella Bellucci right beside her in the number 2 hole.

Tempera was all but ignored in the wagering and went off at 11-1, her spectacular win in the Sorrento a distant memory. To those not close to the situation, her eight-week layoff, combined with the lackluster third in the Del Mar Debutante, gave her the look of a horse going the wrong way. Harty's other filly, Imperial Gesture, had continued to thrive in the mornings, so he and the Godolphin team had decided to enter her as well. The bettors paid little attention, letting her go as the second-longest shot in the field at 53-1.

Speedsters Shesastonecoldfox and Take Charge Lady went to the early lead, sprinting into the teeth of the cold, whipping wind while Bella Bellucci stalked them on the inside in third. Imperial Gesture was next, stuck four wide, with You well placed just to her inside. Espinoza and Habibti had had a terrible start from the rail, stumbling and getting bumped. Now the jock had decided to take her around the entire field. Flores had Tempera right where he and Harty wanted to be, sitting just behind and outside all the speed. As the field approached the turn, the leaders were looking for oxygen and Gary Stevens pushed Bella Bellucci through on the rail. Frankie Dettori had Imperial Gesture moving strongly just outside the tiring lead duo, and for a moment it looked like a two-horse race.

Tempera was even wider than Imperial Gesture and still well within herself, rating kindly for a motionless Flores. Coming off the turn, Flores loosened the reins, turning Tempera loose, and the daughter of

A.P. Indy began a long, determined charge to the wire. Halfway down the lane, Imperial Gesture had the tiring Bella Bellucci measured and forged to the lead, but in the middle of the track, Tempera was rolling. Now it truly was a two-horse race, with both contenders sporting the Godolphin blue. In their box seats, the Hartys were seeing their wildest dreams come true. Flores tapped Tempera twice with his whip and she overhauled her stablemate about 100 yards from the wire, drew away, and crossed the line in front by a length and a half. Imperial Gesture was a clear second, 3½ in front of Bella Bellucci, who held on for third by half a length over You.

The final time, 1:41.49, shattered the stakes record of 1:42.11 set by Countess Diana in 1997, and the mutuel payoffs were just as impressive. Tempera paid $25.80 for a $2 win bet, Imperial Gesture was worth $41.80 for a $2 place wager, and the $2 Godolphin exacta returned $768.

In only their second year racing 2-year-old fillies in America, Godolphin had run one-two in the year's defining event. Ironically, considering the money they had spent at the yearling sales over the past 20 years, nearly a billion dollars, their first Grade 1 win on American dirt had come from a homebred, foaled at Sheikh Mohammed's Darley Stud in Kentucky.

The win was vindication for Harty, who had opened himself up to second-guessing by making the decision to leave Tempera in the barn for the Oak Leaf and train her up to the Breeders' Cup.

"I never imagined running one-two in this race. I have to give all the credit to my help," he said, celebrating with his wife and son. "The biggest single thing I did with Tempera was to have David work her exclusively after the Debutante."

Before Harty turned the trick, only three trainers had ever saddled the top two finishers in the 17-year history of the Juvenile Fillies: Lukas (three times), Baffert, and Nick Zito. Just two years into running his own show, Harty had put his name in the record book alongside three men who had won eight Kentucky Derbies among them. As a bonus, he had picked exactly the right time to beat Baffert head to head in a big race. Baffert had won nearly every battle, but Harty won the war. Gracious in defeat, Baffert congratulated Harty and said, "I'm really happy for Eoin, really glad he finished one-two."

The win was also the first Breeders' Cup triumph for the 33-year-old Flores, who got his start at Caliente racetrack in his hometown of Tijuana, Mexico, in 1984. He broke into the incredibly competitive Southern California jockey colony in 1989 and made a name for himself by being the leading rider five years in a row at the Los Angeles County Fair in Pomona. The Pomona racetrack is as small as Belmont is big and a jockey has to be able to break a horse well and have nerves of steel to negotiate the tight, quirky oval. Flores proved to have both qualities in abundance.

Speed is king is Southern California, and Flores's knack for getting horses out of the gate and into high gear in a hurry got the attention of top trainers, including Baffert, who began using him as one of his main riders in the late 1990's. Harty, of course, was Baffert's chief assistant at the time, and he and Flores got to know each other well, bonding in the early mornings. Due in large part to his success aboard Baffert-trained horses, Flores won more races (208) than any Southern California jockey in 1999, and captured his first two riding titles that year, at Santa Anita and Del Mar. As a result of their work with Tempera, the Irish son of a trainer and the Mexican son of a jockey reached the pinnacles of their respective professions together.

"The whole idea Eoin had was to come into this race fresh, and it worked beautifully," said Flores. "The outside post helped a lot, and when I got her to settle in the early part, I knew we had a good shot because of the way she's been finishing her works in the mornings. She's only raced five times and as she gets more experience, she'll be even better."

Working for Godolphin leaves little time for reflection, and Harty had less than an hour before it was time to saddle his two colts, Essence Of Dubai and Ibn Al Haitham, for the Juvenile. In the interim, two Breeders' Cup streaks were broken.

When 9-1 shot Squirtle Squirt won the Sprint, Bobby Frankel snapped a string of defeats that had grown to 38 after both Flute and You lost to start the day.

"I looked at this horse as my fourth-best shot on the day. You can never figure this game out," sighed the native New Yorker before hustling away to saddle Starine in the Filly and Mare Turf.

Going into that very next race, Frankel's main client, Juddmonte Farms, was winless in 30 Breeders' Cup starts, a record run of big-race futility. Only the late Allen Paulson, with 32, had had more Breeders' Cup starters, and he had won six times. Juddmonte had two horses left: European invader Banks Hill in the Filly and Mare Turf, and the Frankel-trained Aptitude, the morning-line favorite in the Classic.

As the field turned for home, Banks Hill was sitting in perfect position, tucked just behind the two early leaders. Suddenly, the French-raced filly accelerated and in a blink, the race was over. The winning margin was 5½ lengths, but it felt like 20. The win was especially sweet for Khalid Abdullah because he bred Banks Hill himself, the ultimate accomplishment for a man who prides himself on his breeding acumen. Banks Hill was the third Breeders' Cup winner for France's top trainer, Andre Fabre, and his first since 133-1 shot Arcangues shocked the field in the 1993 Classic.

It was a breathtaking performance, and one cheered loudly by the thousands of Europeans in attendance. The 2001 Breeders' Cup had figured to be Europe's best shot at sticking it to the Americans, and with Johannesburg in the Juvenile, Fantastic Light and others in the Turf, and Sakhee and Galileo in the Classic, they were set up to do just that in the day's final three races. The cold, windy weather closely resembled the conditions their horses, and fans, were accustomed to overseas. The much-anticipated Juvenile was next.

Despite his problematic post, Officer was the solid 3-5 favorite of the large crowd. The superstar, as Baffert had referred to him in the days leading up to the race, looked every bit the part in the paddock. He was on his toes, his coat gleaming in a shaft of sunlight. Baffert appeared a bit more nervous than usual, feeling the weight of the moment. Habibti had been a complete disappointment, and his big hope in the Sprint, El Corredor, had run just as poorly. For the quote-a-minute trainer, who had been feeding off the presence of the huge, hungry international press corps all week, it was all up to Officer.

The bettors gave only Came Home at 5-1 and Johannesburg at 7-1 any real chance to spring the upset, despite the fact that no favorite had even hit the board in the first four Breeders' Cup races. Michael Tabor, his hands kept warm inside a pair of gloves, watched intently as Aidan

O'Brien saddled the unbeaten Johannesburg. Tabor, known for making hefty wagers on his horses, whispered something to John Magnier, who allowed a small smile to form on his lips. Magnier never took his eyes off the Kentucky-bred son of Hennessy they had purchased the previous September, while next to him, his wife, Sue, co-owner of the colt, was in constant motion trying to keep warm.

Harty, still on a high from the Juvenile Fillies, saddled his pair without much fanfare. As usual, Essence Of Dubai was a handful, full of himself and acting as if the paddock were his own personal playground. Ibn Al Haitham was more composed, and when Harty hoisted Flores aboard the jet-black colt, the jockey gave him a nod indicating he thought all systems were go. The tote board showed otherwise. Ibn Al Haitham was close to 100-1 and Essence Of Dubai more than 30-1. If the Godolphin colts were about to follow in the footsteps of the fillies, the tote board figured to get quite a workout.

Simon Crisford and John Ferguson huddled together in their expensive long black overcoats, hoping for lightning to strike twice.

"So far so good," said a smiling Crisford with a wink, rubbing his hands together before heading up to the owners' box. With Fantastic Light on deck in the Turf and Sakhee looking to make racing history in the Classic, Godolphin was in a position of strength and they knew it.

When the gates opened, Officer got off a step slowly, forcing Victor Espinoza to make a quick decision. He chose to push Officer into the fray, hustling him up to battle for the lead. To his inside, Siphonic broke quickly from the rail, and on the far outside, Came Home had done the same. Johannesburg reacted poorly to the unfamiliar starting bell, but recovered nicely. As is often the case at Belmont, the inside was not the place to be on Breeders' Cup Day. No horse that had run on or near the rail on the dirt had come close to winning, but that was where Espinoza and Officer were stuck. Baffert's worst fears, the ones that caused him to pound the table in frustration at the post-position draw, were coming true.

Jerry Bailey and Siphonic were in an even more difficult spot, inside and just behind Officer, who was engaged in a speed duel with his West Coast rival, Came Home. The two were cutting out a testing pace, running into the teeth of the fierce headwind. Sitting just behind the pacesetters, drafting like a race car, was Mick Kinane aboard Johannesburg.

The colt was clearly having no problem with his first dirt-racing experience and itching to run, but Kinane had a firm hold, happy to let the two favorites break the wind for him.

Harty was not pleased with how his colts were faring. Essence Of Dubai, who had surged into third approaching the turn, was already fading, and he was not a colt that thrived on adversity. Ibn Al Haitham was seventh, in the front of the second group, but showed no signs of making any real move on the leaders. Kinane still had a strong hold on Johannesburg, but as the field turned for home, he had nowhere to go as his colt was blocked behind a four-horse wall.

Officer stuck his head in front of Came Home as they straightened out for the stretch run, but he was not able to gain much of an edge. After having things all his own way in five small fields, he was finally in a dogfight and struggling. Meanwhile, Siphonic, stuck on the dead rail, kept to his task and actually poked his head in front, making it a three-horse battle for supremacy at the quarter pole. As the three unbeaten American colts slugged it out, Kinane, spotting some daylight in between the tiring Came Home and French Assault, asked Johannesburg to go through the hole.

Immediately, the colt lowered his head and burst between the two, taking dead aim on Officer and Siphonic. Within 10 aggressive strides, Johannesburg had blown by them as well and was in full flight for the wire. Siphonic had no answer for Johannesburg's surge, but battled on gamely, putting away both Officer and Came Home. Cooked by their early duel into the wind, the two favorites had nothing left.

From the back of the pack, closers Repent and Publication, both bred to relish the longer distance, were making up ground with every stride. Johannesburg was out of reach, but Repent flew past all the other early leaders to finish a clear second, a length and a quarter behind the winner. Siphonic, in a tremendous display of heart, hung on for third, a little less than a length ahead of the onrushing Publication. Two lengths farther back, Officer, French Assault, Came Home, and longshot Saarland finished as one, more than five lengths behind the winner.

The Irish fans began singing even before native son Kinane and Johannesburg crossed the wire, ecstatic at having beaten the Americans at their own game. Irish flags were unfurled, and there were people scurrying all over the track, trying to join in the celebration. As usual, Aidan O'Brien was the calm within the storm, waiting patiently for his horse to come back. The trainer was smiling, but he was also careful not to get too excited, lest the colt return with some sort of a problem. When Kinane indicated that Johannesburg was as fit as a fiddle, even the taciturn trainer allowed himself to get a little carried away as the jockey pulled out an Irish flag of his own and waved it at the screaming crowd.

About 50 yards down the track, a disappointed Harty and crew waited for their duo. Essence Of Dubai had faded to last after making his little midrace move, and Ibn Al Haitham checked in ninth, their respective efforts as bad as the fillies' had been good. After seeing the horses had come back sound, Harty stated matter-of-factly, "They just weren't good enough. Essence is a bit of a head case. He seemed to resent running out there today. The maiden just couldn't keep up."

Baffert, meanwhile, waited for Officer. When Espinoza hopped off, the two engaged in an animated conversation. Baffert did most of the talking, and Espinoza did a lot of shaking of his head. A few minutes later, a resigned Baffert said, "Especially with the headwind, when I saw them cooking down the backside, I didn't like that at all. He didn't break well and actually came back with paint on his shoulder from banging into the side of the gate. I don't blame Victor, the horse was really keen to run. It wasn't our day. Officer's still a good horse, but I'm very disappointed. The winner looked awesome."

As soon as the Juvenile was over, Derby dreams took center stage. Second-place trainer Kenny McPeek, his bald head shining in the fading light, sported an ear-to-ear grin when asked about Repent's performance.

"See you in May," he said confidently. "This horse is going to be a big part of the Triple Crown."

Kent Desormeaux felt the same way after getting off French Assault. The French Deputy colt ended up sixth, just a nose behind Officer, and, as predicted by his brother, in front of both Godolphin colts.

"I had a wonderful run. I think my brother and me will be entertaining them the first Saturday in May."

His brother agreed. "Kent said there's no doubt he's a Derby horse, and he should know. In American racing we all feel like we have to be on the lead. The winner had never gone past three-quarters of a mile until today, but he was taught to rate. My hat's off to his trainer."

David Hofmans, justifiably proud of Siphonic, said with a grin, "He ran a great race. He was stuck down inside, the worst place to be. Jerry [Bailey] told me he'd pay his own way to ride him in California."

Regarding the plans for Johannesburg, John Magnier was not talking. Michael Tabor, basking in the glow of his first Breeders' Cup winner one day before his 60th birthday, did warm to the subject.

"Well, we really want to enjoy this first, but sure, the Derby is definitely an option. I've won one and I'd dearly like to win another, so we'll talk to Aidan, see how the horse is doing, and make a decision over the winter. We could run him in America once before the Derby, or maybe just keep him in Ireland and give him a prep in Europe. That's all to be decided, but he proved today he's a champion. The Derby or the English classics, not a bad issue to have to tackle, no?"

Halfway across the world, Sheikh Mohammed had to be shaking his head. Until the following May, all the talk about the Kentucky Derby was going to focus on a colt being trained overseas, but it was not going to be his. He had spent over a hundred million dollars just in the past few years to put himself in precisely that position, but all the winter attention and publicity was headed to Ireland, home of his arch-rivals.

The only consolation for Sheikh Mohammed was in the clock. Tempera (1:41.49) had run much faster than Johannesburg (1:42.27). Applying the formula that one-sixth of a second equals one length, Tempera might have beaten the colts in the Juvenile by almost five lengths. The fact was that on October 27, 2001, Tempera was the fastest 2-year-old in the world. If she could repeat the feat six months later, his Kentucky Derby dream would become a reality.

Harty spoke about the Kentucky Oaks as the logical spot for Tempera the next spring, but he does not make the decisions. "The boss" makes the decisions. The respective performances of his 2-year-olds over the course of the spring, summer, and fall of 2001 pointed to Sheikh Mohammed having quite a bit to ponder through the winter and into the spring.

If he wanted to win the Oaks, Imperial Gesture might well be good enough. She was plenty talented, experienced, and bred to handle the little bit of extra distance she would face the day before the Derby at Churchill Downs. Going by the clock, she too ran faster than the colts on Breeders' Cup Day.

His two most experienced colts finished well up the track in the Juvenile, giving no indication that they were Derby caliber. The other top Harty-trained 2-year-olds were either talented but not as accomplished (Janadel, Classicist), sprinters (Sunray Spirit, Future Minister), inexperienced and immature (King's Consul, Dubai Tiger), or coming off a serious injury (Sleeping Weapon). Many in the Godolphin camp believed that Dubai Destination was also a serious Derby hope, but he had yet to try the dirt and missed what was to be his final start of the season in the October 20 Dewhurst with an injury.

That left Tempera. Harty knew she was the best filly in his barn in June. Her performance on October 27 proved she was not only the fastest 2-year-old filly in America that day, but the fastest 2-year-old, period. In addition, his decision to change her training and focus on getting her to relax in the early part of a race was perfect for the Derby. With five races under her belt, the experience and toughness issues had been accounted for in full. As far as going a mile and a quarter was concerned, both sides of her pedigree indicated that she would run all day. The fact that she was a product of Sheikh Mohammed's bloodstock operation in Kentucky would only make a Derby victory that much sweeter.

Charlsie Cantey, who has covered every Kentucky Derby for television since 1986, said Tempera was just about the best-looking horse she saw at the Breeders' Cup.

"She ran as good as she looked, she's bred to run long, and if she matures and keeps improving, she could be a Derby horse. Considering how women are second-class citizens in Dubai," Cantey noted, "just think of the irony if Tempera does win the 2002 Derby. Sheikh Mo finally gets what he wants, and it was a filly that gave it to him."

Crisford and Ferguson had only a minute to spend with Harty after the Juvenile, as Fantastic Light was already in the paddock, being closely watched by bin Suroor. The field for the 2001 Turf was one of the weakest in years, and Fantastic Light was the deserving 7-5 favorite.

The only question about the globetrotting 5-year-old was his poor recent record at the mile-and-a-half distance. He had lost his last seven starts going 12 furlongs, although he had run well nearly every time. The decision to run him in the Turf meant Dettori would have his hands full getting Fantastic Light that final, testing 220 yards.

The top American hopes were front-running With Anticipation, Bobby Frankel's equally speedy Timboroa, and the classy but distance-challenged Hap. The likelihood that the two front-runners would duel into the wind and wear each other out meant the race set up perfectly for the Europeans, especially Fantastic Light and Coolmore's distance specialist, Milan.

Godolphin and Coolmore were once again leading the way on a big racing day, but for the first time, they had taken center stage in America. Each had already won once, and with their best horses yet to run, the battle was about to be joined. It was Fantastic Light and Sakhee against Milan and Galileo, all four of whom were homebreds. Questions abounded about the talented quartet. Could Fantastic Light stay the 12 furlongs? Could Milan, totally lacking in early speed, get in gear fast enough to get there in time? Had Godolphin made a grievous error in pulling the last-minute switch? Was Sakhee coming back too quickly after such an impressive win in the Arc? Would Galileo be able to put aside his breeding and take to the dirt?

As expected, With Anticipation broke on top and went right to the lead, but he was pressured every step of the way by both Timboroa and Canada's big hope, Quiet Resolve. As the lead trio broke the cold, whipping wind, Dettori had Fantastic Light placed perfectly in fifth, right alongside Sheikh Hamdan's horse, Mutamam. Milan, as usual, was lagging well back in the pack.

At the mile mark, Edgar Prado went for broke on Timboroa, sending him into the lead. Neither With Anticipation nor Quiet Resolve was able to keep up, but Fantastic Light, who had worked his way into second on his own, was just waiting for Dettori to ask him for his kick. When Dettori moved his hands and gave Fantastic Light the signal that it was time to get serious, the race-tough, mature horse lengthened his stride and went right after the leader. Mick Kinane had sent the same signal to Milan, and he responded too, but lacked the instant acceleration of his rival. When Fantastic Light got to Timboroa's throat, he blew by him and set sail for the wire, kicking well clear of the field. Dettori had fully committed to the move and was working hard to get his horse a big enough cushion so that even if he did tire late, he would be too far in front to get caught.

Finally, with 220 yards to go, Milan was in high gear and it was a two-horse race. Milan was really flying, but Fantastic Light was not backing up. Steadily, the son of Sadler's Wells closed the gap on the game Godolphin horse, running what was likely his final race. Dettori took one glance back to see who was coming after him, but the wire was less than a hundred yards away and he knew he was home. Fantastic Light crossed the line three-quarters of a length in front, with Milan six clear of Timboroa.

Saeed bin Suroor was a very happy man, having seen the first leg of what he hoped would be a historic late double go exactly as he had planned. The trainer had done a superb job with Fantastic Light, and this win capped off a sensational season that consisted of six races in four countries, with four Group or Grade 1 wins and two seconds. The win also meant he had locked up his second consecutive Emirates World Series title. The competition, which features 12 races contested in 10 countries, beginning with the Dubai World Cup and ending with the Hong Kong Cup, was created and funded by Sheikh Mohammed. His Daylami had won the inaugural version in 1999, so it was the third straight triumph for a Godolphin horse in the competition, which he set up to put an international spotlight on his horses.

Meanwhile, Dettori shamelessly milked the crowd, slowly returning Fantastic Light to the winners' circle. The jock, an unabashed self-promoter, was also making the cheering crowd wait for his famous flying dismount. As bin Suroor beamed, Dettori posed for the winners'-circle pictures, then directed the trainer to move the horse slightly to the left, where he would have room to land. As the applause built to a crescendo, Dettori leapt in the air, his arms reaching for the sky, a smile creasing his handsome face from ear to ear.

The Godolphin celebration, however, was short-lived. There are no breaks in the Breeders' Cup schedule, and the marquee race of the day, the $4 million Classic, was only 25 minutes away. The sheikhs had taken the risk of running Sakhee on the dirt, and now it was up to the horse to validate that controversial decision. Not only had an Arc winner never won the Classic, none had ever even tried.

Coolmore was hoping Galileo could give them the Classic win that Tiznow had denied them last year. Their Giant's Causeway had fought with the California-bred all the way down the interminable Churchill Downs stretch, only to lose the photo by a head. During the furious battle, Kinane had briefly lost the reins nearing the finish line and many blamed the jock for blowing the race. Having won the Juvenile and finished second in the Turf, the 42-year-old with the red, well-lined face was looking for redemption.

Dettori was looking for some redemption as well, having been pilloried by the international press for his ride on Godolphin's Swain in the 1998 Classic. Told to keep his mount as far from the competitive Silver Charm as possible, Dettori had whipped Swain left-handed through the stretch despite having the horse drift across the track and close to the outside rail. Swain lost the race by only a length, and to this day, many bettors claim Dettori's ride was one of the worst in big-race history.

Tiznow was back to defend his title, but had not shown his usual speed and desire in his two prep races, finishing third in both. In addition, he had become quite ornery in the mornings, refusing to train until he was good and ready, bewildering both trainer Jay Robbins and jockey Chris McCarron.

"Well, he's given us some sleepless nights trying to figure out what he's thinking, but the last week here at Belmont he's been a little better every day, so we're hopeful he's ready to run well," was all the taciturn Robbins said the day before the race. The trainer had even considered slipping the horse a shot or two of vodka the previous weekend to calm him down.

"It's an old-school move," he admitted, "using a little alcohol to keep them calm, but when he did better the next few mornings I let the idea pass."

The race favorite, however, was yet another Frankel trainee. Aptitude, second in both the Kentucky Derby and Belmont in 2000, had improved dramatically in the summer of 2001 with the addition of blinkers, plastic eye cups that partially block a horse's peripheral vision.

Since horses' eyes are on the sides of their heads, they can see nearly everything behind them, as well as what is in front or to the side. They sometimes become distracted during a race, losing their momentum at key points, and those momentary lapses often mean the difference between winning and losing. Blinkers force a horse to look straight ahead and help the high-strung animal concentrate solely on running.

"The blinkers have got him focused and into the race earlier, plus he's just matured and become the horse I always thought he would," declared a confident Frankel on Friday morning.

The post-position draw had been more than kind to the Europeans, as Sakhee was in post 6 and Galileo just to his inside in post 5. Tiznow and Aptitude had both drawn poorly, getting the number 10 and 12 posts, respectively. Due to Belmont's massive size, mile-and-a-quarter races on the dirt start awkwardly, on the clubhouse turn, giving a distinct advantage to horses drawn inside. Everyone drawn wide is forced to either take back immediately or go very wide down the backstretch, neither of which is a preferred option. Jockeys Jerry Bailey (Aptitude) and Chris McCarron (Tiznow) had their work cut out for them. Between the two of them, they had accounted for seven of the 17 Classics.

As expected, Belmont specialist Albert The Great, a game fourth in the previous year's Classic, went right to the front, where he was joined and quickly passed by a Lukas longshot named Orientate. The two set a solid pace. Tiznow was keen to run, and McCarron had him looming large on the outside of the lead duo, the white blaze on his face bobbing up and down smoothly. Galileo and Sakhee were side by side in fifth and sixth, with Galileo just inside his rival. Aptitude was in seventh, but as Frankel had feared, he was stuck way out in the middle of the track, losing a ton of ground.

After six furlongs, Orientate was fried. Albert The Great inherited the lead and was running well within himself, a length clear of 18-1 shot Guided Tour. Tiznow was still third, three wide and just loping along easily. Kinane began to ask Galileo to pick up the pace as the field headed into the turn, but the horse failed to accelerate as he had in all of his previous seven starts on the grass. Dettori sent Sakhee the same message, and as Fantastic Light had done half an hour earlier, the Godolphin colt quickened immediately. Dettori took his mount wide, staying away from the dreaded rail and any traffic trouble. As Sakhee emerged on his flank, Tiznow was moving well too, but not as fast as the Godolphin colt.

The field straightened away for the stretch drive and Sakhee was going full speed, his head low and his stride long. Albert The Great was doing his best down on the rail, but he could not match Sakhee's powerful move. In between the two, Tiznow was plugging away, but he did not have the burst to go with Sakhee either, and the Godolphin colt opened up a half-length lead.

"When Sakhee went by me with so much momentum, I thought I was running for second," said McCarron afterward. Tiznow never gave up, however, and slowly, almost imperceptibly, began cutting into the lead. Dettori had the whip out early on Sakhee, while McCarron, ice water in his veins, kept calm, driving Tiznow with just his hands. With a hundred yards to run, the margin was only a neck, and McCarron finally went to the whip.

"He's been very strong-willed lately, so I had it in my head I wasn't going to force him to do anything," said the 46-year-old Hall of Famer, "but at the sixteenth pole I thought, 'I've got to do something.' I hit him and he just jumped forward."

The two horses raced as a team to the finish, Tiznow's head held much higher than that of his rival, who was still low to the ground and giving Dettori everything he had. The equine warriors hit the wire together, and the photo sign went up on the board. Announcer Tom Durkin had boomed, "Tiznow wins it for America!!" and indeed it did appear that Tiznow had gotten his white-blazed nose there first, but the photo-finish camera was going to have to confirm it.

The huge crowd had been on their feet throughout the race, and their cheers grew with every stride. When the horses reached the wire in the fading New York light the sound was deafening. There was much discussion back and forth about who had actually won the race, but most agreed it was Tiznow. When the "Photo" sign on the tote board was replaced by Tiznow's number 10, chants of "USA, USA" began, and American flags seemed to pop up from every corner of the massive facility.

It was the second straight year the California-bred colt had thwarted a challenge from Europe; first Coolmore, then Godolphin. The unforgettable finish put a patriotic cap on top of what was an emotional day for all involved, from the Breeders' Cup executives to the extra security personnel, through those working with the horses and finally the fans themselves. It was a day none would ever forget.

"That horse has a head like a dinosaur," said a disappointed Dettori after dismounting. "My horse gave me everything he had, but he didn't have the propulsion he does on the turf. We got beaten by a horse that is just very, very tough. I'll tell you what though, you never go against the boss. He's always right."

Crisford, ever the voice of positivity, added, "He ran a fabulous race. So close but so far, but he lost nothing in defeat." Having immediately talked with his boss via cell phone, Crisford added, "Sheikh Mohammed just said to me, 'The picture is now clear why we chose to run him in the Classic.' He was inched out but it was a very good effort. He's done for the year and we'll talk to Sheikh Hamdan about future plans. He loved the main track and gave everything he had."

Despite the narrow loss by Sakhee in the Classic, Godolphin had their best Breeders' Cup ever, highlighted by the wins from Tempera and Fantastic Light. Their horses earned $2,640,000, and after subtracting expenses and money earned by the jockeys, trainers, and grooms, that meant just over $2 million went into the NTRA Charities-New York Heroes Fund, which distributed the money in November.

Coolmore had a fine day as well, highlighted by Johannesburg's win in the Juvenile, which capped off his undefeated season. In addition, Milan had taken second in the Turf and Bach had run third in the Mile. Tabor, O'Brien, and Kinane had already pledged 10 percent of any Breeders' Cup winnings to September 11 relief funds weeks earlier.

There is rarely any time to rest for the Godolphin team, and after the Breeders' Cup they headed straight to Australia, where their Give The Slip lost a photo finish in that country's biggest race, the Melbourne Cup. Four days later they were in Singapore to saddle Kutub to victory in the Singapore Cup, completing what bin Suroor called "a period where I feel like I'm on a wheel that just keeps spinning and never stops."

Harty was on the go too, flying back to California, then to Kentucky to saddle Janadel to finish a decent fourth in the one-mile Iroquois Stakes at Churchill Downs on November 4. He decided to back off of

Sleeping Weapon, who was not quite ready for his comeback race, and was also unable to get Classicist a third chance to win a maiden race.

After returning to California with Janadel, he supervised the move to put the entire group into quarantine around November 10. Once their 30 days were up, they were put on a plane and flown back to Dubai to prepare for their 3-year-old seasons. Harty would never train the horses again, but he claimed that mattered little to him, as a whole new crop of 2-year-olds, over $50 million worth, would be waiting when he arrived in Dubai in early January.

In Europe, flat racing goes on hold until April, meaning all the talk is about the first classics, the 1000 and 2000 Guineas. The stirring performance and record of Johannesburg meant that in 2002, there would be much discussion about the Kentucky Derby as well.

In America, there is only one race that captures the hearts and minds of everyone involved in Thoroughbred racing, and winter and spring are all about the process of determining who will make it to Churchill Downs.

Judging by their rather lackluster performances as 2-year-olds, there was much work to be done if a Godolphin colt was going to win that 128th Derby on May 4, 2002.

13

A Matter of Time?

"The Kentucky Derby is a more difficult race to win than I first believed," stated Sheikh Mohammed, his hands clasped behind him as he relaxed in the Longchamp paddock the day before the 2001 Prix de l'Arc de Triomphe. A week earlier, Simon Crisford had guaranteed that if asked about his bold 1999 prediction of winning the Derby by 2002, his boss would stand behind the statement. He didn't.

"This is only our second year with the entire program in place, but it doesn't matter really because if we don't win this time we'll be back and keep coming back until we do," said the sheikh, adding with a slight smile, "We will win the Derby, praise be to Allah, but I will no longer say when it will happen."

As to why he thought that the challenge was bigger than he had first imagined, Sheikh Mohammed responded with a question.

"There are what, 30,000 foals each year in America?" Told the actual number was closer to 36,000, he nodded and smiled. "That is a very large number and we have only a few horses and are competing against the best owners and trainers in America for the race they all want most to win. It is not easy, but things that are easy bring little satisfaction. We have trained horses in Dubai and won races all over the world and are very confident in our team and our ability." He added that he would have been running horses in the Derby much earlier than 1999 but his English trainers wanted no part of it, so he had to wait until he had his own operation in place.

Of all the 2002 Godolphin Derby colts, Essence Of Dubai's win over a weak field in the Norfolk provided the high-water mark, clearly not the big jump forward that everyone involved had hoped for from the previous year. To add to their dismay, the fact that Johannesburg, who belonged to Coolmore, was the most-talked-about Derby horse from outside America was especially galling. Sheikh Mohammed wanted all the publicity he could get for Dubai, and the idea was that when his 2-year-old colts returned there in the winter, a few would have established themselves as major Derby players. Had they done so, it would have guaranteed tremendous interest in their development at 3, and all the inherent publicity that went along with it. Instead, Coolmore ran one horse, one time in America and secured exactly what Sheikh Mohammed had spent more than $30 million to achieve.

Godolphin's 2002 Derby hopefuls were to follow the same schedule as those of the past two years. Bin Suroor began working with the entire group in late December after they reacclimated to Dubai, and by mid-January he had separated the pretenders from the contenders. On January 19, the deadline for early Kentucky Derby entries, Godolphin paid the $600 fee for 17 horses. Essence Of Dubai, Ibn Al Haitham,

Janadel, King's Consul, and Dubai Tiger made the cut, as did the talented filly Tempera. Their top two European 2-year-olds, Dubai Destination and Naheef, were nominated as well.

They were to begin running in a few trials against one other in late January, February, and March, all in preparation for the UAE Derby on March 23, but according to John Ward, trainer of 2001 Derby winner Monarchos, the September 11 attacks would make Sheikh Mohammed's task of getting his horses ready for top competition more difficult.

"I know quite a few people who worked for him in Dubai who ain't going back in the spring of 2002," insisted Ward. "I think he'll have a tough time getting exercise riders and the like. I saw tapes of three and four years ago and the folks they had there then were not high quality, so if a lot of people stay in America and they have to use those types of folks again, it'll hurt those horses."

Eoin Harty was nonplussed by Ward's comments, saying firmly, "Sheikh Mohammed pays extremely well, and if he has to pay a little more to get some people to go back, he will."

No matter where they do their preparations, all Derby entrants have always been equal in that none has run a mile-and-a-quarter race. The top four Derby prep races are all a mile and an eighth, the same distance that Express Tour covered when prepping in the 2001 UAE Derby at Nad Al Sheba. It is that grueling final 220 yards, that journey into the unknown, that forces the young horses to push themselves farther than ever before, that has helped make the race such a singular test over the years.

As D. Wayne Lukas said with a smile, "The Derby is unique for many reasons, but one of the biggest is that it's an athletic event you really can't prepare for. The horses simply haven't run that far in competition, and you can look at pedigrees all you want, but until they do it, you just don't know. Plus you can't create the atmosphere of 150,000 people screaming at the top of their lungs, starting with that long walk in front of the stands to the paddock. Add it all up and it's one helluva tough assignment."

Starting in 2002, the glorious uncertainty of that final furlong was no more. Sheikh Mohammed decided to lengthen the UAE Derby to a mile and a quarter. He has made many adjustments to his assault on the Derby, but none bigger, and more controversial, than the one to lengthen his personal prep.

"Our horses have all hit the wall at the mile mark so far, so we wanted to get a better gauge on their ability to get the distance before we decide which ones to put on the plane to Kentucky," is how Crisford explained the decision. The Godolphin racing manager added that it was Sheikh Mohammed who made the final call, and the sheikh confirmed it.

"We want to know which horses are able to get the mile and a quarter before we send them to America. After the UAE Derby, there will be no questions about that."

When told about the change, Bob Baffert was incredulous.

"Really?" he asked. "That seems pretty stupid to me, but it's their business so they can do what they want. Can't imagine anyone from over here will be trying for that two million bucks after hearing that."

Richard Mandella said only, "Seems a lot to ask of a 3-year-old in March, but nobody's ever tried it before so we'll have to wait and see."

Running the UAE Derby at a mile and a quarter means Sheikh Mohammed, again playing by his own rules, has taken away a slice of something that made the Derby so special. Only time will tell if his experiment forces those in charge of scheduling the American preps to follow his lead or if he indeed has asked too much of his still-maturing horses.

Lukas, for one, thinks he understands exactly what the sheikh is doing, and why.

"He's going to throw all he's got at that race in late March and see what comes out of it. A couple of them will have no problem with the distance, and those will be his Derby horses. The rest will really struggle. I could have run Charismatic a mile and a quarter easily in March, but Grindstone never would have made it. It totally depends on the horse. When their race is over, he'll know who can get the distance, and if he loses a couple colts for a few months in the process, he's got by far the deepest talent pool in the game, so he can afford it. Tell you what, if he wins two or three in a row, you'll see someone carding a mile-and-a-quarter Derby prep race in America pretty quick."

The decision also meant that the Godolphin 3-year-olds would be running the same distance on the same day as the older horses in the

Dubai World Cup, setting up a solid context for comparison. If the winner of the UAE Derby were to run within a second of the World Cup winner, he would have to be considered a strong Derby candidate, possibly even the favorite. If the UAE Derby winner ran a time nowhere near that of the World Cup winner, the opposite would also be true. As of late January, Sakhee was pointing for the World Cup, as was E Dubai, guaranteeing a top-quality race if either one ran.

In America, the trail leading to the 2002 Kentucky Derby would run through the same places, with many familiar faces. During the first three months of a racehorse's 3-year-old season, he either matures and accepts the increased training and pressure, gaining weight and growing stronger by the day, or levels off. The job of the trainer is to apply the right amount of pressure and be objective about how he feels the horse is responding. It is the trickiest assignment in the sport, and one that has stymied the best minds in the game for more than a century.

Several of the top 3-year-olds of 2002 were to spend their winter and early spring in Florida or Louisiana, led by the Kenny McPeek-trained duo of Repent and Harlan's Holiday. Breeders' Cup Juvenile runner-up Repent returned to action with a win over a sloppy track in the November 24 Kentucky Jockey Club Stakes at Churchill Downs and was being pointed to the $1 million Florida Derby on March 16. McPeek has done the Derby dance once, saddling Tejano Run to finish second behind Thunder Gulch in 1995. He expected Repent to make his 3-year-old debut in Louisiana, while Harlan's Holiday, winner of the Iroquois Stakes in November at Churchill Downs, would stay in Florida.

Cynthia Phipps's Saarland, trained by Claude "Shug" McGaughey, won the mile-and-an-eighth Remsen Stakes in November, then was given a break. He returned to training in Florida, and was being pointed toward the Wood Memorial at Aqueduct. Being a son of 1990 Derby winner Unbridled out of a mare, Versailles Treaty, that won the mile-and-a-quarter Alabama Stakes, Saarland looked like a colt who would relish the Derby distance. The Phippses are the last of America's racing royal families still going strong in the 21st century. Heading into the 2002 season, they had bred seven Derby starters since 1936, but had never won the big one, with their best finish a second by Ogden Phipps's Easy Goer in 1989. McGaughey had been the Phipps stable's trainer for well over a decade and Easy Goer's second was his best finish from five Derby starters.

Siphonic stamped himself as the top 3-year-old on the West Coast at the end of 2001 with a strong three-length win in the December 15 Hollywood Futurity, showing the ability to rate kindly in the process. However, he stumbled badly at the start of the mile-and-a-sixteenth Santa Catalina Stakes in mid-January at Santa Anita and could do no better than second. David Hofmans said Siphonic would likely race only twice more before the Derby: March 2 in the mile-and-a- sixteenth San Felipe Stakes and April 6 in the Santa Anita Derby.

"I want him fresh for the Derby," said the soft-spoken Hofmans. "I always think back to what Billy Turner did with Seattle Slew, choosing to bring him in fresh. You have to remember how quick those next two Triple Crown races come up on you."

Bob Baffert, meanwhile, was digging deep into his bench, and finding little to get excited about. After having unleashed his usual complement of talented 2-year-olds at Del Mar, headed by the brilliant Officer, Baffert seemed poised for another strong Run for the Roses. Just four months later he announced on local television that even he was interested in buying a talented 3-year-old if anyone was willing to sell.

The Hollywood Futurity brought Officer's Derby hopes to a crashing halt. The colt made a menacing move around the turn, loomed dangerously in midstretch, then hung in the final 100 yards, exactly as he had done in his previous two-turn start, the Cal Cup Juvenile. Like so many precocious 2-year-olds over the years, Officer just was not up to stretching his brilliant speed around two turns. Much to the dismay of Baffert, Mulhall, and Salman, he would not be seen on the Triple Crown trail.

Another pedigree casualty was Came Home, who would be pointed for sprint races in 2002. His connections, however, still had a possible Derby hopeful; their California-bred son of Smokester, Earl Of Danby, had won his first two starts impressively.

Without one American colt that towered above the opposition as Point Given had in 2001, the 2002 Derby figured to be a wide-open affair, meaning that all 3-year-olds who had shown flashes of brilliance, even if only in winning a maiden race, had a shot. A win by a late-

developing 3-year-old would not be a surprise, in light of the fact that
the last three Derby winners had no more than a maiden win to their
credit as of February 1 of their 3-year-old season.

The nominal favorite, Johannesburg, was expected to travel a path
that had yet to lead to success in the Derby, although when Aidan
O'Brien calls the shots, history has a way of being rewritten. There were
10 Group 1 races for 2-year-old colts run in Europe in 2001. O'Brien-
trained colts won nine. Illustrating the depth of the Coolmore juvenile
band, he did the heretofore impossible with five different colts. Johannesburg won three, Rock Of Gibraltar two, and Balingarry, Hawk Wing,
Century City, and High Chapparal one apiece. The juvenile dominance
helped propel O'Brien to 23 Group or Grade 1 wins on the year, breaking the record of 22 set in 1977 by Vincent O'Brien and tied by Bob
Baffert in 1997.

In doing so, he completely outclassed the larger Godolphin operation. With or without Johannesburg, Coolmore was better prepared
than anyone in the history of European racing to dominate the 2002
European classics. Their incredible depth also put them in the perfect
position to send Johannesburg to Churchill Downs for a date with history. The risk was minimal, the potential reward astronomical, and they
had plenty of talented horses to run in the 2000 Guineas as well. They
were, however, in uncharted territory regarding how to prepare the colt
to climb the Everest of equine mountains, and their European prep
options were slim.

In 2001, Aidan O'Brien had Galileo, Milan, and Mozart start their
racing season on April 16 at Leopardstown, only a few miles from his
stables in Ireland. Johannesburg would be familiar with the course,
having won the Group 1 Phoenix Stakes there as a 2-year-old. The race
Galileo and Milan ran in was a mile and a quarter, an awfully ambitious
one-and-only Derby prep. Mozart ran in the one-mile Guineas Trial, a
more logical, conservative choice for Johannesburg, but one that would
leave him short on conditioning. Either race would give the colt a little more than two weeks to the Derby, a quick turnaround almost
exactly like the Arc-Classic one made by Sakhee. It would mean Johannesburg would have no American prep, and time for only one real workout over the Churchill surface.

In England, the only logical spots were at almost exactly the same time, at Newmarket. There would be two races on April 18, both of which had been used previously as Kentucky Derby springboards. Citadeed ran in the seven-furlong European Free Handicap as his lone tuneup for the 1995 Kentucky Derby, where he finished ninth. That same year, Eltish, who had run second in the Breeders' Cup Juvenile the previous fall, used the mile-and-an-eighth Fielden Stakes as his sole Derby prep. The Juddmonte colt then ran a decent sixth in the Kentucky Derby, which was won by Michael Tabor's Thunder Gulch. The nine-furlong distance seemed ideal for Johannesburg, and he had romped over the Newmarket course as a juvenile, so his connections already knew he would like the ground.

The next day at Newmarket, there would be a one-mile Group 3 race that was also used by a Kentucky Derby starter, and one with an interesting history. In 1991, a colt bred by John Magnier and Vincent O'Brien in Ireland was bought at a Tattersalls yearling auction by their old partner, Robert Sangster, on the advice of Demi O'Byrne. Sangster then named the colt Dr. Devious, in honor of the veterinarian.

The colt won three of his first five starts at 2, but before the Group 1 Dewhurst, Sangster sold him for $400,000, then watched as the colt crushed the Newmarket field. Dr. Devious began his 3-year-old season in the one-mile race at Newmarket in mid-April, then known as the Craven Stakes, and finished a fast-closing second. Afterward, he was sold to weight-loss guru Jenny Craig, who paid $2.5 million for the colt as a Kentucky Derby gift to her husband, Sid. Ridden by Chris McCarron, Dr. Devious finished a decent seventh in the 1992 Derby, behind upset winner Lil E. Tee. Told by trainer Ron McAnally that Dr. Devious would be better off back on the grass, the Craigs promptly sent him back to England, where the colt cruised to victory over the Epsom Downs turf in the English Derby, beating, among others, a top-class Sangster colt.

The only other non-American option for Johannesburg would be to fly him to Dubai for the $2 million UAE Derby, where he would face off against the cream of the Godolphin 3-year-old crop. The Coolmore crew did nominate Johannesburg to the race, but the odds of their actually shipping into Sheikh Mohammed's backyard to go a mile and a quarter that early in the year seemed as long as the race itself.

The best finish by a horse prepped in Europe was the second by Bold Arrangement in 1986. He was brought to America by trainer Clive Brittain, and the two arrived just a few days before the Blue Grass, the next-to-last year that prep was run just nine days before the Derby.

"You have to have a tough horse to do the travel and run on the dirt, and he was as tough as I've had," recalled the Brittain, sitting outside the jockeys' room at Newmarket. "The travel was different then. He had to stay in quarantine in New York for 48 hours as soon as we arrived and I couldn't see him. His body temperature really shifted during that time, but thankfully we were able to get it back to normal before the Blue Grass. He ran a wonderful race there and probably would have won with a better trip. In the Derby I thought he ran a winning race again, but Bill Shoemaker did a masterful job with Ferdinand so we had nothing to be ashamed of finishing second. It was a wonderful experience for me, but it was very difficult on the horse, so I vowed not to go back unless I absolutely felt the horse could withstand the travel, the dirt, and the crowds. It was awfully loud at Churchill Downs."

Michael Tabor is very familiar with American racing, and has a good relationship with trainers around the country, as evidenced by the presence of $4.5 million yearling purchase Shah Jehan, who scored one win in four European starts in 2001, in Lukas's Santa Anita barn. Lukas and Aidan O'Brien have developed a good working relationship in the past few years, with Lukas often leading the Coolmore string onto the track for Breeders' Cup workouts. Tabor knows firsthand what it feels like to win a Derby, and nobody in the world knows better than Coolmore what a Derby win would mean for Johannesburg's value as a stallion.

American prep-race possibilities included the Wood in New York and the Blue Grass. The Wood was a shorter trip, but the Blue Grass required only one plane ride, then a 90-minute drive down Interstate 64 to Louisville. Both races were scheduled for the same day, three weeks before the Derby.

Tabor made it quite clear that whatever road they chose was ultimately up to Aidan O'Brien, subscribing to the theory that the man who best knows and understands the horse should be the one making the key decisions. It is a theory that led Warren Wright to hire Ben Jones, jump-starting the Calumet dynasty. More recently, Bob and Beverly Lewis did the same with Baffert and Lukas and won two Derbies in three years. Fusao Sekiguchi let Neil Drysdale call all the shots, and the trainer turned the fragile Fusaichi Pegasus into a Derby winner.

Sheikh Mohammed knows all of those stories. He also knows what he wants, and that takes precedence. He wants credit and publicity, and his ego and desire to promote Dubai will never allow him to relinquish his role as the decision-maker regarding his horses. That is especially true now that he has everything he believes he needs just minutes from his home. In light of the events of September 11 and what has been learned since about the role the laissez-faire mentality of Dubai's ruling family played in paving the way for terrorism, there is now more pressure than ever on him to put Dubai in a positive light. If the tiny emirate is to prosper when the next generation of Maktoum men take control, which is likely to be right about the time the oil is due to run out, a strong tourist trade and the presence of Western businesses are a must.

Clearly, money has never been an issue in Sheikh Mohammed's Derby quest, and neither, apparently, has time. It was a Godolphin mantra that if they did not win in 2002, they would be back, and would continue to run in the race until they won it. Either Sheikh Mohammed would one day join the exalted inner circle of Derby-winning owners, or he would eventually break C. V. Whitney's 0-15 record of Derby futility. To many observers, the actual outcome almost did not matter. The only thing more intriguing than success is epic failure, and Sheikh Mohammed was marching forcefully toward one or the other. His expensive, single-minded quest to put his stamp on America's most prestigious horse race meant that if a Godolphin horse did win the Kentucky Derby, it would have done so Sheikh Mohammed's way.

Bibliography

Alexander, David. *A Sound of Horses*. Indianapolis, Kansas City, New York: The Bobb-Merrill Company, Inc. 1986.

Anthony, John Duke. *Arab States of the Lower Gulf*. The Middle East Institute. 1975.

Baffert, Bob, and Steve Haskin. *Baffert: Dirt Road to the Derby*. Lexington, Ky.: The Blood-Horse, Inc. 1999.

Bagan, Joe. *Lukas at Auction*. Denver, Co.: Sachs-Lawlor Company. 1989.

Bolus, Jim. *Run for the Roses: 100 Years at the Kentucky Derby*. Hawthorn Books. 1974.

Buchanan, Lamont. *The Kentucky Derby Story*. New York: E. P. Dutton & Company. 1953.

Chew, Peter. *The Kentucky Derby: The First 100 Years*. Boston: Houghton Mifflin Company. 1974.

Crist, Steven. *The Horse Traders*. New York: W. W. Norton & Company. 1986.

Drape, Joe. *The Race for the Triple Crown*. New York: Atlantic Monthly Press. 2001.

Hervey, John. *Racing in America; 1665-1865.* 2 vols. The Jockey Club. New York: The Scribner Press. 1944.

Hewitt, Abram S. *The Great Breeders and Their Methods.* Lexington, Ky.: Thoroughbred Publishers Inc. 1982.

Hollingsworth, Kent. *The Kentucky Thoroughbred.* Lexington, Ky.: University Press of Kentucky. 1976, 1985.

Livingston, Bernard. *Their Turf: America's Horsey Set and Its Princely Dynasties.* New York: Arbor House. 1973.

Longrigg, Roger. *The History of Horse Racing.* New York: Stein and Day. 1972.

Media Prima. *The Maktoums and Their Horses,* Vol. 1. Al Ghurair Printing and Publishing House, Co. LLC. 1997.

Nack, William. *Secretariat: The Making of a Champion.* New York: Da Capo Press, Inc. 1975.

Nyrop, Richard F. *Area Handbook for the Persian Gulf States.* The American University. 1977.

Reid, Jamie. *Emperors of the Turf.* Macmillan London. 1989.

Robertson, William H. P. *The History of Thoroughbred Racing in America.* Englewood Cliffs, N.J.: Prentice-Hall, Inc. 1964.

Robinson, Patrick, and Nick Robinson. *Horsetrader.* HarperCollins. 1993.

Thompson, Laura. *Newmarket.* Virgin Publishing. 2000.

Willett, Peter. *Makers of the Modern Thoroughbred.* Lexington, Ky.: University Press of Kentucky. 1984.

Winn, Colonel Matt J., and Frank G. Menke. *Down the Stretch: The Story of Colonel Matt J. Winn.* New York: Smith and Durrell. 1945.

About the Author

Jason Levin has written about sports, including horse racing, since 1987, but spent the early 1990's working as a teacher and trainer for the Institute of Reading Development before turning to writing full-time in 1996. He has loved horse racing ever since the 1970's, and he was lucky enough to have witnessed first-hand the brilliance and determination of Forego, Affirmed, and John Henry. Most recently, he was the horse-racing and boxing writer for FOXSports.com, and is currently a regular contributor to *HorsePlayer* magazine, *Basketball Digest,* and the Breeders' Cup/NTRA website. A graduate of the University of California, Santa Barbara, he has written screenplays, short stories, and numerous magazine and newspaper articles. This is his first book.